ARCHITECTURE
AND ANARCHISM

Paul Dobraszczyk

ARCHITECTURE
AND ANARCHISM

Building without Authority

ANTEPAVILION
in association with
Paul Holberton Publishing

CONTENTS

PREFACE

On the afternoon of Sunday 30 August 2020, some 50–odd riot-equipped police entered the premises of Antepavilion at Columbia Wharf in Hackney. Alleging a breach of the English law introduced in the wake of the Coronavirus pandemic, they came to prevent a show of solo ballet dancing which had been running for eight consecutive weekends on a pontoon moored on the Regent's Canal. This was DistDancing, a free pop-up performance created by dancers whose regular work had been brought to a halt by the COVID-19 restrictions that saw theatres and other venues close for over a year. Its stage was the raft of NATO pontoons that were the intended platform for the 2020 Antepavilion commission. As the police shut down the sound system and threatened to arrest the organizers, the crowd on the opposite bank of the canal chanted in unison: 'Let them dance!'.[1]

Two days before, Hackney Council had issued a Stop Notice and Enforcement Notice under the Town and Country Planning Act 1990. These notices criminalized the display of 'art installations' at the Wharf, as Antepavilion and its predecessors had been doing for over 20 years.

In turn, the Stop Notice reinforced an injunction obtained by emergency application to the High Court a week before. This was to prevent the launch of a group of full-scale fibreglass sharks mounted on floats in the Regent's Canal created by architect Jaimie Shorten. Four of the planned five sharks were already floating in the canal alongside the Wharf when the injunction was served.

The sharks were inspired by the famous Headington Shark in Oxford – installed in 1986 by American immigrant Bill Heine in the roof of his modest, newly purchased 1850s terraced house. Created by sculptor John Buckley, it was his comment on the civilian casualties of American air raids on Libya by F111 squadrons stationed at local US air base, Upper Heyford, on the day he completed the

The Headington Shark, Oxford, pictured in 2019 after it was officially sanctioned and restored

purchase.[2] The shark precipitated a protracted planning battle. The then chair of the Oxford Planning Committee was quoted as saying: 'I am against narcissistic, Disneyland fantasy and I will fight with every drop of my blood to see that it is torn down from the roof.'[3] The shark itself was eventually granted planning consent following a public inquiry in 1991 by the Secretary of State. The planning inspector famously said: 'it is not in dispute that the shark is not in harmony with its surroundings, but then it is not intended to be in harmony with them.'[4]

Jaimie Shorten's *Sharks!* installation at Columbia Wharf in August 2020, with the previous year's Antepavilion competition winner, Maich Swift Architects' Potemkin Theatre, seen on the rooftop behind

Shorten's *Sharks!* upped the planning ante by having the sculptures sing politically poignant songs about Brexit and give lectures on important themes in contemporary architecture and urbanism. *Sharks!* was the winning design of the annual Antepavilion commission, established in 2017 to promote independent thought and symbiotic creativity in the fields of art, craft and architecture.[5] It responded to a brief that called for an exploration of 'the tension between authoritarian governance of the built environment and aesthetic libertarianism'.

The competition was conceived and sponsored by heritage and alternative architecture specialist property company Shiva Ltd. The Council argued that the installation represented a 'material change of use of the land to mixed use' that had not obtained its permission, even though Shiva had been using the site for the production and display of art since the mid-1990s. The Council had previously served notice in 2019 for removal of two of the older Antepavilion structures, arguing that they caused 'visual harm' because they didn't fit in with the character of the local 'conservation area'.[6] The case against *Sharks!* went to the High Court, whose judgement on 18 September 2020 was inconclusive and the litigation is ongoing. The ruling deferred to the established English law principle that local planners are sovereign in matters of 'planning judgment' and thus outside the remit of the High Court. The dispute must therefore be resolved by the usual channels, namely either the granting or refusal of planning permission – precisely the mechanisms that were being challenged by Antepavilion.[7]

For proponents of the Antepavilion projects – and 200 letters of support were submitted to the Council in protest at its Enforcement Notice – the actions of Hackney Council highlighted the absurdities of the British planning system, particularly the way in which it stymies genuine creativity in favour of the kind of sterile uniformity that characterizes what passes for 'development' in cities today. They also drew attention to the arbitrary nature of many planning regulations, the way in which this inevitably results in subjective decisions being made by petty officials with little or no claim to be arbiters of good taste. For many, the actions of the Council seemed churlish – a mean-spirited reaction against a spontaneous self-organized attempt to enliven the public realm. For four years, the Antepavilion projects have put innovative temporary structures on public display on a previously derelict canal-side warehouse. It now houses artists' studios and hosts all kinds of public events, including exhibitions and performances – a vital corrective to the decay of the public realm as more and more urban space is financialized.

The research that resulted in this book was commissioned by Antepavilion in late 2018 as a way of drawing attention to myriad projects, past and present, that key into its libertarian ethos and desire for much more diverse and self-organized forms of architecture (what this book calls 'anarchist architecture'). Antepavilion highlights the stark gap between the explicitly authoritarian way in which the built environment is generally governed and the kind of aesthetic liberation that is vital to a full human flourishing in cities. The projects illustrated here provide a window into some of the results where such authoritarianism has occasionally not held sway; and what might be possible if it could sometimes be held at bay. They also draw attention to the differing forms of libertarian politics that undergird them. Taken as a whole, they're meant as an inspiration to build less uniformly, more inclusively and more freely.

ACKNOWLEDGEMENTS

Writing this book has been immensely challenging but also enjoyable and liberating. It would not have been possible without the support and trust of Russell Gray who, as the director of Shiva Ltd, principal sponsor of Antepavilion, continues to practise a radically different form of property investment in London. It goes without saying that we desperately need more people like him in that line of work.

Many people other than the author are involved in the creation of books and this is particularly so in this case. In almost every project that I visited while researching for this book, it was the people who stood out for their openness, generosity and kindness. Of these, I want to particularly thank Jon Broome, Lara Eggleton and Stefan Skrimshire, Clemens Mackensen, Hoppi and Tao Wimbush, Ben Cummins, Paul Bradbury, Martin Rosenkreutz Madsen, Jan Lilliendahl Larsen, and Nadia and Clarissa at Agrocité. Along the way, Tim Waterman, Simon Springer, Dan Fitzpatrick, Tom Dyckhoff, Morag Rose, and Paul Graham Raven have been generous in their advice and support of the research. Encouragement and contacts have also been provided by Matt Smith, Rachael Kiddey and Chuck Morse.

The final stages of writing coincided with the extended COVID-19 lockdown in Spring 2020. During this time, embracing the spirit of collaboration that is at the heart of anarchist thinking, many others provided input on the writing, including Ruth Kinna, Simon Sadler, Joan Grossman, Folke Köbberling, Jon Broome, Todd Mecklem, Paul Bradbury, Jenny Pickerill, Brian Rosa, Patrick Weber, Anthony Ko, Will Jennings, Peter Kraftl, Timothy Miller, Katherine Tyldesley, Bradley L Garrett, Stefano Portelli, Rahul Mehrotra, Ken Lum, Ian Lambot, Robert Houston, Janine Wiedel, Marco Casagrande, Stephen E Hunt, Aaron Bryant, and Kate Evans. Many also generously contributed images that so enrich the book as a whole. This process had taught me so much about the value of collaboration in writing and to trust more fully in the openness and generosity of others.

Finally, I'm grateful, as always, to my wife Lisa and daughter Isla who have been patient yet again with my obsessions and absences.

Paul Dobraszczyk

INTRODUCTION architecture and anarchism

As architecture in cities in the Global North becomes increasingly commodified, sterile and elitist – part of a global capitalist system where urban space is equated with profit for a tiny few – there is a pressing need to transform what is meant by value in building. There is also an urgent requirement for urban construction to become less destructive – currently it's a major driver of climate change and global resource depletion. Within this culture of urban crisis, there is still a lack of willingness to think more broadly about who makes cities and for whom they are built.

The production of urban space is always a multi-faceted activity. Cities are vast agglomerations of private and public, human-created and 'natural' spaces governed by myriad formal and informal laws and social codes. Thought of in this way, architecture isn't so much a discrete activity derived from professional expertise, but rather a whole field of opportunity for the many, an arena of possibilities rather than one for the implementation of formal plans. This is architecture from the ground up, a fully participatory architecture that promotes liberty for the many rather than the few.

It is what this book calls an 'anarchist' architecture, that is, forms of design and building that are motivated by the core values held by 'mainstream' anarchism since its emergence as a distinct kind of socialist politics in the nineteenth century. These are autonomy, voluntary association, mutual aid, and self-organization through direct democracy. As will become evident, there is a vast range of architectural projects that can been seen to reflect some or all of these values, whether they are acknowledged as specifically anarchist or otherwise. This book argues that anarchism, broadly conceived, can and already does play an important role in infusing the built environment with emancipatory potential.

This book brings together 60 projects from the Global North that illustrate anarchist values in action. These values are evident in projects that grow out of romantic notions of escape – from isolated cabins to intentional communities. Yet, in contrast, they also manifest in direct action – occupations or protests that produce micro-counter-communities. Artists also produce anarchist architecture – intimations of much freer forms of building cut loose from the demands of moneyed clients; so do architects and planners who want to involve users in a process normally restricted to an elite few. Others also imagine new social realities through speculative proposals. Finally, building from the ground up is, for some, a necessity – the thousands of migrants denied their right to become citizens, even as they have to live somewhere; or the unhoused of otherwise affluent cities forced to build improvised homes for themselves.

The result is to significantly broaden existing ideas about what might constitute anarchism in architecture and also to argue strongly for its nurturing in the built environment. Understood in this way, anarchism offers a powerful way of reconceptualizing architecture as an emancipatory, inclusive, ecological and egalitarian practice.

Anarchist trajectories

In September 2020, soon-to-be-ousted US president Donald Trump described the cities of Portland and New York, among others, as 'anarchist jurisdictions' – incendiary

11

rhetoric typical of Trump and intended to deepen the divisions between conservatives and liberals in the US. By invoking the 'A' word against his opponents, Trump keyed into simplistic associations of anarchism with destruction and disorder to justify a punitive withdrawal of federal funds.[1]

At its heart, anarchism is a politics of thought and action that reflects the original meaning of the ancient Greek word *anarkhía* meaning 'the absence of government'. All forms of anarchism are founded on self-organization, or government from below, predicated on a radical scepticism of unaccountable authority and hierarchy in favour of bottom-up self-organization. It is not disorder, but rather a different order created from below on the principles of autonomy, voluntary association, self-organization, mutual aid, and direct democracy.

As a form of political thought and practice, anarchism is multifaceted and has a long history. Anthropologist David Graeber has argued that the gift economies of early human societies – and some surviving ones – were, *de facto*, anarchist because they worked on the assumption that inequality was socially destructive.[2] Others have drawn attention to anarchist tendencies in the world's major religions: for instance currents of anti-authoritarianism, pacifism, and libertarianism in Taoism, Islamic Sufism, Sikhism, Buddhism and Christianity. Even when anarchism was first named and formulated as a specific political project by French philosopher Pierre-Joseph Proudhon in 1840, with his declaration that 'property is theft!', it was in the light of a belief that anarchist principles of voluntary association, mutual aid and self-organization were not new but forms of behaviour that were as old as human societies themselves.[3]

Proudhon was reacting to the increasing centralization of power in nineteenth-century cities as industrial capitalism took hold. In the second half of the century, anarchism was closely aligned with an emergent Marxism – the libertarian arm of socialism championed by Mikhail Bakunin and defined by an aggressive stance against any form of authority.[4] After an irrecoverable split with Marx at the International Workingmen's Association in 1872 – largely over conflicting attitudes towards the role of political parties and the state in the future emancipation of the proletariat – anarchism developed its own trajectory as a libertarian form of socialism. The acts of violence committed by anarchists in the late nineteenth and early twentieth centuries were strongly associated with republicanism.[5] They were a reflection of the increasingly militant stance adopted by some after 1872, even as others, like Leo Tolstoy, embraced radical pacifism and spiritual freedom as the foundation of their anarchist politics and practice.[6]

From the mid-nineteenth century onwards, anarchism's distinctiveness as a form of politics resided in its emphasis on practice rather than theory. Whereas variants of socialism often have their origins in individual thinkers (for example, Marxism, Leninism, Trotskyism, Maoism), the various 'isms' of anarchist politics mostly reflect distinct kinds of practices, examples of which include anarcho-syndicalism, anarcho-communism, insurrectionism, anarcha-feminism, co-operativism, individualism, platformism, eco-anarchism, even anarcho-capitalism.[7] Although it's problematic to generalize about such a wide range of anarchist practices, they tend to cohere around certain ideological faultlines: either collective or individual notions of liberty; anti- or pro-capitalist stances; non-violent or violent forms of resistance; separatist or engaged communal life; secular or spiritual. As Graeber has argued, what unites the majority of anarchists is less a coherent body of theory than a shared attitude, 'one

The Banana House in Christiania, Copenhagen, built in 1985
by two itinerant German architects, Axt & Kelle

might even say a faith; the rejection of certain types of social relations, the confidence that certain others would be much better ones on which to build a liveable society'.[8] This emphasis on practice has often led to anarchism being seen as Marxism's poorer relation, borne out most clearly in the overwhelming reliance on Marx's theoretical writings in left-leaning academic discourse as opposed to that of significant contemporaneous anarchist thinkers such as Bakunin and Proudhon.[9]

The highpoint of European anarchism was arguably its important role as an anti-fascist movement in the 1930s. For example, the widespread control of economic life by workers, and the collectivized living and cultural liberation that emerged in Catalonia and Aragon during the Spanish Civil War, represented a brief flowering of anarchist practices on a large scale, until they were mercilessly crushed by Franco's fascist forces in 1939 (with international backing from the communist Soviet Union).[10] In the 1960s, anarchism became more prominent as a global social movement espousing personal autonomy and direct democracy, perhaps most notably in the wave of student protests that occurred in European cities in 1968, and later in the Zapatista uprising in Mexico and the Piqueteros in Argentina in the mid-1990s, which saw the widespread establishment of popular assemblies as models of democratic self-organization.

Anarchist historian Ruth Kinna has identified a range of more recent developments that Graeber termed 'small "a" anarchism', namely practices like direct democracy and consensus-based decision-making that derive from anarchist traditions but which their practitioners don't necessarily label as anarchist.[11] Many of these – for example the Transition Network, based in the UK – are connected with an emerging green politics that sees planetary survival as only achievable by means of a broad-based, grass-roots anti-capitalist project, with initiatives by local communities in towns and cities across the world combating the effects of climate change through mutual aid and passive and sustainable methods of living.[12] At the same time, though, other groups continue to draw more directly on the rich legacy of anarchist thought and practice, perhaps most notably the Rojavan revolution in northern Syria that has seen Kurdish forces based there form autonomous cantons that together make up a self-governing, multicultural confederation directly inspired by the work of American anarchist Murray Bookchin and his concept of social ecology.[13]

Anarchist spaces

Many of these historical and contemporary examples of anarchism in action demonstrate that, as a political project, it is intimately bound up with architecture.

Anarchism has inspired countless efforts at establishing intentional communities, radical and revolutionary agendas and various forms of direct action. Intentional communities founded on anarchist principles – this book considers such diverse examples as Christiania, Slab City, La ZAD and Grow Heathrow – have all featured self-organized forms of building. On the one hand, this includes the re-appropriation of existing structures, usually rehabilitating abandoned buildings or restructuring others for common usage; on the other, the building of entirely new structures to accommodate individual liberty and a radical change in social organization. For example, in Christiania, established in 1971 in the centre of Copenhagen, residents first squatted abandoned military buildings, converting them into communal homes, before others self-built their own houses in an extraordinary diversity of styles and materials. Even temporary anarchist projects – for example, protest camps – require rudimentary forms of building: the construction of makeshift shelters and basic infrastructure.

The importance of the built environment in anarchist projects was recognized by late nineteenth-century anarchist thinkers Élisée Reclus and Peter Kropotkin, who were also pioneers in the study of geography.[14] They argued that the centralized power and organization that came with industrial modernity had increasingly imposed an artificial uniformity on the built environment, whereas decentralized, local forms of government led to greater diversity. Although both decried the exponential growth of industrial cities and the corresponding depopulation of rural areas, Reclus in particular nevertheless argued that it was only in cities that a full flowering of human diversity was possible. Cities were 'collective organisms' that thrived only when each 'cell' was healthy.[15] In a different vein, Kropotkin's focus was on building networks of small-scale autonomous communities, drawn from the libertarian socialist society imagined in William Morris's utopian novel *News From Nowhere*, first published in 1890.[16]

In both forms, this 'organicist' thinking was an influential precursor to the radical town planning of Patrick Geddes, who knew Reclus, Kropotkin and Morris. In *Cities in Evolution* (1915), Geddes stressed the importance of cities' connectivity to their larger geographic regions and empowerment at a local level.[17] This devolved view of urban governance, which came directly from anarchist principles, was a radical counter to the increasing centralization of power in both industrial cities and global ones like London. Modernization and development meant the consolidation of informal and localized power into city-wide municipal authorities, official bodies that, over time, would come to oversee and regulate an ever greater scope of the built environment, both above and below ground. This gradual tightening of centralized power led to an increasingly ordered city – cleaner, more efficient, with rising standards of living for the majority. What was once the responsibility of individuals and communities was, over time, ceded to professionals, who were able to bring increasing expertise and refinement, but at the expense of individual autonomy.

Yet, this equating of progress with order was paradoxically dependent on the continued existence of disorder to give it validity. Moreover, no matter how much power is centralized, control of the built environment is only ever partial and selective, given how cities have not only increased in scale but also in their complexity. Jane Jacobs's pioneering study *The Death and Life of Great American Cities* (1961) cast a forensic eye on everyday urban life that most modernist planners and architects ignored – for example, the informal comings and goings of people during the day on a typical New York street. She concluded that formal and informal uses of urban space

Multiple informal additions to the back of a Victorian terrace in Stoke-on-Trent, 2020

exist side-by-side and that 'failures in city neighbourhoods are ultimately failures in localized self-government' and not in top-down planning.[18] In *The Uses of Disorder* (1970), Richard Sennett gave this everyday self-government in cities a specifically anarchist interpretation. In order to counter the strong desire for security that is willing to sacrifice freedom in return, Sennett argued for an urbanism that is freed from state regulation and control, one that is ceaselessly changing through a process of confrontation and negotiation, all undertaken by citizens themselves. Assuming that underneath the desire for security lay a host of unfulfilled desires (made apparent in the apathy and boredom of the suburbs), Sennett argued that resistance to disorder has to be overcome at the level of individual psychology before it can become a collective, organizing principle for building and living in cities.[19]

In a different vein, in the 1972 book *Adhocism* – a rallying cry against the authoritarianism of architectural modernism and post-war urban planning – Charles Jencks reckoned that around 80 percent of the human-made world isn't designed by anyone and is 'reconstituted *ad-hoc* for specific purposes'.[20] There's nothing inherently surprising about this – after all, only around 5 percent of the built environment is actually designed by architects; what was unusual was Jencks's call for greater freedom of participation. Condemning the totalizing order imposed by modernist planning, he argued instead for the complex order that would emerge from giving individuals more freedom and the legal and financial means to shape their own environments. Jencks argued that the advantage of this informal method of ordering over totalistic planning was that it allowed people to learn from mistakes. He pushed for a renewed sense of creativity towards the everyday built environment that would see a flowering of the burgeoning do-it-yourself industry beyond the borders of privately owned homes. To a degree, the recent proliferation

of so-called 'DIY urbanism' – for example, shipping containers repurposed as places of leisure and commerce or grass-roots initiatives like pop-up parks or urban farms – provides a concrete realisation of Jencks's call to users to reconstitute informal spaces in cities. At the same time, Jencks's thesis has been revisited by Roman Mars and Kurt Kohlstedt in their popular podcast and book *The 99% Invisible City*, although with more of an emphasis on simply noticing these spaces rather than actively reconstituting them.[21]

The question this book asks is why the freedoms we have to organize and govern how we use urban spaces are so curtailed when it comes to more radical forms of self-building, namely ones that are less about providing alternative forms of consumption than asserting a politics of genuine transformation that empowers citizens. Planners and architects are usually quite happy to pay lip service to this basic idea of user empowerment; yet, they rarely allow it to challenge their own status as the expert arbiters of design. Recent grass-roots global movements like Transition Network and Extinction Rebellion are increasingly recognizing that the current model of urban development is actually hugely destructive environmentally and socially. As part of their sustainable agenda, these movements restructure urban governance at a local level along anarchist principles of self-organization, mutual aid and direct democracy.

While the focus in this book is on sites and projects in the Global North – what is perceived as the 'developed' part of the world – it also questions the overly schematic geographies of Global North and South and, consequently, the idea of development itself. A few of the sites included here do this themselves: the Open City in Chile demonstrates a level of architectural sophistication rare even in developed countries; Tahrir Square in Egypt is included because it inspired the global Occupy Movement in 2011; Kowloon Walled City in Hong Kong because, although demolished over 30 years ago, it nevertheless remains a potent influence on popular culture across the globe; Auroville, in India, because it's a genuinely international intentional community. Finally, the Calais Jungle – a migrant camp established in 2016 – demonstrates that today's national borders don't reflect the reality of the incessant and growing number of people that are mostly travelling from the Global South to the North. All of these sites – and many of the others too – question the distinction between those who self-build out of necessity and those who do so by choice.

Seeds beneath the snow

Perhaps the most significant figures to make a strong link between anarchism and architecture were the American critic Paul Goodman and, above all, British writer Colin Ward. Goodman's pioneering 1947 book *Communitas* traced utopian visions of urban planning back to William Morris and Patrick Geddes, seeing in garden cities the potential for the development of an autonomous, community-led urbanism.[22] Ward's reputation rests on his prolific output from the 1940s onwards. In over 30 books, he investigated an enormous range of social practices that he regarded as anarchist – in housing, work and leisure, urban policy, architecture and design; and he wrote lucidly about everyday subjects such as community allotments, holiday camps, housing co-operatives, and how children perceive and engage with cities.[23] Throughout his work there is a strong belief in anarchism as an always present but often latent force in social life that simply needs nurturing in order for it to grow. Ward argued for a way of building that was focused on changing 'the role of citizens from recipients to participants, so that they too have an active part to play' in the building of towns and cities.[24] In this view, revolution is conceived as already embedded in the here and now – an emergent process from below rather than transformation imposed from above.

Ward was drawn to practices that exemplified this taking back of control by citizens; examples of which included instances of mass squatting, such as the seizure of empty properties by tens of thousands of ordinary people immediately after the Second World War;[25] and the self-built chalets constructed in their thousands in the early twentieth century by urban citizens wanting a rural retreat and taking advantage of small plots of land being sold off at the time.[26] He was a tireless advocate of self-building as a viable form of urban development, and found in the work of architect Walter Segal a model of how this might be applied in British cities. Ward also drew attention to participatory forms of urban design, citing the example of Black Road in Macclesfield in the 1970s, where local architect Rod Hackney defied the council's demolition order for a row of Victorian terraces by empowering residents to undertake renovations themselves.[27] In this example, Ward was pointing the way to a much wider emphasis today on participation in architecture, the work of practices like the Turner prize-winning collective Assemble applying these principles to a much wider remit of projects, from the renovation of the Granby Four Streets in Liverpool to the creation of temporary structures like a pop-up cinema in an abandoned petrol station in London in 2014. Although

Terraced house being renovated in Cairns Street in 2015, part of Assemble's ongoing Granby Four Streets project in Toxteth, Liverpool

Assemble are not claiming to be anarchists, they nevertheless place great emphasis on the long-standing anarchist principles of mutual aid, affinity, solidarity and equality – all of which refuse capitalism's insistence on competition and hierarchy.[28]

Ward's emergent understating of anarchism has been criticized by more aggressive 'insurrectionary' anarchists, such as Alfredo Bonanno, as overplaying the transformative power of latent practices – that it ends up disempowering citizens because it removes any need to intervene or engage with existing conditions.[29] Some have even gone so far as to suggest that contemporary capitalism is a perfect bedchamber for anarchism – a completely deregulated market allowing autonomy for the elite few, where the state retreats and wealthy entrepreneurs exercise power from their secure enclaves. Gaining most traction in the US in the laissez-faire culture of Silicon Valley, and as expounded by Murray N. Rothbard, anarcho-capitalism abandons the collectivist vision of mainstream historical anarchism in favour of a highly individualized form of freedom, often termed libertarianism.[30] It's one of the reasons why many socialist thinkers such as eminent urbanist David Harvey are highly suspicious of, if not outrightly hostile to, anarchism as a political project. But behind this legitimate critique lies a belief that some forms of hierarchy and private monopolies must be maintained if a new socialist society is to emerge; that a small group of enlightened people must continue to hold on to the reigns of power lest the revolutionary ideals be relinquished by the lethargic masses.

Ward disagreed profoundly with this idea of revolution as a top-down process because, in fact, it actually ended up reinforcing existing hierarchies of power. Instead, he saw revolution as an emergent process that is already evident in the world, observable in practices of all kinds. At heart, this is a resolutely optimistic (critics would say naive) vision of human nature as rooted in a desire for freedom that is always collective. In his observations of ordinary people working allotments, building houses, seizing private property and embracing their freedom to dwell, Ward envisioned a revolution not as a clean break with the past but rather as a fundamental condition of reality that simply needs nurturing. The drawback, of course, is that it underplays the overarching structures of power that are always seeking to circumscribe or prevent the emergence of more autonomy. In short, there are dangers in both 'emergent' and 'insurrectionist' formulations of anarchism: the former risks falling into conservatism; the latter into vanguardism, namely an elitist disdain of all but the most strident forms of activism.[31]

Building together

The participatory practices of building celebrated by Ward have fed into an important countercurrent within recent architectural writing, the most wide-ranging study to date being *Spatial Agency: Other Ways of Doing Architecture*, a book and website published in 2011.[32] The project provided a thorough overview of practices working to involve people more actively in architecture. Arguing that design professionals need to embrace a much wider remit than building alone – what might be broadly called the 'social' – *Spatial Agency* picked up and expanded on ideas developed by architects from the 1960s onwards, such as John Turner, Lucien Kroll, John Habraken, Giancarlo de Carlo,

Christophe Alexander and Walter Segal.[33] Embracing all manner of participatory practices in over 200 separate instances, from the community architecture movement of the 1970s and 1980s, intentional communities like Christiania in Copenhagen, to DIY urbanism, *Spatial Agency* aimed ambitiously to redraw the entire field of architectural production, changing the role of architect and planner from designer/overseer to facilitator, and architecture from a 'matter of fact to a matter of concern'.[34]

Although the authors never spelt out directly the politics of such a transformation, implicit in it is the breaking down of hierarchies embedded so strongly in the architectural and planning professions. In calling for a new kind of architecture based on 'mutual knowledge ... founded in exchange, in negotiation, out of hunch, intuition', *Spatial Agency* clearly drew on the kind of anarchist practices celebrated by Ward.[35] What limited its impact, though, was that its message was aimed squarely at the very audience the authors were seeking to move away from, namely 'specialists', either in terms of practice or research. A broadening of the language used to talk about architecture and cities is also needed, one that speaks clearly to those whose participation is being sought. What this requires is a wholesale shift in the organization of design, one in which non-professionals are given a voice to speak, write and picture an architecture they desire. This is especially important in a world in which words like 'participation' are regularly used by developers and municipal authorities as simply a way of ticking boxes and hiding the true motives of continued control from above.

A participatory architecture may seem difficult even to imagine, let alone build, but its contours can already be felt in existing everyday urban environments, such as allotments – ubiquitous spaces in many cities across the world and made up of land that has been set aside by local authorities for residents to grow food in exchange for a nominal annual rent. As Colin Ward and David Crouch have demonstrated, allotments are examples of common spaces within cities – sites that are deliberately kept outside of the market, either by municipal authorities or citizens themselves.[36] They are filled with more-or-less provisional structures – an array of readymade or self-built sheds and greenhouses, interspersed with small open plots littered with improvised structures for growing food, as well as receptacles for composting. Although there are often strict rules about what is and isn't permitted on allotments (for example, in the UK and most other countries in the Global North, you cannot build any form of permanent dwelling), they are nevertheless urban environments that encapsulate the merging of formal and informal participatory practices of building and space-making in cities. Each plot-holder – steward rather than owner – has to negotiate both private and communal concerns. Individual territory is clearly important, but always in the context of co-operation that works effectively through skill-sharing – and mutual aid. Most allotments also feature common structures – from repurposed shipping containers to community centres – built according to consensus and a voluntary pooling of resources. Allotments also display, more than private or public gardens, a meld of the human and non-human – a hybrid 'productive' landscape that is neither natural or artificial, but a blend of both. Far from a romantic vision of rural idyll, allotments demonstrate both a nurturing and an antagonistic relationship of the human and non-human, with certain kinds of 'nature' (food-producing plants) clearly prioritized over others (slugs and snails, for example).

The characteristic pattern of spatial agencies in allotments can be extrapolated, in the imagination, to encompass the whole urban environment. A radically reconfigured model of urban land tenure – leased to owners from a central land trust or holders with a common,

Allotment structures at Green Lane, Stockport, 2021

progressive vision – would replace purely private land ownership and speculative building. Here, the boundaries between the private and public would be decided informally by users themselves. Some building would be the responsibility of individuals – perhaps living spaces conceived more as temporary structures that could be moved or reconstituted when necessary – and some would be collective – structures where resources are pooled and shared for the common good. This loose form of spatial organization would require participation at every level, the demands of which would be offset by its basis in community and stewardship rather than individual assets and ownership – in effect a sharing of both strengths and weaknesses. Architecture, in this scenario, would emerge organically from the needs at hand, and incrementally as those needs develop and change over time – building as the embodiment of social rather than financial value.

What would be removed would be any dictatorship of need based on the interests of a small group or groups. The self-made city would need to grow out of the local – the very smallest scale of inhabitation – but the model of organization could foreseeably be scaled up to whatever level is deemed as necessary, so long as its basic principles of social rather than financial value are adhered to.

As with many anarchist projects, this vision may be objected to as utopian – unrealisable because it pushes too hard against existing forms of power and vested interests that define how cities are made and governed. But, as Ruth Levitas has elucidated, utopian thought is important because it foregrounds underlying values and commitment; it is a protean tool for clarifying principles and processes rather than creating a literal blueprint for the future.[37] It is also primarily concerned with the imagination. As I have argued elsewhere, imagination is key in how we 'pre-experience' alternative futures; it opens up spaces of possibility that offer a whole range of outcomes that can never be predicted with any degree of certainty.[38] Yet, there is also a characteristic concreteness to the anarchist imagination – pointing out existing tendencies that can be nurtured and past precedents that can be drawn upon. This is a gradualist utopianism: an unfolding future of 'an endless variety of communities, associations, networks, projects, on every conceivable scale, overlapping and intersecting in ways we could imagine, and possibly many that we can't'.[39] What this future city would not be is anything like a state.

Freedom and ecology

Allotments also reflect a radically different kind of ecology at work from that which orders the conventional built environment. In *The Ecology of Freedom* (1985), anarchist social theorist Murray Bookchin argued that an ecological society can only come about once social hierarchies have been abolished. By focusing on the life of early societies, he showed that human domination of nature only evolved after social hierarchies had emerged.[40] In this reading, hierarchy is a human invention that we have also imposed on nature – in effect, an explicit reversal of orthodox Darwinism – and, more and more today, scientists are beginning to realise that the non-human world may indeed be one characterized by mutual aid or symbiosis rather than the Darwinian struggle for survival. Bookchin argued that the sense of wholeness or completeness in nature is achieved through a full realisation of its diversity – the abundance and excess that so often characterize 'pristine' natural environments, but one which is now drastically curtailed as a result of human dominance. People have not only stifled nature's diversity by exploiting it so ruthlessly; they have also prevented their own development into a fully diverse social whole.[41]

The implications for architecture within this view of ecology – what Bookchin termed 'social ecology' – are far reaching. In this reading, an ecological architecture is not only one that sits more lightly on the earth (consuming less in its construction and in the energy used for inhabitation), but is also part of a social ecology that achieves maximum diversity alongside and not at the expense of that of nature. It would mirror and complement nature's example in achieving fecundity through interdependence and not in spite of it.

Small-scale realisations of such an ecological architecture can be found in thousands of eco-villages across the world: places like Lammas in rural Wales where 'development' is recast as a meld of the human and the non-human. In an eco-village, the building of structures for human inhabitation – whether communal spaces, individual homes, storage spaces, even toilets – is not separated from the development of the non-human environment. Indeed, the basic philosophy underpinning low-impact development is precisely that articulated by Bookchin, namely that one can never cleave human activity from nature: both are bound up together in a dynamic and interdependent relationship. Many self-builders in eco-communities speak of their homes as a 'second skin': the very fabric of the structure has grown with them over time.[42] Even the conventional infrastructures of water supply, waste removal and electricity – things most urban inhabitants take for granted – are given new meaning when built autonomously. And those who live in eco-communities also learn that what humans build and what nature provides are far from separate worlds. Just like Bookchin's pre-modern societies, eco-communities show that an ecological architecture grows out of nature rather than being disconnected from it. And, as demonstrated at Lammas, the richness of building can also enhance that of the nature from which it is derived.

Eco-communities are small-scale – a few dozen residents in the majority of cases; a few hundred in an exceptional few. How, therefore, can ecological architecture become integral to larger built environments, on the scale of towns, cities, even megacities? Developed-world cities have gargantuan ecological footprints, far beyond what can realistically be called sustainable; for example, in 2003, it was estimated that London requires nearly 49 million global hectares to sustain it – 300 times its geographic area, or twice the size of the United Kingdom.[43] How can self-organized building even mitigate, let alone transform, this destructiveness? Clearly the massive structural forces that shape cities today must be challenged and overhauled – over-consumption, grossly inflated land values, the monopolization of development, a financial system that concentrates wealth rather than disperses it, cronyism and hypocrisy in planning policy (to name but a few).

David Harvey has drawn attention to the problem of scale in many radical projects, arguing that 'patently good solutions at one scale (the "local" say) do not necessarily aggregate up (or cascade down) to make for good solutions at another scale (the global, for example)'.[44] Underlying this question is an assumption that politics should operate through vertical hierarchies rather than the kind of horizontalism that is at the root of anarchist projects. Simon Springer has countered Harvey by arguing that 'the delusion of scale is that it represents a theoretical distraction, a drawing away from the grounded particularities of the everyday'.[45] This argument is rooted in a belief that social hierarchies originate in precisely the kind of abstract thinking that Harvey employs, that the tightening of centralized control in modern cities has created an increasing conceptual distance between government and its subjects. In calling for a 'flattening' of these vertical hierarchies of scale, Springer, like Colin Ward, proposes a prefigurative anarchist politics that is grounded in everyday practices,

in the materiality of sites, and in the making of space for autonomous decision-making. Practical encounters, rather than theoretical abstractions, would keep such a politics grounded; instead of the delusion of top-down control, anarchist projects create 'multiple sites of horizontal activity and autonomous resistance' that grow the revolution from within. Rather than seeing these as elements of a hierarchy of power, as is generally the case in urban governance, it might be possible to see their relationship in terms of a non-hierarchical confederacy of multiple, linked approaches, as outlined by Bookchin in his 1993 book *Urbanization Without Cities*. The key is to build from the ground up a new kind of value system in cities – one that doesn't pit humans against nature or each other but rather embraces a greater commons that is seen as owned by all (and that, of course, includes the non-human).[46]

The right to the city

In 1967, French sociologist Henri Lefebvre wrote 'The Right to the City', an essay subsequently seen as prophetic of the popular uprisings in Paris and other cities in 1968 that saw a near-revolution in urban life towards more egalitarian ends.[47] Recently reappraised by David Harvey and Peter Marcuse in light of the Arab Spring revolutions and Occupy protests of 2011, Lefebvre's argument is a powerful advocation of equality: of the need to break down and transcend the hierarchical ways in which space is organized in cities.[48] In this reading, everyone who lives in a city should be able to participate in the making of its spaces, whether that right is exercised at the level of decision-making or actual building (and everything in between). Lefebvre argued that urban inhabitants do not 'earn' this right by virtue of any accident, whether a result of their nationality, class, ethnicity, gender, or income, but rather because they all inhabit the city, that is, their everyday lives are defined by its spaces and structures. This is potentially a powerful democratic antidote to the forms of authority based on wealth, nationality, technocratic expertise, and even electoral popularity that are characteristic of the way in which cities are generally governed.

But how does such a right exercise itself in practice, given the bewildering number and diversity of urban citizens; and can it really offer an effective counter to the powerful neoliberal form of capitalism that is doing the very opposite to what Lefebvre intended? Lefebvre argued that organization from the bottom up has to start in what he described as the 'holes and chasms' of the city, namely spaces and structures that escape the control of the powers that be, one example being abandoned buildings.[49] These are places where experimentation is possible with projects that advocate and enact reconnection with alienated urban spaces, promote use value over exchange value in those spaces, develop alternative economies of recycling and gifting, and promote collaboration across the social spectrum.[50] In recent years, there's been a focus on how DIY or 'guerrilla' urbanism has taken advantage of such spaces precisely in order to experiment with alternative approaches – examples of which included in this book are the community urban gardens Agrocité in Paris and Prinzessinnengärten in Berlin. But these might also be co-operative forms of housing and business, community land trusts, self-organized buying and selling; parkour, skateboarding and urban exploration; re-occupied abandoned buildings; and the protest camps of the Occupy movement and, more recently, Extinction Rebellion. These highly disparate practices are, as Lefebvre rightly foresaw, difficult to unite into an overarching politics that could indeed challenge the dominant ways of city-making.

Indeed, DIY urban practices have been accused of being far too reluctant to foreground their politics, perhaps unsurprisingly given their often tenuous hold on the spaces they appropriate.[51] For to do so would put them in confrontation with existing forms of authority – power that often allows their practices to exist in the first place. As Lefebvre argued, to create an egalitarian city requires someone, or some group, being able to make public claims on behalf of these myriad small-scale tactical interventions in the city. This need not mean the kind of political representation that characterizes most democratic forms of governance, but rather a recognition that operating at different scales in cities requires different forms of organization. There could be different levels of effect rather than of power, where stepping-up in scale signals both a lessening in the direct participation from those at the bottom – necessary to mitigate the exhaustion that is often the result of direct participation – but also a concomitant increasing in the power of the values they want to see realised. What will be key is how a radical form of accountability is held by those few that are chosen to represent the many, something that our existing political systems are precisely failing to do.

This is really a question of how the good city is imagined and how willing urban inhabitants are to participate in making it become a reality, however large or small, local or global their contributions may be. As Lefebvre also argued in his concept of 'heterotopia' (very different from Michel Foucault's better-known idea), a libertarian city cannot emerge from any conscious plan, but rather more out of what people do in their everyday lives: how they imagine and sense their urban environment and what kind of meaning they seek in it.[52] Mirroring the insights of Ward and Springer, this is an emergent city that allows different kinds of emancipatory spaces to be created, ones which appear and disappear at every moment. For Lefebvre, the spontaneous coming together of people in everyday urban life already heralds the myriad possibilities of collective action to create something radically different. What is

Interior of Tao and Hoppi Wimbush's self-built house at Lammas, Wales, 2019

required is an imaginative scaling across what's already there in order to realise the same values of commoning that emerge from these everyday acts of liberation.

Resistance and refusal

Changing value in architecture – making it work towards more libertarian, participatory, ecological and egalitarian ends – will not happen without a great deal of resistance from those who seek to maintain their control over it. Almost all anarchist projects end up in confrontation with the state. This may be violent – for example, the brutal suppression of the 1871 Paris Commune, with tens of thousands of executions, or the crushing of revolutionary Barcelona by Franco's fascists and international backers in 1939. But it is just as often coercion by different means. As the story of Antepavilion demonstrates, those who

hold power will use every available means to target and suppress those who would dare to challenge them. No wonder that many who choose to self-build do so completely out of the spotlight – isolated rural sites that can remain invisible to official scrutiny. But even the most well-hidden structure or community inevitably depends on some kind of wider approval, most often neighbours willing to turn a blind eye. And those pioneers who choose to engage with the planning authorities – for example, the Lammas community in rural Wales – have no easier a ride. With hard-won expertise in planning law and a willingness to be scrutinized at every turn, not to mention skills of diplomacy in winning over neighbours, those trying to self-build legitimately have to commit all of these resources to have any chance of changing the laws that bind them, except in exceptional places like Almere in the Netherlands, where self- and custom-building have been

One of the many unconventional living spaces built at Oosterwold, Almere, 2016

actively promoted since 2011 by the municipal authorities in the Oosterwold district of the city.[53] Assisted by Dutch design firm MVRDV, residents have been given a great deal of freedom to build as they want, within a collectivized vision of municipal responsibility that, although unacknowledged, has its roots in anarchist ideas of autonomous, socially driven urbanism.[54]

There's a melancholy irony in the fact that many of those who choose to try and build more sustainably end up being subject to an almost pathological level of official scrutiny that none of us with carbon-guzzling lifestyles are ever forced to bear. When any action is openly set against the dominant power structures, it will inevitably bear a heavy burden of responsibility, even as those powers pay lip service to the very things they are stifling so effectively. If many choose to hide from such scrutiny by building in remote places, those that do it in cities, like Antepavilion, are always highly exposed. Even with resources – whether money, tenacity or time – fighting the authorities can become a full-time occupation and it has to be done entirely on those authorities' own terms. But herein also lies hope, namely that those with resources might use them to ends serving other than vested interests. Galvanizing property developers, landowners, planners and civic officials to act differently is a critical, if chronically understated, part of enacting progressive change in the urban environment. What often prevents this is the lure of resistance as the only form of opposition, a stance that has a tendency to foreclose the hard graft of long-term negotiation and messy compromise that produces any effective form of social change.

A broader appeal might be made if we substitute the word 'resistance' for 'refusal'. Refusing to participate in any form of domination – of each other and of nature – is clearly a long-term project that relies as much on denial as it does on the extent of our individual resources to be able to make such decisions. At this level, judgements are hard to make, the effectiveness of our actions difficult if not impossible to measure, the extent of our powerlessness always more pressing than our awareness of agency. This is a weak form of power, if indeed it is power at all. But the goal of any anarchist project is not to seize power; it is to dissolve it.

In the late Ursula Le Guin's allegorical science-fiction work *The Dispossessed* (1974), the moon of the planet Urras has become host to an anarchist society, namely hundreds of thousands of renegade Urrastians fleeing persecution. This new world, Anarres, is gradually terraformed by its inhabitants but, as time passes, its anarchist principles become hardened into legalistic rules, with the novel's hero, scientist Shevek, becoming victim of this rigid conformism. Coming to a realisation that anarchism is a transformative process that never ends, always at work challenging the human desire for status, Shevek accepts his own position of weakness as paradoxical proof of its strength: 'we know that there is no help for us but from one another, that no hand will save us if we do not reach out our hand. And the hand that you reach out is empty, as mine is.'[55] This radical disavowal of individualism is central to the anarchist vision of the dissolution of hierarchies.

For architecture and cities to become part of this emergent reality, they must involve all those who have a stake in their development. In place of architecture as professional expertise is, in David Harvey's words, an 'insurgent practice, where all are potential agents of design and building'.[56] This is a resistant practice because it simply refuses to close down opportunities and possibilities presented by reality itself, however constricting it may seem. It is, in Harvey's estimation, 'an imaginative vision that both projects new futures and also embraces their imperfections'.[57]

This is not to understate the weight of authoritarian systems of planning and design that characterize urban environments; or, concomitantly, the need for people and organizations to resist that dominance at a structural level. But perhaps there is much more freedom than we generally realise. When the protest group Extinction Rebellion took over the streets of London for a few days in April 2019, they not only brought the issue of climate change to the fore; they also radically transformed the way the city functioned. Even if it was only a short-lived intervention, extraordinary appropriations occurred: a road bridge became a garden; a boat was moored in the middle of a traffic intersection; the centre of government a free public space; a park a camping ground in the heart of the city. Of course, these actions did not change the politics and power relations of urban planning; but they did have a powerful impact on the imagination of the city. If anarchism is indeed a latent force, then perhaps anarchy is also a condition already present within the built environment. In this reading, architects and planners would act as facilitators rather than designers – curators of the spatial agency that is everywhere waiting to be released. Cities would be built from a process of exchange, where everyone can be architects because everyone already has something valuable to contribute.

Gazebo being erected by Extinction Rebellion protestors in Parliament Square, London, April 2019

I. LIBERTY

Freedom is the precondition for acquiring the maturity for freedom, not a gift to be granted when such maturity has been achieved—Noam Chomsky, *On Anarchism* (2013), p. 8

At the root of anarchist thinking and practice is the upholding of freedom as a basic human right. In some circles, the freedoms promised by self-governance are a way of separating oneself from others – arguments for decentralization and autonomy are becoming more and more evident in contemporary right-wing politics. For example, anarcho-capitalists want freedom from regulating authorities in order to maximize the benefits they postulate – or perhaps personally derive – from the free market.

More progressive forms of anarchism, which are still rooted in the socialist politics that emerged in the nineteenth century, equally see freedom from authority as critical, but in this case this is for the creation of a better society – one that is more equal, just and sustainable. It is a collective vision that is fundamentally optimistic about people's ability to govern themselves and to govern themselves well. At root, this is about radical forms of placemaking – of building both structures and spaces to frame a renewed social life. Too often, freedom in architecture is simply equated with individual self-build projects (for example, in the long-running *Grand Designs* television series), obscuring the ways in which building is always part of the construction of a larger social and environmental whole.

This opening section uses eight sites to think through the relationship between freedom and architecture. Six pieces focus on intentional communities, from the permanent and long-lived (Christiania, Auroville and Slab City) to the temporary and ephemeral (Burning Man, Rainbow Gatherings and the Kumbh Mela). Embracing the secular and spiritual, the large and the small, these communities ground emancipation in the practical reality of living together, and of building as a communal endeavour. These are communities that negotiate, each in their own ways, the delicate balance between freedom and control.

The other architectural projects explored in this section – the Hundertwasser-haus and the Holzmarkt – speak of that balance in the context of design and use; and of the relationship between architect and inhabitant. These range from libertarian approaches to form – the curvy lines of the Hundertwasser-haus – through to materials and function (the Holzmarkt). What links them is a distinctly counter-modernist vision of design as organic and subject to evolution.

Christiania, Copenhagen, 1971–

Part of the nineteenth-century military buildings in Christiania that have been converted into co-operative housing

With over half a million visitors every year, Christiania in Copenhagen is the city's third largest tourist attraction. A self-governed 'freetown' of around 900 residents – the largest and oldest of its kind in Europe – Christiania was established in September 1971.[1] Responding to an acute housing crisis in Denmark's capital, local residents tore down the fences of a recently abandoned military barracks, squatted its empty buildings and set up a playground for their children. In the weeks that followed, a call went out for more settlers, and it was soon overrun with young people seeking an alternative and affordable way of living in the city.

Declared a temporary social experiment by the Danish government in May 1972, the 85–acre lakeside site has been subject to numerous attempts by Copenhagen's municipal authorities to reclaim it as a site for redevelopment, none of which have been successful, mostly on

Two self-built houses on the banks of Christiania's lake

A recently built illegal dwelling in the reed-beds at the northern end of Christiania

account of the large-scale protests that resulted. Even after a court ruling in 2011 upheld the right of the state to the land, Christiania continues to function as a self-governing city-in-a-city. Rather than taking back the site, the Danish government instead chose to 'normalize' it, allowing residents to collectively purchase the land and buildings, provided that any new development would conform with Danish law. In effect, Christiania has become a bona-fide municipal council, albeit one with very different values from those of its official counterpart.

One of the pretexts for the proposed redevelopment in 2011 was the desire to knock-down 66 'irregular' houses in Christiania – self-built homes mostly constructed in the 1980s and 1990s by those who preferred not to live in the old barracks, parts of which date back to the 1830s. These self-built homes are all architectural oddities. Some are merely repurposed caravans, shepherds' huts and gypsy wagons. Others suggest a wild, ad-hoc vernacularism: one house is almost entirely comprised of recycled windows held together within a timber frame; another looks like a cross between a mountain chalet and an orthodox church; yet another is a ramshackle bricolage of timber, glass and scaffolding poles that floats on water.

At the other end of the architectural spectrum, some of Christiania's houses were built by designers, the most famous being the Bananhuset ('Banana House'), constructed in 1985 by two itinerant German architects, Axt & Kelle. The elegant semi-circular shape of this large timber-framed house is supported by the hillside on which it rests. Other design-led homes are characterized by eccentric geometries: both the Pyramiden ('Pyramid') and a hexagonal glass house built on piles on Christiana's lake are reminiscent of the space-age structures designed by Richard Buckminster Fuller in the 1960s.

Remarkably, both the primitive and the refined houses are built mostly from salvaged materials – timber, corrugated metal, sheets of glass, breeze blocks – acquired from Christiania's purpose-built hardware store. Although self-building in the freetown has been outlawed for the past 15 years – a product of government-imposed conditions for the site's continued existence – the many structures that remain are still testament to the fertile diversity of housing that might yet emerge in cities if building controls were placed in the hands of dwellers themselves. Even as the Danish authorities have prevented any new building, residents of Christiania are still allowed to renovate their homes as well as alter their roofs, resulting in a new kind of diversity emerging on the site. And, in defiance of this imposed authority, a few have even built illegal dwellings in the reed-beds at the northern edges of the site and in the water beyond – agglomerations of floating platforms and boats lashed together with rope to form micro-communities.

Christiania's longevity is the result of a form of self-governance that continues to work for its hundreds of residents. Divided into 15 geographical districts – ranging from 50 to 9 people per district – the governance of Christiania operates at two different scales: area meetings reach consensus on 'local' issues pertinent to each district; while common meetings do the same for the whole community. Even though meetings can be lengthy and acrimonious, the consensus model has been in place for half a century. The widely varied models of housing within Christiania – from the individual self-builds to the collective apartments in the old barracks – are always set within this dual-scale governance, moving ceaselessly from the local to the 'global'.

Occupying a prime city-centre site, Christiania has been critical in facilitating wider connections between conventional urban development and radical alternatives, especially as it is visited by so many tourists, even if this is only for the exotic allure of the open selling of drugs (a long-standing and problematic byproduct of Christiania's freedom). Whenever the freetown has been threatened, protests have erupted beyond its borders. But it remains to be seen whether Christiania will be able to hold onto its radical vision, or stagnate in its current role as a tourist site. To continue to develop, it must resist attempts at 'normalization', even in the face of its erasure – and the illegal dwellings built on parts of the site demonstrate that some are prepared to resist any imposed authority. Holding out the hope that its connection to the wider city will continue to save it, as it has done in the past, Christiania's motto remains a powerful mandate of shared vulnerability: 'you cannot kill us – we are part of you.'[2]

Hundertwasser-haus, Vienna, 1977–86

The colourful and curvy Hundertwasser-haus in Vienna shares with Christiania the honour of being the third most visited tourist attraction in its respective city. Conceived in 1977, the building was the result of a long process of often-fraught consultation between the Vienna city authority, Austrian artist Friedensreich Hundertwasser, and architects Peter Pelikan and Joseph Krawina.[3] The city authorities recognized that maverick artist and provocateur Hundertwasser could provide Vienna with social-housing of very different appeal than its interwar modernist apartment blocks. The melding of libertarian principles of design, everyday housing and spectacular aesthetics became a hallmark of Hundertwasser's architectural style and, after the success of his Vienna building, he went on to realise many other projects, including similar apartment complexes in Bad Soden (1990–93), Darmstadt (1995–2000), and Magdeburg (1996–2005), a motorway service station in Bad Fischau (1989–90), and even the District Heating Plant in the Spittelau district of Vienna (1988–92).[4]

Hundertwasser's distinctive style emerged from his pathological hatred of architectural modernism, particularly its emphasis on rational, utilitarian design. Proclaiming that right angles in architecture were immoral, Hundertwasser developed a freer, organic approach to design that drew strongly on Art Nouveau (known as Jugendstil in Vienna) and rejected the modernist notion of housing as a machine for living in.[5] Thus, although the Hundertwasser-haus is built in brick – usually resulting in conventional right-angled structures – it is done in such as way as to create an undulating facade. This was achieved by applying an irregular thickness of mortar at the base of the wall, allowing the bricks laid above to maintain a wave-like arrangement, all the way up to the equally irregular roofline. Hundertwasser distinguished each individual apartment (52 of five different sizes) with coloured plaster on its street-facing wall, the edges of which are deliberately sinuous. Although the windows are conventional rectangles, their right angles are obscured with paint and mosaic tiles. As with Antoni Gaudí's work in Barcelona, the roofline of the Hundertwasser-haus is treated as a distinct environment of its own, its sinuous forms quickly enveloped by vegetation. Hundertwasser even included trees literally growing out the windows of three of the apartments, what he termed 'tree tenants'. Building green walls and forested towers long before these became a popular way of 'greening' urban buildings, Hundertwasser's vision was guided by an ecological approach in which 'nature was given back what the house had taken away from her'.[6]

Although Hundertwasser was a passionate advocate of participation in architecture, his was a very different approach from that adopted by some of his architect contemporaries, such as Giancarlo de Carlo in Italy and Lucien Kroll in Belgium. Residents had no say in the design programme; rather, Hundertwasser believed that, in creating organic architectural forms – undulating interior walls, irregularly tiled bathrooms, or trees growing out of windows – he would release the individual creativity of users that the box-like apartments of modernist tower-blocks extinguished. In addition, he secured 'window rights' for each of the tenants, meaning that they could change anything on the exterior within arm's reach of their windows. Hundertwasser also provided an 'adventure room' for the children of tenants, with an undulating floor to encourage experimentation at a young age. This would teach children to develop what Hundertwasser called their 'third skin' – an organic progression outward from skin to clothes to house that would foster an holistic and highly individualistic way of living.

When the Hundertwasser-haus opened in 1985, 70,000 visitors and journalists queued to see the building and, since then, it's seen an unrelenting stream of visitors, who are attracted also by a nearby shopping precinct and

Façade of the Hundertwasser-haus along Kegelgasse, Vienna

General view of the Hundertwasser-haus along Kegelgasse, Vienna

art museum, both designed by Hundertwasser. As geographer Peter Kraftl has argued, tenants have always had to negotiate the dual role of the building as an everyday living space and spectacular tourist attraction, even though visitors are not allowed to enter the apartment complex itself. Some tenants feel sidelined by the media attention on the extraordinary visual appearance of the building or resent being the object of the tourist gaze; others hold a deep attachment to the building, describing it as being 'alive', its colourful façade offering a joyful contrast to the predominant greyness of Viennese architecture. For residents, the tourist experience itself has become part of their everyday lives, even if, by and large, what they do inside the building is as ordinary as in any other apartment block.[7] Indeed, according to Kraftl, not one of the residents has ever exercised their 'window rights', although many had, over the years, decorated the interior corridor walls with drawings and political slogans.[8]

It's clear that there's a tension between the mundane quality of everyday life in the building and the transformative vision of Hundertwasser, as if the artist simply assumed that everyone would want to be as free to create as he did. Indeed, it seems that as a tourist attraction and postcard image of Vienna, the diversity of the tenants' wishes and desires have been glossed over in favour of a utopian vision distanced from their reality. Freedom for inhabitants means precisely the opposite – allowing their complex, subtle and contrasting needs and desires to take priority over the overarching vision of the designer, however well-meaning it may be.

Auroville, Tamil Nadu, India, 1968–

Hundertwasser's conception of the house as a 'third' layer of skin is based on a spiritual idea of reality as an holistic meld of the individual subject – their immaterial spirit and soul – and the material substance of the world as experienced through the senses. The desire to change the world by the power of this inner spirit has always informed the creation of intentional religious communities. In the Christian tradition, this can be seen in the very first radically egalitarian communities of believers, the medieval monasteries that tried to recover this earlier vision, and the overtly anarchist communes inspired by the writings and practice of Leo Tolstoy. But this emphasis of transformative living underpins all religious communities, whatever tradition they follow. At present, the largest of these is Auroville in Tamil Nadu, India. Home to around 2,500 people from 100 countries, it is an explicitly non-territorial city, where property ownership is forbidden and spiritual liberty a guiding principle.[9]

Based on syncretism (the amalgamation of many religious traditions), Auroville began on 28 February 1968 with young people from 124 separate countries and all 29

Model of Auroville as envisaged by architect Robert Unger in the late 1960s

Indian states each placing a handful of earth from their home-lands in an urn right at the centre of the new city. Auroville's conception actually dates back to 1938, when the spiritual leader Sri Aurobindo Ghose and his spiritual partner Mirra Alfassa, better known as the Mother, commissioned architect Antonin Raymond to design the first reinforced concrete building constructed in India to serve as a residence for the members of their rapidly expanding ashram.

Auroville combined innovative technology with radical social autonomy. Throughout its long history, the community has commissioned unconventional architects to design buildings on the site.[10] These include Roger Anster – in 1971, he built the first houses on the site with huge curving ferro-concrete roofs; and Italian architects Piero and Gloria Cicionesi, who built a temporary school for the community. The Cicionesis also supervised the first stages of construction of Auroville's most startling building, the Matrimandir, a vast golden globe that functions as a meditation and integral yoga centre and is sited at the very centre of the city (and only completed in 2008). The city plan itself was drawn up by French architect Robert Unger – its spiralling structure, known as the 'galaxy concept', radiating out from the central dome in four distinct zones: Residential, Industrial, Cultural and International. Although superficially resembling the garden cities developed by Ebenezer Howard at the turn of the twentieth century, Auroville's founding principle of individual spiritual liberty sets it apart from the rather dour uniformity of garden cities as they were mostly built.

More recently, architectural expression in Auroville has become concerned with sustainability and also in empowering the wider community to build for themselves. In the late 1970s, architect Poppo Pingel pioneered the use of rammed-earth construction in the city; while the American ceramicist Ray Meaker experimented with

Auroville's Town Hall, designed by local architect Anupama Kundoo and completed in 2003

The Sri Aurobindo Auditorium, designed by R. Chakrapani and completed in 1970

The Matrimandir in Auroville, designed by architects Piero and Gloria Cicionesi and completed in 2008

fire-stabilized mud houses, building 20 separate projects since 1985. In this period the Earth Unit was set up in Auroville to provide advice for architects and students to build with mud and earth. The many hundreds of volunteers who visit Auroville each year usually assist in building houses for some of the 70,000 mostly impoverished Tamils in 75 surrounding villages, thus disseminating the sustainable building practices developed at Auroville.[11]

A recent visitor to Auroville has drawn attention to some of the problems lurking behind its reputation as a spiritual haven. In recent years, there have been several reported cases of robbery, sexual harassment and even murder in the area immediately beyond the older part of the city. For some, Auroville's reputation for liberty has been compromised by its administrative rigidity; anyone documenting the city must get clearance from its Outreach Media Centre – hardly in tune with the city's founding ideals. Auroville's numerous self-formed committees have created a situation in which financial accountability has become almost impossible, while the emphasis on individualized spiritual practice can lead to isolation and mental health problems for residents.[12] Yet, in being rooted in an evolutionary notion of human growth and in seeking to expand and move beyond its own exclusive borders (the original plan was for 50,000 residents), Auroville still represents a powerful example of outward-looking liberty. The fact that it continues to endure – and to grow, albeit slowly – indicates that its problems are not overwhelming, but rather that the city is continuing to negotiate the ongoing tension between individual liberty and communal living.

Burning Man, global, 1986–

Making art as a way into freedom has long been the driving force of festivals, flowering with spectacular speed in the early 1970s after the Woodstock Festival (1969) saw music bringing together hundreds of thousands in a decommodified utopian celebration of countercultural values. In recent years, perhaps the most influential demonstration of this is the annual week-long Burning Man event held in the Nevada desert in early September. In countless websites, press articles, numerous glossy books and other publications, the scarcely credible artwork of Burning Man emerges out of the extreme landscape in which it is set. Giant wood and metal sculptures of figures, animals and mythological creatures animate the barren landscape, lit up at night in spectacular technicolour; mysterious abstract sculptures appear like objects deposited by aliens; giant temples a mirage of past historical styles. Participants move around the site on bicycles or in the vast array of 'Mutant Vehicles' that have been a staple of the event for years – many reflecting the post-apocalyptic chic of the *Mad Max* series of films. It's clearly a carnival of excess – or a 'permission engine' as its organisers term it – a place of radical liberation to experiment in whatever way you want to.[13]

Attracting over 70,000 participants in 2019, the event had very humble origins, when Larry Harvey burned a life-size effigy of a man to entertain his son and a few friends on a San Francisco beach in July 1986. After the police intervened in 1990, the event moved to the Black Rock Desert, some 300 miles from San Francisco, under

Giant female figure installed at Black Rock City in 2015

Aerial view of Black Rock City in Nevada, 2012

the invitation of the anarchist art provocateur group Cacophony Society, who were hosting a Labor Day gathering there in early September. In each subsequent year, the number of people who participated doubled, reaching 4,000 in 1995.[14] In that year, the camp began to be known as Black Rock City, organized as a fully equipped temporary settlement, planned around a vast semicircle inscribed with streets but completely erased by desert dust storms afterwards.

Black Rock City is now organized by a limited liability corporation working year-round in San Francisco with 35 staff members and a six-member governing board.[15] As well as applying for permits and liaising with federal agencies and local governments, the company also award grants to dozens of participating artists each year. Most artists –

and there were at least 300 separate installations in 2019 – still need to fund their projects by other means, whether through crowd-sourcing or corporate sponsorship. On the ground at Black Rock City, representatives of the company oversee communications, infrastructure and emergency services, among other city functions; the controversial provision of police officers by the federal authorities mostly accepted if begrudgingly. Today, anyone can attend the event, but they first must pay around $400 for a ticket plus another $100 for a vehicle pass, bring all their own food, water and shelter, and also be prepared for a long wait while their belongings are inspected by the police. Once inside though, the libertarian ethos of the event still prevails – a week-long party that places the highest value on individual self-expression, unbridled hedonism, and a

Art installation titled *Exsuscitare Traiectus* at Black Rock City, 2011

complete prohibition on buying and selling, everything on offer being classed as a gift.

The ethos of Black Rock City has spread globally, with more than 60 like-minded communities and celebrations now held in 26 countries, all under the banner of Burning Man. Indeed, it has now become a brand – the ten principles of Burning Man, published by Harvey in 2004, offering a loose template for those seeking to adopt the name.[16] These bring together the elements of Burning Man that have evolved at Black Rock City, including the gift economy, self-expression, participation, community and what he terms 'Leaving No Trace', which, today, means hundreds of volunteers cleaning up every speck of detritus after the event has finished. Three of these principles use the word radical – Radical Inclusion, Radical Self-Reliance, and Radical Self-Expression – and Burning Man is often presented as a genuinely transformative experience for its participants where other more conventional festivals are simply pale imitations. Such rhetoric emphasizes Burning Man as an avant-garde form of cultural expression, even as this is offset by its principle of inclusion.

In fact, Burning Man is full of such contradictions. Its policy of cleaning up every speck of rubbish demonstrates ecological responsibility; yet, its annual centrepiece – the burning of the ever-larger effigy of a man and many other structures – seems frankly distasteful in a world where climate-change is stoking apocalyptic fires elsewhere. Its principle of inclusion is flatly contradicted by the cost of the entrance ticket alone, but also by the measure of control exerted on the funding of participating artists, with Harvey seeming to have the final say on almost everything. Gifting may produce a radically different kind of experience for participants, but it conceals the vast resources necessary to host the event in the first place. Burning Man does attempt to balance different expressions of freedom, from the excess, abandonment and cacophonous energy that characterize media representations of the festival, to the more contemplative moments offered by the temples, particularly when they are burned the night before the last act of the festival, the conflagration of the Man. Here, participants mourn past losses, relinquish fears and find hope for the future in this quieter ritual of burning.

Many of Burning Man's organizers and participants are drawn from California's Silicon Valley (Google now owns over half the shares in the company). Just as Black Rock City was rapidly expanding, a new kind of utopia was invented in Silicon Valley, namely the cyberspace that promised escape from the strictures and maddening complexities of the 'real' world. There's more than a hint of escapism in the ethos of Burning Man, despite its emphasis on engagement, participation and civic responsibility. Liberation is sometimes spectacular, noisy and excessive; but more often than not, it is hidden from view, experienced in moments of stillness, and quietly unobtrusive.

Rainbow Gatherings, global, 1972–

Rainbow Gathering in Oregon in 2017

The de-commodification that is one of Burning Man's ten principles keys into a long-standing desire of many to escape the relentless world of consumer capitalism. And, in the US, it has its origins in the free festivals movement of the early 1970s. After Woodstock, music festivals became commercialized and there were many in the counter-culture that wanted to continue the example of that original free festival. In the first week of July 1972, more than 20,000 young people converged in a remote forest on a Colorado mountainside for a few days to meditate, chant prayers and play music. This was the first Rainbow Gathering – and they have been occurring every year for one week at the beginning of July in the US since then (and, from the 1980s, in Europe and subsequently in over 20 countries around the world). Entirely funded by donations from participants (who are asked to contribute to a 'magic hat' that is passed round at mealtimes), there is no buying and selling at Rainbow Gatherings and everything is free for those who attend.[17]

The participants at Rainbow Gatherings don't produce any of the spectacular structures that make Burning Man such a photogenic event; rather, it's the principles of organization that take centre stage. For Rainbow Gatherings are at root experiments in non-hierarchical ways of living, their founding ethos grounded in the belief that all individuals can be free if they are simply allowed to be. There's no explicit policy of inclusion, but no-one is ever turned away from Gatherings and everyone is provided for once there. Meals are shared in 'food circles' and decisions made by consensus in 'talking circles'. Similar to the ways in which protest movements like Occupy and Extinction Rebellion organized themselves, Rainbow Gatherings emphasize that it is people themselves, and not the structures they build, that are the bedrock of libertarian forms of social organization. Any recognized Rainbow rules (such as non-violence) come only from one source, the main Council which meets at the annual national gatherings.[18]

Just like Burning Man, Gatherings have developed their own traditions and rituals which give form to the overarching ideal of liberty, whether the decision-making circles themselves, chanting and prayers, or participatory forms of music. But, unlike Burning Man, there is no official organization behind the scenes: the wider Rainbow Family, as they are known, have no leaders, spokespersons or documents, and no membership – it's been playfully called a 'disorganization' with the world's largest number of non-members.[19] What it does have is an ever-changing rota of volunteers (called 'facilitators') who spend weeks setting up the camps and sometimes months afterwards cleaning up and actively restoring and often enhancing the forest ecosystems that they temporarily occupy.

As ethnographers Kirsten C. Blinne and Tenali Hrenak explain, trying to describe the organization of a Rainbow Gathering is difficult because it happens in the moment: what Gatherers learn, they learn from each other, primarily through oral tradition, some of which now exists in published memoirs and web-based resources, but which is always worked out in the context of the Gathering itself.[20] For Blinne, it is the quotidian aspects of the event that are most memorable: 'using a communal shitter, for me, is a major part of the gathering experience from digging the slit trench latrine to clean-up and all the poop that comes in-between.'[21] It is these mundane acts, usually cast out of everyday consciousness, that suddenly take on unexpected significance when carried out in a radically inclusive environment. For these basic human functions would simply not be adequately met without the cooperation of the entire community. And, mostly, the individual camps at Gatherings are centred around food: communal kitchens built from the fallen timber of the forest that form the other end of the excretory processes that unites us all.

The radical inclusion that characterizes Rainbow Gatherings has unsurprisingly led to a good deal of negative press coverage, especially when things go wrong.[22] There have been deaths at Gatherings – homicides even – and isolated cases of child abuse and sexual assault; and local people tend to be hostile to what they perceive as libertarian hippie values – drug use and public nudity for example. There are also participants who refuse to work for the common good, taking the free resources on offer but not giving anything back in return (known as 'Drainbows'). Within Gatherings, security, conflict resolution and emergency situations are handled by the Shanti Sena ('peace army'), who also liaise with state police.

However problematic their policy of radical inclusion, Rainbow Gatherings demonstrate a fundamentally different way of treating those on the edge of society, namely through acceptance rather than suspicion or hostility. Rather than viewing themselves as an enclave set apart from mainstream society (what Gatherers often call 'Babylon'), Gatherings acknowledge that their diversity, in fact, reflects it. What sets them apart is that they try to respond differently by confronting violence and hate with peace and love. Easy to dismiss these as outdated utopian hippie values; yet this prioritization of tolerance over peace is actually a clear demonstration of what radical inclusivity actually means in practice. Rainbow Gatherings embody an anarchism that is supported by a powerful ethical foundation, one that takes seriously the responsibilities that come when we choose to live and act together without leaders.

Rainbow Gathering in Bosnia in 2007

Kumbh Mela, Allahabad, India, every 12 years

It's now commonplace for temporary events like Burning Man and Rainbow Gatherings to accommodate tens of thousands of participants. Even as an ethos of participation is mostly underplayed, a growing number of festivals – whether for music, spirituality, art or any number of other reasons – are organized year round across the world that require permanently staffed organizations to run them. But accommodating millions is another matter and the scale of India's Kumbh Mela festival sets it apart from any of its counterparts. Held every four years since at least the eighteenth century at different sacred riverside sites in India, the Kumbh Mela returns to each one every 12 years, the largest being the festival held at the confluence of the Ganges and Yamuna rivers in Allahabad.[23] The 2013 festival was the largest the world had ever seen; five million devotees were accommodated but it is estimated that up to 120 million visitors came to the site to bathe in the river during the festival's 55–day duration. It was also the first Kumbh Mela to be comprehensively documented, in this case by a research team from Harvard University.[24]

Accommodating such vast numbers of people has resulted in what Rahul Mehrotra and Felipe Vera – two of the Harvard researchers – have called an 'ephemeral mega-city' – a vast settlement that has evolved over the many incarnations of the festival into a sophisticated example of large-scale but short-lived urban planning. The building of such a city, occupying the 23.5 square-metre sacred site known as the *nagri*, is complicated by the fact that, for most of the year, the land is flooded by the two rivers. Planning begins a year before the festival while the *nagri* is still inundated by the Monsoon. This foresight is largely the product of British colonial officials' desire to contain and control the event in the nineteenth century, when fear of disease and other dangers brought a process of rationalization to the organization of the Kumbh Mela. This involved applying an irregular grid over the site

Crowds of pilgrims at the 2013 Kumbh Mela

Pilgrims at the 2013 Kumbh Mela walking to the sacred bathing sites,
with a temporary bamboo temple shown in the background

– similar to the ways in which the British planned their military cantonments in India – and appointing a local magistrate to oversee planning and construction.[25] In 2013, this involved the building of 160km of roads (mostly using steel plates bolted together), 17 pontoon bridges that crossed the two rivers, 14 field hospitals, 35,000 latrines, a comprehensive water and electricity infrastructure, and numerous police stations and watchtowers to keep order.

Funded mostly by India's federal government, this infrastructure is planned well in advance but, because the exact extent of the site is not known until the river waters recede around four months before the festival begins, the grid plan has to be flexible enough to be adaptable to the variable conditions on the ground. Once the floodwaters are gone, the infrastructure is put in place. Thereafter, building materials arrive in huge quantities, almost all of which are provided by private companies in return for a rental fee by participants. These comprise: a mixture of standard-length bamboo sticks that are used to construct almost all of the supporting walls of structures ranging from simple dwellings to hospitals and temples; corrugated iron panels for dividing the camps; and a vast array of multicoloured fabrics to cover the bamboo structural frames. The religious groups who occupy the site for the entire duration of the festival – a plethora of Hindu sects – are divided into camps within the sections of the site specified in advance (14 in 2013). Once the festival ends, everything is dismantled – the building materials either stored for future reuse, recycled back into the local economy or, in the case of bamboo and thatch, left to naturally biodegrade. This waste refertilizes the silt that is then put to agricultural use during the dry months in the years between festivals.

This top-down approach to planning – understandable given the scale of the Kumbh Mela – is offset by the relative autonomy of the various religious groups who attend to organize their own camps. The fact that the building materials are so simple – lightweight and low-tech modular elements like bamboo sticks – means that even unskilled participants can reconfigure structures and spaces to suit their own needs. In addition, centralized planning beforehand is supplemented by on-the-ground participation by officials who meet every evening during the festival to address problems and adapt the structures and spaces. Mehrotra and Vera argue that it's precisely this built-in flexibility that allows the otherwise constrictive grid of the site plan to be malleable: for example, in the ways in which every camp is different in its configuration; and in the many gardens that are created by participants as oases among the incessant crush of pilgrims.

Mehrotra and Vera have also suggested that the ephemeral megacity created for the Kumbh Mela provides a more general example of how architects and planners might adopt a much more flexible approach in creating urban environments; cities that embrace impermanence as a virtue rather than a vice.[26] Indeed, the decidedly low-tech solutions employed for the Kumbh Mela are a powerful counter to the prevailing idea of 'smart' cities in discourse on the future of urban life.[27] In a future when urban landscapes will become increasingly vulnerable to flooding, fire, extreme pollution and overpopulation, the simple and pragmatic technologies used to create the Kumbh Mela might be appropriate ways of confronting and responding to the uncertainty generated by such threats. The sheer size of the festival also provides a unique example of how to negotiate the tension between freedom and control in an urban context appropriate to today's megacities.

One of the 17 pontoon bridges constructed across the Ganges and Yamuna rivers during the 2013 Kumbh Mela

Slab City, California, USA, 1950s–

The grid might be a planning tool that negotiates the delicate balance between control and freedom; but it's more usually associated with an inflexible form of rationality. Such was the case with Slab City in the southern California desert some 200 miles southeast from Los Angeles. Now known as 'the last free place' in the USA, it was ironically once a military settlement, Camp Dunlap, laid out in the Second World War as a gridded settlement appropriate to the harsh disciplinarian life of combat training. Abandoned at the end of the war, it was taken over by squatters and has been continuously inhabited ever since. It's now named after the concrete slabs laid down by the military as foundations for their barracks and other buildings.

Officially designated as public land owned by the state, California has tried many times in the past to sell the 640-acre site, but its harsh desert location – cut off

Welcome sign at the entrance to Slab City

Open-air bar and seating area at Slab City

from the nearest main road and other settlements around the shrinking Salton Sea and close to a military firing range – has made it unattractive to would-be developers. At present, a few hundred people live there, but the population varies wildly according to the time of year. Every autumn, hundreds of 'snowbirds' – mostly retired couples – travel from the northern US states to join the small permanent population in their Recreational Vehicles (RVs), parking on any free concrete slab or other suitable space and departing again once the heat begins to build in April. According to one former resident, Nadine Anglin, the population of Slab City rose to a staggering 6,000 in the winter of 1985.[28] And always there is also a smaller population of itinerants, so called 'bush bunnies' who live temporarily on the edges of the site, either homeless or on the run.

Widely documented because of its longevity, Slab City has become part of a wider cultural imaginary of frontier living and the realisation of personal freedom. Sean Penn's 2007 film adaptation of Jon Krakauer's novel *Into the Wild* (1996) saw its rebel protagonist Christopher McCandless stopping off in Slab City on his way north to an off-grid existence in Alaska; while Ana Lily Amirpour's 2017 Netflix film *The Bad Batch* used the site as a suitable setting for a post-apocalyptic settlement of social outcasts – abandoned in a fenced-off desert enclave (though we never know quite why). Ironically named Comfort, this ramshackle town is dominated by the trade of hallucinogenic drugs that fund its basic infrastructure.

Drawing on different incarnations of the American Dream, these fictions present Slab City as a place of contradictions: home to both outcasts and pioneers living a life of hedonistic excess and hard-edged practicality. As documented in detail by Charlie Hailey and Donovan White, these contradictions are paradoxically inherent to the longevity of Slab City.[29] The site is thoroughly fluid in many different ways. First, although some residents have built their own houses – mostly out of salvaged materials such as timber, corrugated metal, cardboard and canvas – the majority still live in RVs or static trailers, gradually adding to them over the years. Consequently, although some

Dilapidated RV at Slab City, 2007

territories are jealously guarded (even though all who live there are effectively squatters), they are rarely owned for long because the majority of the residents are itinerant. This transience also diffuses conflicts over the long term: if you don't like your neighbour, you can simply move to another part of the site.

What Hailey and White found in Slab City was a place that was constantly evolving: at one moment abandoned, the next inhabited, and vice versa. This lack of fixity led to a strange intermingling of past, present and future – a sense that the linear time we tend to take for granted in conventional cities had been dissolved. In the early nineteenth century, Native American Cahuilla lived on this part of the Colorado river delta where a lake used to exist. During the Second World War, thousands of military personnel briefly trained there for expected desert combat in North Africa. In the present day, RV enthusiasts with enough resources to travel year round live alongside homeless people, drug addicts or those with mental health problems given a sanctuary, and hard-nosed survivalists looking for an end-of-the-world refuge.

At its heart, Slab City embodies a characteristically American take on anarchism – residents have complete freedom so long as they do not impinge upon anyone else's. The shared spaces that have been built over the years, including sculpture gardens, an internet cafe, skate parks, and The Range – a bar and entertainment area that hosts weekly open-mic events – were built without any collective decision-making; rather, by individuals seeking to provide services or start a business. This emphasis on sharing sits uneasily with a frontier ethic of individual self-sufficiency. Yet, in allowing both, Slab City seems to have evolved a way of coping with the contradictions inherent in human behaviour, a loose system of organization that is less about developing collective governance and more about encouraging the initiative of individuals. The longevity of the community indicates that this is one way of balancing the desire for freedom with the need for order.

Holzmarkt, Berlin, 2012–17

Concrete is also the centrepiece material of a more recent experiment in anarchic urban planning, the Holzmarkt development, opened in May 2017 and located on the river Spree near Berlin's Ostabahnhof station. Like many areas of central Berlin after the reunification of the city in 1990, it was waste-ground until requisitioned for creative use by Bar25, a legendary nightclub run by Juval Dieziger and Christoph Klenzedorf. When the site was eventually earmarked for redevelopment, its holding company SpreeUrban made plans for a new luxury development of high-rise office blocks. However, in 2012 this plan was shelved and the plot of land was put out for tender. In a bold move, Dieziger and Klenzedorf reclaimed the site with the help of Swiss pension fund Abendrot, who bought it for €10 million and then leased it back to a cooperative founded by Bar25 supporters.[30]

Working with architects Hütten & Paläste in 2012–13, the central planning concept was for an urban village in which the structures and spaces would be flexible enough to allow for a variety of possible uses and which could be extended and reworked in the future. The architects provided an 'infrastructural backbone' to the site – an agglomeration of several four-storey buildings made from pre-cast concrete elements that were purchased using a component catalogue. This was built for a variety of uses, including a carpentry workshop, music studios, a market and an event and practice space for a circus troupe. The rest of the site would be allowed to develop informally – self-built 'huts' and other structures would provide spaces for a range of small-scale uses, from artists' studios to shops, cafes and bars.[31]

Today, viewed from the other side of the river Spree in Berlin's Kreuzberg district, the Holzmarkt presents a startling counter to what we normally expect of urban redevelopment. Instead of conventional high-rise buildings, with their transparent glass facades and geometric purity,

The principal concrete-framed building of the Holzmarkt, September 2018

Interior of the KaterHolzig nightclub, September 2018

the Holzmarkt is a haphazard jumble of forms that seem to have little visual relationship to their function. Although the concrete structural frame of the core buildings can be found in almost any other modern multi-storey structure, here it has been clad in a wild assortment of materials that seem deliberately anarchic in their refusal of formal and structural integrity. Brick vies with timber, corrugated metal, recycled rubber, and bare concrete painted with murals; the whole linked at various levels by metal and timber walkways. This represents, in stark visual terms, the collision of the formal programme of architectural modernism and an emphasis on the concrete frame as a flexible container for users to fill as they wish: a fact that somewhat ironically recalls one of Le Corbusier's earliest projects, the Dom-Ino House of 1914, in which the fledgling soon-to-be arch-modernist architect attempted (unsuccessfully) to make his fortune by selling two-storey concrete frames and letting buyers fill in their own walls.

As envisaged by the architects, a panoply of self-built structures have sprouted around the core infrastructure. Nearby is a stack of shipping containers repurposed as artists' studios, one of which is clad in recycled beer cans. Further down towards the river are more informal structures, including the KaterHolzig nightclub, a timber-frame building supporting an almost continuous facade of salvaged windows. Smaller structures surround the nightclub – wooden verandas to shelter revellers, sheds functioning as cafés or smaller bars, and a haphazard assortment of street furniture to cater for crowds. Although the site has

only one entrance – an artful 'hole' in a wooden fence fronting the busy Holzmarktstrasse – it remains fully open to all and noticeably absent is any security.

The uniqueness of the Holzmarkt development stems from the way in which it has combined more formal aspects of urban planning with the spontaneity of creative practices that have come to define cities like Berlin in recent years. Although the idea of the 'creative city' has been criticized by some as just another way in which neoliberal elites use artists and other creatives to pave the way for inevitable gentrification, there are crucial ways in which the Holzmarkt development counters this. First, the site cannot be sold on at a profit, a move that clearly prevents landowner Abendrot from being enticed by the standard development model. Second, the architecture itself is completely at odds with the urban futures envisaged by most property developers and municipal authorities: the loose functionality of the concrete frames, the porosity of inside and outside, and the collision of the formal and informal all resist the monolithic visions of profit-driven urban development. Naturally, there are drawbacks: there is currently no permanent housing on the site, which compromises the idea of the Holzmarkt as a self-sustaining urban microcosm; and its continuing evolution is dependent on an idealistic vision of creative practices continuing to flourish and provide revenue. Yet, perhaps such vulnerabilities are part-and-parcel of freer and more informal ways of making cities – unlike the firm, if ultimately illusory, assurances of endless profits for investors in the neoliberal city, there are no such guarantees when one makes the city for oneself.

General view of the Holzmarkt from the river Spree, September 2018

II. ESCAPE

There is some of the same fitness in a man building his own house that there is in a bird building its own nest. Who knows but if men constructed their dwellings with their own hands, and provided food for themselves and families simply and honestly enough, the poetic faculty would be universally developed, as birds universally sing when they are so engaged?
—Henry David Thoreau, *Walden* (1854), p. 36

In the nineteenth century, as the Global North gradually and unevenly industrialized, self-building encapsulated a romantic longing for a more direct relationship between humans and the natural world; and nowhere more so than in the hut that American writer Henry David Thoreau built for himself at Walden Pond in Massachusetts in 1845. Drawing on a rich tradition of self-building that included fishermen's huts, vernacular country villas, and wilderness retreats for writers and hermits, Thoreau cast himself as the modern equivalent of Adam building his primitive hut in the Garden of Eden. From then on, huts became places of retreat – bolt-holes, whether places for heroic contemplation (Martin Heidegger's mountain hut) or summer holidays, the countless *dachas* of the Soviet countryside.

This section draws out the meanings of escape when people choose to build for themselves. It begins by focusing on an historical moment in Britain when large numbers of working-class people were able to acquire small plots of land for building – something which ended dramatically with a change in planning law in 1947. The second piece focuses on a surviving example of just such a development on the edges of present-day Copenhagen – Nokken. We stay in the Danish capital to explore another site of escape, in this case for children: the junk playgrounds that originated in the city in the 1940s and which then spread all over Europe.

The next two pieces explore two roughly contemporaneous countercultural communities in North America: Drop City in the US, perhaps the most famous hippie commune of the late 1960s; and the Maplewood mudflats just outside Vancouver. These two examples serve to illustrate a fecund moment when countercultural communities were truly enormous in their impact. It finishes with three sites that have politicized the act of escaping the city: long-standing squats in France (the ZAD) and the Netherlands (ADM squat) that are fundamentally concerned with developing new ways of living outside of the control of the state.

Taken together, the sites explored in this section challenge us to think again about the romantic appeal of self-building, to see escape as more than simply shutting oneself off from others; rather, it can be a way of opening up spaces so that richer forms of social life can develop. Most of the sites explored here ended up failing in one way of another, either because of internal tensions or external forces. But failure is never the end of the story – there are always vestiges that remain, traces that are waiting to be resurrected to inspire others.

Interior of the replica of Thoreau's cabin at Walden Pond, Massachusetts

Plotlands, UK, early 20th century

View of the Palmers Estate in Laindon, a plotlands site developed in the mid-1930s by a local builder

In the first half of the twentieth century, all across Britain, tens of thousands of self-built houses were constructed – perhaps the only sustained period in British history when house-building was widely in the hands of dwellers themselves. Meticulously documented by Colin Ward and Dennis Hardy in the 1980s, plotlands came from marginal farmland that was divided into small plots and sold off cheaply to buyers wanting to create their holiday homes, rural retreats, or smallholdings.[1] By far the largest concentration of plotlands was in southeast England, reflecting the fact that London provided the biggest market of people wanting to escape the city; but plotlands also sprung up in locations close to every major city in Britain. Self-built house were also put up along the banks of major rivers, such as the Thames, Severn, Wye and Dee; and all around the coast, from Norfolk to Northumberland; Lancashire to Cornwall.

The combination of cheap land (some plots going for as little as £1), widespread availability of prefabricated materials, and the owners' (free) labour and skills, led to the building of a huge array of structures, ranging from appropriated army huts, railway coaches and tram cars to shanties, sheds, shacks and chalets built from timber, brick and corrugated iron. With little or no infrastructure provided by local authorities, many of these communities were effectively off-grid, resulting in their widespread condemnation by middle-class observers as rural slums. In architect Clough Williams-Ellis's 1937 collection *Britain and the Beast*, broadcaster Howard Marshall described the plotlands as 'a gimcrack civilization [that] crawls like a giant slug across the country, leaving a foul trail of slime behind it'.[2] Hardly disguising their misanthropy towards the working-classes, these responses reveal a fundamental conflict in the way in which the countryside was perceived and who was entitled to occupy it. The seemingly anarchic growth of plotlands developments clearly enraged those who believed that the British countryside should be a carefully managed preserve of the few. In the end, it was postwar planning legislation – most importantly the 1947 Town and Country Planning Act – coupled with the fact that landowners were now subsidized to upgrade marginal farmland, that led to cessation of the plotlands as a viable form of development. Today, very few of the original plotlands dwellings remain; they have either been bulldozed to make way for post-war development, or slowly upgraded to blend in with bland suburbia.

The British plotlands flourished at the same time as many other informal settlements in the Global North, such as the numerous Hoovervilles in the USA that sprang up on the edges of almost every town and city during the Great Depression of the 1930s;[3] the Wild Settlement movement in Vienna, which saw the seizure of private land by thousands of homeless citizens after the collapse of the Austro-Hungarian empire in 1915;[4] and the 120,000 self-built huts constructed in the first decades of the 20th century on allotments in Berlin by citizens wanting a place

A surviving plotlands house on the banks of the river Thames near Shepperton

Coastal self-built chalets at Embleton Bay, Northumberland

of escape.[5] Just like the British plotlands, these makeshift landscapes were largely obliterated by comprehensive redevelopment after the Second World War; but they provide an intriguing picture of a multinational pheno-menon that still speaks of an alternative approach to mass housing. As architect Charles Holland has argued, in both Berlin and Vienna, the municipal authorities tried at times to incorporate informal housing into their longer-term comprehensive redevelopment plans. Recognizing and accepting the value of informal settlements in their cities, they sought to facilitate self-build as a way of saving money on labour, while providing funds for materials and installing basic infrastructure. Combining strategic plan-ning with dweller control, such a hybrid model of urban development might yet provide a powerful alternative to the overwhelming dominance of private-sector-led house building that is only fuelling the ongoing housing crisis. The state could, in this way, create new markets for private-sector investment rather than simply trying to cor-rect market failures.[6] However, the result would likely be hybrid landscapes – neither urban nor rural – that would undoubtedly be offensive to many, particularly those that continue to hold the view that the countryside shouldn't be developed at all.

The sad case of Jaywick Sands provides a salutary warning of the dangers of isolating former plotlands set-tlements from mainstream development. In the 2010s, Jaywick was the most deprived ward in England; it was also the largest plotlands site in Essex that developed out of a planned holiday resort for Londoners, built in the late 1920s. After the Second World War, many from bombed-out districts of London moved here permanently.[7] Since then, most of the town's original shacks have been upgraded and connected up to services; yet Jaywick's notoriety led to it being used in the US President Donald Trump's midterm election campaign in 2018 as a particularly extreme example of urban blight; while in the same year, UN officials visited Jaywick as part of an investigation into the effects of austerity on living conditions in the UK. Clearly suffering the ill effects of decades of neglect, the town exemplifies the need for informal settlements to be connected to the formal networks of power – but in a relationship of mutual respect not control or castigation on the part of the authorities. As the documentary film *Jaywick Escapes* (2012) shows, current residents still view the town as an arcadian idyll, despite its undoubted problems. The town still holds its original promise of escape – a life of ease and leisure so often denied to the most vulnerable in society. Yet, it is also clear that not all the needs of a community like Jaywick can be met from within, particularly when that community is already disadvantaged and geographically isolated. To assume that dweller control in housing will solve all social problems is merely wishful thinking or worse – an excuse for the complete abdication of responsibility by the state for its most vulnerable citizens.

Nokken, Copenhagen, 1930–

The plotlands in Britain, and many other informal settlements in European cities, may have come to an abrupt end after the Second World War, but a few still survive on the edges of some cities, mainly as a result of determined community resistance. One of these is Nokken, immediately south of a vast area of urban regeneration on reclaimed land in southeast Copenhagen. Nokken consists of around 120 individual plots of land that are now classed as an urban allotment and protected from any commercial redevelopment. Such protection was hard won – the 100 long-term residents of Nokken resisting plans in the 1990s for comprehensive redevelopment of the area even though the land is now owned by the Copenhagen Municipality.[8]

Founded as a fishing village in 1930, Nokken has slowly evolved into two distinct areas: the principal 'village' where self-built houses are occupied permanently; and a larger area of allotments where smaller structures can be inhabited for only short periods.[9] Strung out on dirt roads enveloped in vegetation, the village could not

be more different than the brand-new apartments just a stone's throw away to the north. Houses range from the wilfully eccentric – a stained-glass clad bungalow sprouting an improvised observatory – to the utilitarian – a hastily repurposed gypsy caravan and shipping container. They also range wildly in terms of size – from single-occupancy dwellings to large family homes. Yet all are visually unobtrusive – a restriction on height being part of the stipulation for Nokken's continued existence.

In the allotment area, the structures are all tiny: single-room dwellings that adjoin gardens, whether purely ornamental or for growing food as in a traditional allotment. These huts, cabins and chalets display the marks of individuality that corporate-led developments can never achieve and sculptures, ornaments and found objects adorn walls and fences. As if to draw attention to this oasis of individual expression, at the entrance to the community is a strange monument: half of a boat's upturned hull in which a framed embroidery sits on top of the dissected innards of a piano. A surrealist collage of juxtaposed elements, this sculpture announces the presence of the unconventional, a built environment that seems to have grown out of the landscape and the materials it has produced over the years.

All around Nokken are strewn a variety of waste materials: a mess that stands in direct contrast to the detritus of the vast construction site at Islands Bryggen. That mess is temporary, to be cleaned up as soon as building is finished and no doubt hidden in a vast landfill site on the edge of the city. By contrast, the wastes of Nokken are made visible – awaiting some future use not yet accounted for. And because the community is not served by standard municipal infrastructure, such as sewerage, each householder has to deal with their own wastes, either in septic tanks or soil-compost toilets.

A repurposed shepherd's hut in Nokken, April 2019

Nokken's self-built houses suggest an alternative form of urbanism to the conventional neoliberal model of comprehensive redevelopment, one that is neither urban nor rural but rather a hybrid of the two. It is development that is grounded in the power of individuals, rather than global corporations, to shape their own dwellings but also in those individuals taking on more responsibilities than conventional home owners. As April Anson has argued in relation to the recent 'tiny house' movement, which has seen large numbers of people embrace small-scale homes as a way of reducing costs and their environmental footprint, this emphasis on both individual freedom and collective living is a hallmark of more radical attempts at alternative forms of urban living.[10] It might be romantic to see Nokken as a community that stands in heroic resistance to the encroaching juggernaut of neoliberal speculative urbanism; yet, the decision by some to choose an alternative, and to fight for it, reveals how the tension between freedom and responsibility can be successfully negotiated.

Art installation at the northern edge of Nokken, April 2019

A self-built house in Nokken, Copenhagen. In the background
are new apartments built on Islands Bryggen, April 2019

Junk playgrounds, global, 1943–

London's first permanent adventure playground, on a two-acre
council site in Faraday Road, Notting Hill, 1965

Copenhagen is also home to the world's first, and oldest surviving, junk playground – a place of escape for the city's youngest inhabitants in the northern suburb of Emdrup. Junk playgrounds were first proposed in 1931 by Danish landscape architect Carl Theodor Sørensen, after he had observed children playing on construction sites and junk-yards. However, Sørensen had to wait 12 years before he was able to build one on the Emdrupvænge housing estate.[11] A six-foot-high bank of mud and vegetation was raised to keep noise levels down and to hide the play-ground from the surrounding housing estate. Emdrup's first play leader, Jon Bertelsen, supervised the hundreds of children of all ages and social classes who visited to site each day in its early years.

As recounted by Bertelsen in his diaries, the Emdrup playground started with just heaps of detritus and mounds of earth as the first play materials. The children began by digging caves into the earth and assembling their own houses from the assorted junk on offer. Over time, these makeshift shacks marked the territories of indi-vidual groups of children while, at the same time, com-munal structures – for example, a police station, hospital and shared wigwam – were constructed by the children as places for monitoring the evolution of the site and for intervening in disputes. No individual structure lasted for long – the huts were intermittently demolished and rebuilt for different owners and to new designs. As Bertelsen put it, 'in children's play activities the process of construction, the completed result and the eventual pulling down are all stages of equal importance'. One of Bertelsen's last acts as director of Emrup in 1947 was to participate in the demoli-tion of the 20m-high wooden tower built by the children, after it was reported by concerned locals that children kept falling off it.[12]

Initially, the idea of junk playgrounds failed to gain much traction but, after British landscape architect

Lollard Street Adventure Playground in Lambeth, London, 2019

and playground campaigner Lady Allen of Hurtwood visited Emdrup in 1945 and published an article on the site in *Picture Post* in 1946, a whole range of projects were implemented across Europe. In Britain, Lady Allen had observed children playing on the many bomb-sites that scarred British towns and cities in the 1940s; she argued that, rather than bar children from these sites, they should simply be made safe for play activities. The numerous playgrounds that opened in Britain in the 1950s – the earliest ones in Camberwell (1948) and Clydesdale (1952) in south London – were simply junk playgrounds by another name – Lady Allen simply substituting the term 'adventure' in response to criticism of the word 'junk' as symptomatic of bad behaviour.

Lady Allen's passion for adventure playgrounds was informed by wider debates on the best ways to rebuild and renew British cities after the destruction of the Second World War. The playground in Lollard Street (begun in 1955 and still in operation today) was built on a bomb-site within view of the Palace of Westminster – a demonstration to government officials as to what participatory rebuilding might actually look like. In direct contrast to most architects and urban planners, Lady Allen held the radical view that reconstruction should be carried out with the participation of the general population. Indeed, many of the adventure playgrounds she inspired derived from local initiatives by parents, the playgrounds themselves supervised by volunteers. This might be read as a prescriptive form of participation that was, on the one hand, designed to prevent delinquency in children; and, on the other, an antidote to the otherwise totalitarian dominance of urban planning in the post-war period.[13] Yet, in photographs of playgrounds, such as those taken by Swedish play leader Svane Frode in the 1970s, the extraordinary juxtaposition of the anarchic structures built by children with the rational geometries of modernist housing blocks, offers a powerful visual testimony of the radically subversive methods of design that might be brought to bear on cities.

Colin Ward argued in 1961 that adventure playgrounds represented a potent example of a 'free society in miniature', offering, as they do, concrete examples of both built and social structures created entirely from the bottom up. Drawing on accounts by play leaders, Ward argued that the apparent disorder of playgrounds was in fact a product of their organic evolution. As play leader Jack Lambert recounted, the structures made by children often began their lives as jealously guarded territories – signs of a tribal mentality; but quickly evolved into constituent parts of a fledgling community. Ward celebrated the messy aesthetic of these makeshift structures as evidence of a deeper form of beauty – a beauty of process rather than of product, of the coming together of a 'multitude of varied forces and influences of every kind, following their own course'. He saw the spontaneity and creativity of children as qualities that lie dormant in the adult world – a world that is 'devoted to competition and acquisitiveness'. In short, the adventure playground was a potent model for an altogether different kind of city.[14]

Of course, Ward's anticipated anarchist society has never materialized out of these examples set by children. In seizing on the adventure playground as a model of freedom, he underplayed its crucial role in reining in potential delinquency – as much a form of control as any other; and also the fact that many of the original playgrounds were only meant as temporary stop-gaps before

Self-built structures from the 1980s at the Emdrup playground in 2019

more conventional development took over. And successive rounds of Health and Safety legislation have meant that the ones that remain, such as Lollard Street in Lambeth, have had to make compromises between free and structured play. While the emphasis is still on freedom, the play structures are now provided by specialist companies rather than built by the children themselves, even though the junk that surrounds them still speaks more of a 'loose parts' approach than the ritualized play of swings, climbing frames and roundabouts. In Lambeth and many other urban areas, playgrounds have seen their local authority funding taken away, meaning they're now run as charities. But the adventure playground has also seen something of a revival in the USA, where the benefits of spontaneous outdoor play are being celebrated as an antidote to childhoods cut short by new media and parental paranoia.[15] Yet, even as the oldest adventure playground at Emdrup remains committed to the principles on which it was founded, today it is a very tame version of what it once was. The children who play there now are forbidden to build new shelters for themselves; instead, they're allocated one of the few remaining self-built structures from the 1980s that survive as reminders of a different age.

Drop City, Colorado, USA, 1965–73

The great social and political upheavals in the United States in the late 1960s saw tens of thousands of intentional communities being set up across the country and particularly in its wilder Western states, where planning laws were looser and the climate more benign. This exodus of young people was provoked by the Civil Rights Movement, disillusionment due to the Vietnam War, and a burgeoning environmentalism that feared the excesses of capitalism and abhorred the spiritual bankruptcy of consumerism.[16]

Even though the artists' commune Drop City was very small in comparison with some of these other communities – only 15–20 permanent residents on six acres of scrubland just outside Trinidad, Colorado – and had only short-lived success (founded in 1965, it was abandoned by 1973), it nevertheless gained an unmatched profile and influence, mainly on account of its recognition by such luminaries as Buckminster Fuller (who bestowed on it his Dymaxion Award in 1966) and countercultural icons Stewart Brand, Lloyd Khan and Steve Baer, as well as retrospective first-hand accounts of life there.[17] More recently, Drop City has been the subject of academic reappraisal, a documentary film, and a book-length account.[18] Despite its popular reputation as a failed experiment – a hippie commune that quickly disintegrated – it remains a unique example of the realisation of technical structures by amateurs, combined with libertarian social ideals. It was also one of the first places where renewable energy sources were harnessed – a large solar collector was constructed from used car mirrors that provided electrical power and passive heating for Drop City's domes.[19] Such was its influence that it led to many other communes being founded on similar principles, most notably Libre, also in Colorado, the Lama Foundation in New Mexico, and Amereida in Chile, all of which still exist today.

The array of structures that comprised Drop City, c. 1969

Still from Joan Grossman's film *Drop City* (2012) showing a solar panel being fixed to one of the zomes, c. 1970

Drop City was best known for its buildings: ten multi-coloured polyhedral structures that were variants on Fuller's geodesic domes, which he had been developing since the late 1940s. Initially actively supported by Fuller himself, Drop City's houses quickly mutated into something else, namely zomes – irregular polygonal structures designed by Steve Baer and built by him and other residents. Inspired by the polyhedral structural forms of crystals, the zomes at Drop City, such the Cartop Dome and the Complex (both built in 1966), gave the site its unique visual identity. As illustrated in Baer's publication *Dome Cookbook* (1968), the timber-framed structures were clad with panels cut from redundant automobiles, lending them a formal quality that fused mechanical engineering with ad-hoc expressionism.[20] The Complex was the most ambitious structure realised, comprising three 34ft-wide rhombic-icosa-dodecahedrons fused together to form a kitchen, living room, study, storage area and bathroom. Cheaper and easier to assemble than Fuller's precision-engineered geodesic structures, zomes reached a wide audience with Baer and others' publications, most notably Lloyd Khan's bestselling *Domebook* (1970), *Domebook 2* (1971) and *Shelter* (1973).[21] Effectively DIY manuals, these publications saw a veritable dome-building craze develop across the United States in the early 1970s, resulting in hundreds of thousands of both Fuller's and Baer's models being built by amateurs. As Khan readily admitted when he stopped publishing his *Domebook* in 1971, the results

View of the Complex at Drop City and an earlier geodesic structure on the right, c. 1966

were often lacklustre to say the least. With their pleasing geometries, domes may look easy to build; but even the most basic models require a knowledge of geometry that simply isn't necessary for more conventional self-builds, where right angles are the norm.

Beyond the spectacular aesthetics of Drop City's domes and zomes was a much more grounded attempt to rebuild communities from the bottom up. In calling itself a 'city', despite its small scale and tiny population, Drop City was clearly aiming much higher than most eco-communities do today (most now call themselves 'villages' precisely to make such a distinction). In building domes, the Droppers were trying to create an architecture that could be replicated anywhere – prototypes for a potentially infinite number of replica Drop Cities that would rebuild urban society from the bottom up in a vast network of dispersed communities. Drawing inspiration from portable, indigenous forms of building practised by Native Americans, Drop City espoused a new kind of urban architecture that would emerge from the salvaged wastes of its excessive carbon-based consumerism.

Despite the fact that Baer later likened the salvaging of redundant cars and other industrial materials to a negative form of parasitism – feeding on what you hate – the incorporation of urban detritus marks out the structures of Drop City from more recent eco-houses. These tend to focus obsessively on using 'natural' materials that can be renewed, an active disengagement from conventional urban building materials, such as brick, concrete and steel.[22] By reconfiguring the very things that they turned against, the builders of Drop City maintained the connection of the rural and the urban by showing how the city's cast-offs could be made useful once again. The cars-cum-domes were in fact commodities turned on themselves, redeemed because forced to become part of a much larger ecological and mental world. The breadth of this vision and its intrinsic engagement with the urban is what keeps Drop City relevant today, despite the fact that nothing remains of it.

Maplewood mudflats, Vancouver, Canada, 1940s–71

Sometimes, even when self-built communities like Drop City are physically erased, they are miraculously resurrected in other forms. During the 2010 Winter Olympics in Vancouver, artist Ken Lum exhibited 1/3 scale models of three ramshackle wooden shacks at the base of what was then the city's tallest skyscraper, the Shangri-la Hotel. The exhibit referred to a long history of squatted settlements on the intertidal mudflats that surround Vancouver on three sides. The model shacks were scaled-down replicas of homes lived in by writer Malcolm Lowry in the 1940s and 1950s, and the marine researcher and co-founder of Greenpeace Paul Spong and artist Tom Burrows in the early 1970s.[23] Lum invited Vancouver's residents to think about the meaning behind his juxtaposition of shacks and luxury hotel. Both embodied different notions of escape: the shacks representing escape from urban life, with its rigid planning laws and powerful elites; the hotel, the libertarian ideals of neoliberal capitalism – conspicuous luxury and freedom from want for the wealthy few. As Vancouver continues to gentrify at a rapid rate, the question of which kind of libertarian politics will prevail in the future is an urgent and pressing one for all of the city's inhabitants.

Lum's shacks have been subsequently relocated to the Dollarton mudflats north of the city, close to where they originally stood. Now a nature reserve, in the late nineteenth century, these lands were mostly home to Native Americans who were gradually evicted and erased from historical memory, even as they still claim ownership today. By the 1930s, when Malcolm Lowry moved into one of the shacks, there were some 538 people living on the waterfront in either shacks or boats or a mixture of the two, taking advantage of the fact that Dollarton lay outside the administrative jurisdiction of the city of Vancouver. Lowry makes little mention of Native American rights to the land in his stories where the mudflats feature,

Shacks and boats in Finn Slough, Vancouver, 2018

Still from Sean Malone's 1972 film *Living in the Mud* showing
Paul and Linda Spong's house on the right

most notably *October Ferry to Gabriola* (published posthumously in 1970). Indeed, his utopian understanding of the community – which he called Eridanus in reference to the underworld river in Virgil's *Georgics* – rests on a wilful blindness to others' claims upon what he regarded as 'free' land.[24] Lowry didn't stay long enough to see the bulldozing of the shacks by Vancouver's municipal authorities in 1958, but he inspired another, shorter, era of inhabitation in the early 1970s.[25]

Documented in two short films – *Mudflats Living* (Robert Fresco & Kris Paterson, 1972) and *Living in the Mud* (Sean Malone, 1972) – the Maplewood mudflats became home to around 25 people who were disillusioned with modern urban living and the escalation of property prices during Vancouver's construction boom of the late 1960s. As these films show, the structures that emerged were built

to adapt to the shifting landscape of the intertidal mudflats. Elevated on wooden piles and linked by makeshift gangways, the houses themselves were constructed from salvaged materials – principally discarded timber from commercial logging, and windows, doors and corrugated metal from urban landfills. Paul and Linda Spong's house was perhaps the most sophisticated structure: a two-storey building with a startling and colourful bricolage of materials, ornamented with driftwood sculptures; while artist Willie Wilson's house was surrounded by a vast array of materials salvaged from the city's dumps – to be either reused or given away to others. In this small community, young countercultural artists mixed with older-generation squatters who had survived the earlier demolitions in the late 1950s. But when the bulldozers arrived again on 18 December 1971 – at the behest of the mayor's Grosvenor

Plan to incorporate the area and build a new commercial development on the site – most of the residents watched as their homes were torched – the artist Tom Burrows recording it for posterity as a piece of performance art.[26]

Dollarton was incorporated as part of Vancouver but the mayor's plan for redevelopment never materialized and the area is now a sanctuary for wild birds, with Lum's replica shacks the only thing that references its turbulent history. However, other areas of Vancouver's intertidal zone continue to lie outside of municipal jurisdiction, providing spaces for alternative forms of urban dwelling. At Finn Slough in the southern suburb of Richmond, a small community continues to evolve in a collection of self-built houses standing on stilts or floating on water and linked by narrow boardwalks. Artist Glen Anderson is one of the residents and, like Willie Wilson and Tom Burrows before him, collects driftwood to make sculptures. Ownership of the land here is a conflicted issue – in the face of a lack of legal clarity, residents contend that they live on Crown land and should therefore be subject to a Crown lease; while property developer Steve Smith is trying to prove that he owns the land in order to build luxury apartments.[27] For the moment, such ambiguity allows for an alternative mode of habitation to continue but, judging from the histories of the other settlements, it is clearly one that hangs in the balance and is unlikely to be able to withstand the pressures of property speculators or an inflexible municipal authority.

If current predictions about the likely impacts of climate-change are right, the rest of this century will see the inundation of many low-lying coastal cities by rising sea levels, including Vancouver. If more land in cities becomes intertidal, then buildings will either need to be moved or adapted. In this context, Vancouver's mudflat communities provide a significant, if small-scale, demonstration of

Ken Lum's installation *From Shangri-la to Shangri-la*, installed outside the Shangri-la Hotel in Vancouver in 2010

how to live more flexibly with ever-shifting tidal waters. If the standard model of urban development argues for cities to be protected from encroaching waters by defensive structures, alternative models seek a more accommodating relationship with the intertidal zone, allowing parts of the city to return to the wetlands they once were. Yet, even the most optimistic proposals don't suggest how we might continue to inhabit these zones, instead offering a romantic vision of reclamation by nature that wilfully ignores the pressing need for more affordable housing in cities that will only grow more urgent as urban land disappears.

La ZAD, Notre-Dames-des-Landes, France, 2009–

Watchtower built by squatters next to a roadblock
at one of the entrances to La ZAD, 2013

The threat of violent destruction is ever present for those who build communities outside of the law. In the first week of April 2018, over 2,500 armed French riot police, together with armoured vehicles and demolition machines, attempted to level a vast protest camp spread out over 2,000 hectares: the site of a proposed airport at Notre-Dames-des-Landes near the city of Nantes. The subject of fierce opposition since it was first put forward in 1957, the airport plan had finally been shelved by the French government in January 2017. Yet, the protestors, who had occupied the site since 2009, remained, their existence as an anarchist commune – up to 250 strong in 80 separate collectives – becoming much more grounded in developing alternative, sustainable ways of living than simply a protest against airport expansion. Having already tried to evict the squatters in a major police operation in early October 2016, but being met by 40,000 additional protestors from all across France, the police, using tear gas, stun grenades and rubber bullets, returned in April 2018 in much greater numbers and with a blanket ban on news reporting of the eviction. Protestors' footage of the eviction suggests a war zone – the police vehicles demolishing many of the dozens of self-built structures in seconds, the black-clad protestors wearing gas masks fighting the police in darkness using molotov cocktails, slingshots and even lasers.[28]

The occupiers had named the site La ZAD – *zone à défendre,* meaning 'zone to defend', a subversive reworking of the acronym used to describe sites for redevelopment in France (*zone d'aménagement différé,* meaning 'designated construction area').[29] La ZAD began as part of the global Camp for Climate Action protests in 2009 – an occupation that was both an explicit protest against airport expansion and also an opportunity to develop greener lifestyles. It is one of the largest and longest-lasting protest sites in recent history and has become legendary in activist circles,

Bar and communal space built at La ZAD, 2013

inspiring similar occupations across Europe, including Grow Heathrow in London, the Hambach Forest anti-coal mining protest camp in Germany, and another opposing the proposed storage of nuclear waste in the Lejuc Forest near Bure in northeastern France.[30]

The many structures built at La ZAD derive from evolving tactics of occupation. The earliest homes were treehouses that drew inspiration from the UK anti-roads protests of the 1990s. Later, particularly after the removal of many treehouses in the 2013 police operation, more substantial structures were built, including an infirmary, a timber-framed barn, information centre, meeting rooms, climbing wall, brewery, library, bakeries, boxing gym, pirate radio station, and a play centre for children. Around the edges of the site were barricades and several observation towers that served as look-out posts for any signs of police activity.

Straw-bale house under construction at La ZAD, 2013

In his documentary film about La ZAD, made during the failed 2013 eviction attempt, Jean-François Castell interviewed a wide range of supporters of the occupation, including local farmers, politicians and protestors themselves. It revealed that a whole network of people, both inside and outside La ZAD, were essential in sustaining the occupation: food and building materials were regularly brought in by local residents; and farmers helped blockade the site during the eviction attempts.[31] A critical tactic on the part of the police in the most recent eviction attempt was to cut off these networks. In the year leading up to it, protests in support of the site were curtailed and the press were not allowed to access the site. Yet, as reports from ZAD residents show, the zone continues to exist, albeit much reduced – the remaining structures still inhabited, some of the destroyed ones rebuilt. Meanwhile, the ideals behind the occupation are dispersing elsewhere, waiting to reappear as protestors recover and regroup – and parallels have already been drawn between La ZAD and the 2019 *Gilets Jaunes*, or 'Yellow Jacket' protests, in Paris and elsewhere.

The French government clearly feared such a larger solidarity emerging. One of the most powerful moments in Jean-François Castell's 2013 film about La ZAD is when a local farmer speaks about why he supports the occupation, even as La ZAD's permaculture practices directly challenge his own industrial methods of farming. What this farmer recognized was the power of 'fraternity' that had developed between people of widely differing views – one that, to him, was a powerful and hopeful vision of the future. Witnessing the police operations of 2013, another local resident in his 70s was reminded of his time serving in Algeria 50 years previously, when he evicted people from their land in the name of what he termed 'something futile'. It is these larger connections – when an ostensibly narrow form of protest suddenly reaches out more widely – that the French state feared. When solidarity cuts across normally hostile interests, a truly inclusive revolution might begin.

ADM squat, Amsterdam, 1997–2019

La ZAD, like all squatter communities, is under constant threat of eviction. In the Global North, squatting often begins as a form of protest – against environmental destruction in rural areas or the lack of affordable housing in cities; but, if a squat endures, it can quickly become an autonomous community. In cities, this sometimes amounts to a form of escape from within, creating micro-enclaves of freedom.

Until it was evicted and destroyed in January 2019, the ADM squat on the redundant Amsterdamse Droogdok Maatschappij shipyard in northwest Amsterdam had, for 21 years, enacted just such a radical transformation of urban life. With around 125 residents scattered over 42 acres, ADM was the largest squat in Amsterdam, and probably the Netherlands as a whole.[32] The city of Amsterdam has a long history of squatting – beginning in the late 1960s and reaching a high point in the late 1970s and early 1980s, when upwards of 9,000 people were occupying hundreds of vacant buildings around the city. After several violent evictions in the early 1980s, numbers decreased and those that remained became increasingly militant, assailed in the 1990s by a tightening of the law against squatting as well as the gentrification that has continued to this day. As a consequence, more peripheral sites became favoured by squatters attempting to forge an alternative urban life that didn't demand the confrontational stance that inevitably sapped the energies of their city-centre counterparts.[33]

In October 1997, several dozen squatters arrived on trailers and boats to take over the former office building of the shipping company who owned the site. Turning the office units into living spaces, the community gradually expanded beyond this building, with many new residents living in caravans, trailers and makeshift houses built from salvaged and donated materials. A former warehouse was repurposed as a workshop for the creation of

The front of the repurposed office building of the ADM shipping company, 2015

Entrance to the ADM squat, with a metal sculpture created by the community shown on the left, 2018

artworks, many of which were scattered over the site until their removal in 2019. Since 1998, ADM has hosted the annual Robodock festival, the Jetlag Experimental Circus festival, and alternative knowledge sharing events such as the Futurological Symposium. Despite the squatters' long history of artistic production and their provision of public events (often without any payment in return), the city mayor and Dutch law courts ordered them to leave by Christmas 2018. With only a temporary reprieve, the police and private security finally evicted all the residents in early January 2019 – a handful of them relocating to a much smaller site provided for them by the city authorities.[34] The ADM site will now be redeveloped by its new owners Chidda Real Estate, who will likely build high-end offices and apartments.

As part of their transformation of the industrial site, ADM residents planted hundreds of trees – now recognized as an ecological imperative in the mitigation of climate-change (but at ADM, these trees were also destroyed by the developers). Over the years, the squatters also created a new ecology of building. For example, when part of the former office building was demolished by its owner in 1998 – an attempt to take back possession soon after the squatters moved in – the residents decided to incorporate the ruin into their renovations, leaving broken pieces of concrete hanging from the damaged wall and patching over the gaping holes left. By integrating destruction into creation, ADM residents kept that violent history visible in the very fabric of the building, thereby bringing together two things normally kept well apart.

ADM's unofficial spokesperson, and one of its original residents, Hay Schoolmeesters, has ruefully remarked that the alternative culture pioneered by the community has now entered the mainstream in hipster culture.[35] In Amsterdam, this has been most dramatically realised in the fate of another former shipyard close to the city centre, the NDSM Wharf development. Here, what was once another vibrant squatter community has been thoroughly cleansed of its social autonomy. The squatters have been evicted and young 'creatives' have moved in. There's now an array of cultural events and festivals designed to appeal to consumers looking for an alternative vibe. This is now the acceptable face of urban freespaces – places where a surface aesthetic of autonomy conceals a much more conventional set-up of hierarchical control by commercial interests.

The Brainwash Cinema installed at ADM during the 2009 Robodock festival

III. NECESSITY

Everyone should be able to build, and so long as this freedom to build does not exist, the planned architecture of today cannot be considered an art at all .... Only when architect, bricklayer and occupant are a unity, i.e. one and the same person, can one speak of architecture. Everything else is not architecture but the physical incarnation of a criminal act—Friedensreich Hundertwasser, 'Mould Manifesto' (1958)

It is generally the case that the millions of urban inhabitants who self-build in the Global South do so by necessity. Migrating from rural poverty, they cannot afford the inflated prices of land or property in cities; and municipal or national governments will not help to house them. By contrast, it is assumed that those who self-build in the Global North do so by choice, often because they have greater resources than those who live in houses designed by others. However, making such a stark dichotomy between necessity and choice obscures how each term is always in fact relative to the individual concerned. For example, as is clear in the above quotation, for artist Friedensreich Hundertwasser, freedom to build was not a choice but a necessity, clearly the result of some inward drive that most of us lack.

This section questions what counts as necessity and choice in relation to self-organized building. As the first piece on the Paris zone shows, not long ago, in many cities in the Global North, the poor lived in similar conditions to those in cities in the Global South today. As the second piece demonstrates, these conditions also persist in migrant camps – places where the assumed division between 'developed' and 'developing' unravels. All over Europe today, migrant camps challenge us not only to think beyond national borders but also whether terms like necessity and choice are helpful in coming to terms with the sheer scale of global migration and its diverse

and complex causes. In a different vein, places like Dignity Village in Portland show us that migration and homelessness are two sides of the same coin of an exclusionary politics that characterizes most cities in the Global North. The third piece offers an excursion to the infamous Kowloon Walled City in Hong Kong, once the most densely populated place on Earth and one that was largely unplanned and unregulated. This historical oddity reminds us that places built through necessity can attain astonishing levels of richness and diversity, contrary to the conventional logic of urban planning and design.

Two articles on social centres (squats that are run as cultural venues) question what counts as necessary in terms of cultural provision in cities. Social centres generally allow for a much greater range of creative expression than government-provided equivalents. They work to foster and connect highly diverse cultural practices and often embrace different kinds of politics. They reformulate freedom as both choice and necessity and wed it incontrovertibly into the buildings and spaces of the urban.

The final piece on scaffolding shifts the idea of necessity to architectural materials themselves. Scaffolding is a necessity when buildings are created or altered, but, in the case of the anti-roads protests at Claremont Road in 1994, it can also be reconfigured into a tool of dissent.

The *zone*, Paris, 1840–1944

For over a century, a 250m-wide strip of land encircling Paris was effectively a shantytown. This was a no-man's land – *terrain vague* – between the city, its ring of fortifications and entrance gates (*portes*), and the burgeoning suburbs (*banlieue*) beyond. Declared a *zone non aedificandi* (non-building zone), its impoverished residents, known as *zoniers*, lived in a chaotic assemblage of caravans and self-built huts. Despite being obliterated at the end of the Second World War, Paris's *zone* is a powerful reminder that some cities in the Global North were once not so different from those in the Global South today. Paris's *zone* was effectively an informal settlement that encircled the formal city just as countless self-built *favelas, barrios, callejones, bustees* and *gecekondus* now form rings around many cities in Brazil, Colombia, Mexico, India and Turkey respectively.[1]

Although the population of the *zone* fluctuated, by the time of the 1926 census it was at least 42,000, many of whom had moved there from central Paris, provincial France or neighbouring countries. It was a place where impoverished factory workers lived alongside ragpickers, gypsies and carnival performers, with the occasional riches-to-rags victim or soon-to-be famous person (the guitarist Django Reinhardt spending part of his childhood there). Some residents owned their properties; the majority were tenants. Throughout its long history, the *zone* attracted a great deal of attention from other Parisians, particularly from the 1860s onwards, when the modernization of the city under Baron Haussmann heightened the stark contrast of the impoverished *zone* and the luxury of the new boulevards and department stores. At once a place that repulsed and attracted, the *zone* was intensely scrutinized by both public officials, who condemned it as insanitary and unsightly, and artists and writers, who found its otherness alluring. In the first decade of the twentieth century, the celebrated photographer Eugène Atget

Eugène Atget's photograph of a *zonier* at Porte d'Ivry, 1912

captured some of the most evocative images of the *zone's* many self-built shacks – chaotic assemblages of salvaged materials, often decorated with discarded toys, dolls and other cast-offs collected by the residents. Some of Atget's photographs also show animals – a strange and unsettling collision of waste and nature that spoke powerfully of the hidden detritus of the City of Light, with its escalating levels of consumption.[2]

Atget's photographs also strongly appealed to the Parisian Surrealists in the 1920s and 1930s, who saw in them an exotic and disorderly urban environment totally at odds with the rational geometries of Haussmann's Paris. The Surrealists experienced the strange juxtapositions of objects in Atget's photographs of the *zone* in the flea markets that were an important part of its economy. Discarded and broken objects – commodities no longer valued by their owners – created an alternate reality: the

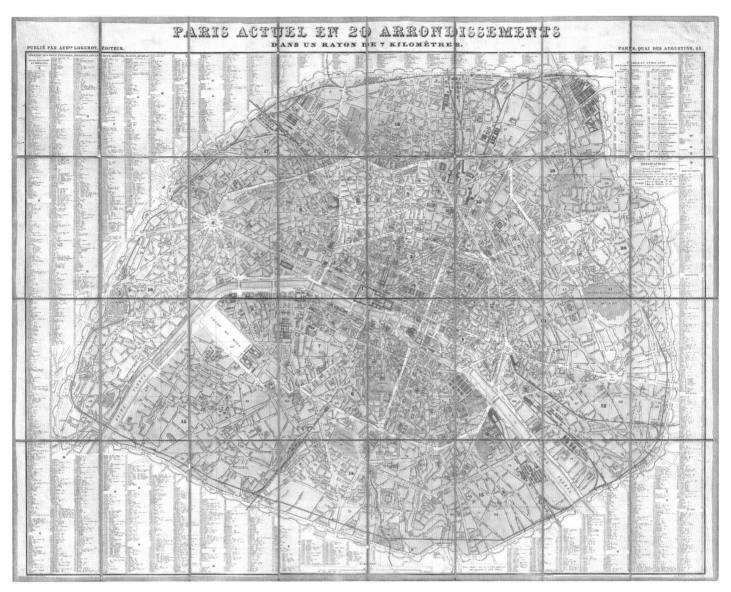

Logerot Map of Paris, published in 1887, showing the fortifications of the city and the *zone* immediately beyond

Surrealist dream-world of unconscious desires turned into real-life tableaux. But in romanticizing these objects, the Surrealists downplayed the harsh living conditions and precarious existence of the *zoniers* themselves, something which Atget's photographs explicitly drew attention to.[3] It's a tendency that still pervades attitudes towards informal settlements in the Global South – a valuing of the perceived resourcefulness and freedom of slum dwellers that prioritizes their energizing effect on privileged outsiders rather than the crushing reality of living on or below the breadline.

Under the German Occupation of 1940–44, plans were drawn up by the Vichy government to create a greenbelt around Paris that would see the razing of the majority of the informal houses and other structures in the *zone*. In 1949, photographer Robert Doisneau and novelist Blaise Cendrars published *La Banlieue de Paris*, an elegiac portrait of the disappearing *zone*, now romanticized as a vanishing remnant of old Paris. Although the greenbelt was only ever partially realised, the fate of the *zone* was sealed after the Second World War by the construction of the *boulevard périphérique*, the motorway that now encircles the city and which was finished in 1973. Thereafter, the land between the city limits and the mushrooming *banlieue* was gradually filled in with a mixture of commercial, residential and leisure developments.

Despite its disappearance, the *zone* lived on as a word that continues to resonate powerfully in French culture. The unprecedented riots that engulfed the suburbs of many French cities in the autumn of 2006 revealed the almost complete separation of the core of historic cities like Paris from their impoverished *banlieue.* The rioters – mostly disaffected youths rebelling against the government's proposed watering-down of employment rights – called themselves *zonards* in memory of the outcast inhabitants of the original *zone*.[4] At the same time, the creation of La ZAD in 2008 in countryside northwest of Nantes saw the application of the word to describe an occupied territory as a place of protest.

From the 1990s onwards, the site of the original Paris *zone* has also seen the return of makeshift settlements created by the homeless and migrants from Central and Eastern Europe, Africa and, more recently, Afghanistan, Iraq, Syria and Sudan. Building shelters underneath the concrete flyovers of the *boulevard périphérique*, these encampments are always only temporary, being quickly dismantled by the police, only to reappear elsewhere.[5] They demonstrate that the Paris *zone* is still a *terrain vague*, an edgeland that cannot be erased however much the city around it modernizes. They also show that the forces that produced the original *zone* are still very much present, but now on a truly global scale.

Calais Jungle, France, April 2015–October 2016

Migrants are targeted by the authorities of nation states because they reveal that borders are artificial constructs that don't fit the reality of a globalized world. The long-standing official policy in France and elsewhere in Europe has been the destruction of migrant encampments and the dispersal of their residents, even as some of these camps have lasted for years. Yet, there have also been some attempts by the state, charities and NGOs to accommodate migrants on a more permanent basis, for example the Sangatte camp established by the Red Cross near Calais in 1999 but shut down in 2002 on the orders of the then French interior minister Nicolas Sarkozy. Another attempt at state intervention in April 2015 led to the building of a vast container camp 7 km outside Calais to house around 1,500 migrants in regimented rows of repurposed shipping containers. However, in between this camp and the Jules Ferry Centre set up for accommodating women and children, a large shantytown developed, what would become known as the Jungle.

During its 18–month existence, the Calais Jungle became a *cause célèbre*, attracting an enormous amount of public interest and press coverage, as well as many thousands of dedicated activists, charity workers and curious visitors from across Europe.[6] With over 10,000 residents comprising 25 nationalities – the largest groups being Sudanese, Afghans, Kurds, Eritreans, Ethiopians, Syrians, Egyptians and Iranians – the Jungle became the biggest informal settlement in Europe. When the local authority demolished part of the camp in March 2016, its population density briefly became the highest in the world: at 800 people per hectare it was double that of Cairo or Manila. The Jungle developed a sophisticated network of social spaces, including 72 businesses (documented in July 2016), several churches and mosques, and schools and cultural spaces set up by volunteers and NGOs. Architectural students at the Ecole Nationale Supérieure d'Architecture

Welcome centre at the Calais Jungle, January 2016

de Paris-Belleville carried out an in-depth study of these structures, making drawings of the entire encampment as well as individual restaurants, shops, religious buildings and dwellings.[7]

These drawings show an extraordinary range of makeshift buildings. The construction materials were mostly basic – recycled timber, nails, large tarpaulins and insulating textiles – but the range of functions was as broad as in any conventional urban environment. Restaurants were often the largest structures, employing small teams of builders and grouped along the camp's main street; religious buildings were identifiable by their distinctive forms – mosques planned around the mihrab; churches on the Latin or Greek cross depending on the nationality of their congregations. This diversity was a direct reflection of the cosmopolitan nature of the camp, demonstrating how extreme precarity and privation do not preclude vital forms of inhabitation.

Tents in the sand dunes of the Calais Jungle, September 2016

Many of those who visited the Jungle or lived alongside migrants found it to be an exciting experimental space in which new kinds of social relations were being fostered, whether between the distinct groups of migrants themselves or betwen those who supported them. Largely outside of the control of the state, and in direct contrast to the regimented life imposed on migrants in the nearby container camp, the Jungle became much more than merely a transitory place of survival. Street art adorned many of the structures, including a work by British artist Bansky, who also donated building materials from his Dismaland theme park.[8] Architect Sam Jacob created a 1:1 model of a migrant's dwelling using a 3D scanner, exhibiting it at the 2016 Venice Biennale – a decision prompted by his desire to preserve 'a moment in the rapid, ephemeral flux' of migrant life.[9] As recognized by

two government representatives who visited the Jungle in December 2015, this clear sense of solidarity between migrants and privileged outsiders, coupled with the effective self-management of the camp, caused 'great disquiet' and was probably the main reason why the camp was cleared in October 2016, the migrants removed in buses to reception centres across France.[10] Thus a return once again to the policy of destruction and dispersal – an increasingly desperate attempt to keep these unwanted residents out of the public gaze in order to limit the solidarity that emerged in the 'Calais moment'.

The Jungle was just one of many thousands of migrant camps that have been a feature of European border zones and big cities since the 1990s, including Idomeni (2015–16) located on the border between Greece

Tents and other structures in the Calais Jungle adjacent to the
official container camp, January 2016

and Macedonia, Patnas in Greece (1996–2009), and other
camps in northern France like Norrent-Frontes (2012–17)
and Grande-Synthe (2004–17). And, across the rest of the
world, the number of people living in some of kind of
camp is estimated at 17 million, including at least six million who have fled the Syrian conflict since 2011.[11] With
the coming prospect of the displacement of tens, if not
hundreds, of millions more by the ravages of climate
change, there is an urgent need to radically rethink how
migrants are accommodated in the largely affluent Global
North. A policy of concealment will be untenable once the
numbers become too large. Despite the obvious despera-
tion of many of the Jungle's residents, they and those who
supported them showed that self-organization is possible
even on a fairly large scale and with few resources.

St Michael's Church in the Calais Jungle, February 2016

Dignity Village, Portland, USA, 2001–

Migrant settlements like the Calais Jungle are part of a wider network of informal camps for those without homes; in the US, these have sometimes themselves been called jungles. Dating back to the rise of modern industrialism in the second half of the nineteenth century, homeless camps emerged on the outskirts of cities as 'way stations for a new proletariat of migratory and seasonal workers'.[12] These reached a peak in the Depression era, when shanty towns (invariably called Hoovervilles, after US president Herbert Hoover, who was widely blamed for the economic downturn) were built on the edge of almost every city and town.[13] Largely disappearing during the Second World War, when the entire US economy and its citizens were mobilized for the war effort, homeless camps only emerged again in any numbers during the Reagan presidency in the 1980s. The new neoliberal economy Reagan inaugurated slashed federal funding for cities and largely removed the safety net for those on the edge of homelessness. As numbers of people on the streets spiralled, so did an increasingly draconian police response – the removal of hundreds of homeless shelters by riot police in Manhattan's Tompkins Square Park in 1991 being the most high profile example of many such brutal evictions.

View of the range of structures self-built in Dignity Village in September 2020

Adobe and timber house in Dignity Village, September 2020

In recent years, particularly after many thousands of people were left homeless after the collapse of the sub-prime mortgage market in the US in 2007, these camps have become more tolerated. In the case of Dignity Village, on the edge of Portland, this has resulted in full acceptance through legalization. Dignity Village was founded in 2001 after a year-long wave of protests by groups of the city's unhoused population against the effective criminalization of homelessness by the municipal authorities.[14] The protest started in December 2000 with the setting up of an encampment of tents – named Camp Dignity – under a motorway bridge in the centre of Portland. The municipal authorities responded by continually moving the population on to other sites. After a year of constant evictions, the authorities finally donated a plot of city-owned land on the edge of Portland adjacent to a prison, a composting facility and the city's international airport. This move was meant to be temporary – the site was far from ideal being six miles from the city centre. Yet, over the course of 18 months, tents were replaced by rudimentary shelters, all self-built by the residents with the help of many volunteers. In 2020, Dignity Village housed around 50 permanent residents; with many others living there temporarily. In 2004, the community was sanctioned as an official tiny house village by Portland City Council.

The 34 miniature cottage-style buildings built by the residents of Dignity Village are typical of the recent tiny house movement in the US, where planning regulations are more relaxed for 'temporary moveable' homes under 400 square feet in size (those in Dignity Village are around 200 square feet). Some are decidedly ramshackle – timber-framed structures patched together from salvaged and donated materials, such as tar paper, roof tiles and wood panels; others are more sophisticated, for example a Swiss-style chalet with large eaves and a veranda at the front. The central communal structure – a domed meeting hall for the Village's governance – was built from recycled windows and solar panels; and other structures and services include a community cycling centre and kitchen, an electricity-generating windmill, toilets, showers, computer room and raised-bed gardens for growing food. The ethos of the community thus brings together sustainability and social justice in a unique way.

Self-building is clearly a significant part of this ethos; but it's just one element in the 'dignity' the village imparts to its residents. The ad-hoc homes are set against conventional ways of housing the homeless in the US, principally in shelters that are run on strict disciplinary lines. The self-organized 'Out of the Doorways' movement that spawned Dignity Village was a protest against the way the shelter system patronized homeless clients. Forsaking charity models for self-empowerment, the protest politicized the unhoused, transforming them from passive recipients of charity into active place-makers.[15] The freedom that the residents of Dignity Village have achieved may seem commonplace by conventional standards; but it is radical in its politics – each resident has an equal voice in governing the community and all members enjoy equal protection.

The model pioneered by Dignity Village has been taken up in cities across the US and elsewhere. In Portland alone, five additional homeless communities have been founded since 2011 and dozens exist on the edges of other US cities; but legalized camps like Community First! (Austin, Texas) and 'Opportunity Village' (Eugene, Oregon) are far outnumbered by illegal ones constantly at risk of eviction.[16] Clearly, the model offered by Dignity Village will only work for a limited number of participants; and its rhetoric of self-sufficiency threatens to legitimize public-sector abandonment of those without homes. There is widespread concern that these new forms of legal camps represent a quick-fix, low-cost solution to the complex causes of homelessness; that they sidestep the problem of providing adequate housing on a long-term basis. Yet Dignity Village also demonstrates that a transformative political practice begins with place-making, however rudimentary that may be.

Group of self-built homes in Dignity Village, September 2020

Kowloon Walled City, Hong Kong, 1846–1994

Until it was demolished by the British Hong Kong administration in 1994, Kowloon Walled City was a tiny lawless enclave (0.1 square miles) within the city with a scarcely believable population density of 3.2 million people per square mile – the greatest the world has ever seen. Photographs and documentary films made in the 1980s and early 1990s show an almost solid mass of buildings – around 350 individual high-rise structures broken up into thousands of tiny, modular spaces for the City's 40,000 or so residents.[17] In between the buildings was a warren of extremely narrow and almost perpetually dark streets, crammed with improvised infrastructure and filled with detritus. This was an unplanned built environment that nevertheless seemed to realise, *in extremis*, Le Corbusier's modular ideal: the minimal living space pushed to its dystopian limit – a real-life version of J.G. Ballard's 1957 story 'The Concentration City', or the human equivalent of the alien Borg cuboid structure first seen in *Star Trek: the Next Generation* (1989).

Although the demolition of Kowloon Walled City was agreed by the British and Chinese authorities in 1987, the long period it took to actually clear the site gave it a sustained period of high visibility. Originally a military fort under Chinese jurisdiction, the Walled City was annexed by the British colonial authorities in 1899 but remained largely untouched by the rest of Hong Kong as a diplomatic concession to the Chinese. In the early twentieth century, it became a shantytown of wooden shacks with a population of around 2,000 by the time the Japanese occupied Hong Kong in 1941. The resumption of British rule saw a huge influx of refugees from China – a product of the Cultural Revolution. The population of the Walled City grew exponentially and, by the late 1960s, its shacks and low-rise buildings were being replaced by concrete-framed high-rises as private developers sought to capitalize on its unique territorial status.[18] The new buildings were usually simply upwards extensions of older ones, leading to an organic high-rise city unlike any other in the world. The result was the Walled City that was documented by architectural researchers, filmmakers and photographers – at once an anarchic form of self-organized urbanism – for a time, a hotbed of vices like gambling, prostitution and opium smoking – and a slum-like urban hell – the dark twin of a rapidly developing Hong Kong. Yet, for some residents, the Walled City was also a refuge, a place where one could live cheaply, with a strongly developed community, and with minimal interference from the government.[19]

One of the most powerful images of the Kowloon Walled City is a longitudinal cross-section drawn by Japanese architect Hitomi Terasawa, published in the book *Large Scale Illustrated Kowloon City* in 1997 and partially rendered as a 3D image in the *South China Morning Post* in 2013. Unlike conventional architectural drawings, these renderings depict not only the structural frame of the buildings but also the minutiae of everyday life in this superdense built environment. The modular spaces are not only filled with inhabitants – residents, diners, shop owners, manufacturers, even pets and racing pigeons – but also furniture, laundry, machines, a temple, plumbing, wires, signs, bicycles, and umbrellas. Because the Walled City was so dense, its internal arrangements were largely invisible, linked by secretive multilevel walkways that meant you could traverse the entire city without ever touching the ground. These images open up that vast interior, at once making it legible but also showing its cacophonous density of materials, products and people. They paradoxically brought into the light this city of darkness – an obsessive engagement borne of the knowledge that it would soon be completed erased.

After demolition was completed in 1994, the Walled City was replaced with a park that turned the history of the site into a sanitized form of heritage. Although

Cutaway axonometric view of part of Kowloon Walled City drawn
by Adolfo Arranz and published in the *South China Morning Post* in 2013

Aerial view of Kowloon Walled City in 1989

remnants of the City were retained, most notably the nineteenth-century *Yamen* (magistrate's office) and part of one of the gates to the fort, it mostly erased its more recent history along with the memories of its residents. Its afterlife has been felt more strongly in the imagination, from the cyberpunk futuristic vision of *Blade Runner* (1982) and the early novels of William Gibson to Japanese manga and video games such as *Call of Duty: Special Ops* (2019). It's even inspired a partial reconstruction: the Kawasaki Warehouse in Japan, an amusement arcade housed within a painstaking replica of part of the Walled City, which was open for a decade until 2019.[20] These afterlives are mostly nostalgic paeans to an anarchic urbanism that seems so appealing in contrast to the sterile conformity of much contemporary urban development. Yet, the Walled City has also been incorporated into attempts by younger residents of Hong Kong to resist Chinese authoritarianism. In the youth-led ACG (Action, Comics, Gaming) practices in Hong Kong, protagonists dress up as their favourite manga characters from the Walled City-inspired *City of Darkness*

series (2000–11) and then act out scenarios in the Walled City park itself. Drawing on the identity of the City as a place of political, social and cultural refuge, these game-players use fictional incarnations of the past to subvert the sanitized memory now offered by the park.[21]

No less important is the way in which the memory of the Walled City has fed into more direct expressions of protest to Chinese erosion of Hong Kong's democratic history, ranging from the Umbrella Revolution occupations in 2014 to speculative architectural projects like Anthony Ko's *An Activist Artefact* from 2017. Both of these very different responses envisage a bottom-up occupation of the city that draws inspiration from the self-organized world of the Walled City. It's not that these reflect the 'reality' of the City any more than more commercial media do; but rather that they take one aspect of its history to bolster a vision of a new kind of city, one that is freed from authoritarian control, whether that lies in the hands of government, developers, financiers or others to come.

Recreation of part of Kowloon Walled City in the Kawasaki Warehouse, Japan, 2014

Forte Prenestino, Rome, 1986–

Military sites that fall out of use seem to lend themselves to illicit occupations – in addition to Kowloon Walled City, this book also references three other examples: the Paris *zone*, Christiania, and Slab City. Military strategy often changes quickly in times of war; and its technologies are always at the cutting edge, making them particularly vulnerable to obsolescence. Ancient cities are often littered with abandoned defences – walls or forts left over from the age before aerial warfare made them defunct. On the eastern edges of Rome, one such site – Forte Prenestino – has been occupied for over three decades by squatters who have turned it into a social centre – *centro sociale*. Originally built in the 1890s as a military fortress in the Centrocelle suburb, Forte Prenestino was abandoned in the 1960s. The former fort itself is a sprawling warren of tunnels over three storeys. Situated on eight acres of land, it's the largest social centre in Europe and one of around 34 in Rome and dozens more in larger Italian cities like Milan, Turin, Genoa and Naples.[22]

Social centres are abandoned urban spaces that are squatted by activists intent on developing forms of social and cultural production that are outside of commercial and institutional settings. Although they are present in many cities across Europe, Italy has the greatest concentration. One of the reasons for this is a long tradition of self-organization that began in the industrial factories in the north of the country in the 1960s and, later, developed into a more militant movement – known as Autonomia Operaia (Workers' Autonomy) – in the 1970s.[23] The apex of this movement saw workers and students uniting against Italy's series of coalition governments (when the Communist Party formed an alliance with the Christian Democrats) in the late 1970s in opposing capitalism, consumerism, and a hierarchical organization of society. In September 1977, 70,000 people attended the Congress Against the Repression in Bologna, creating a festival of radical self-expression, with painting, dancing and singing spontaneously arising out of huge makeshift camps in the city's squares, parks and gardens.

Although squatting was never a significant aspect of Autonomia, it framed the culture around which the first generation of social centres were set up in Milan and Turin – they were places to develop autonomous forms of cultural production for workers in keeping with their ideals of self-management. Yet, Autonomia's emancipatory ideals were quickly overshadowed by the violence of groups like the Red Brigade, who kidnapped and murdered the former prime minister Aldo Moro in 1978. Unsurprisingly, brutal state suppression followed. In the late 1970s, hundreds if not thousands were arrested and Autonomia's centres of cultural production, including radio stations, bookshops, printers, and information centres, were largely shut down.[24]

Despite its apparent demise, Autonomia inspired a new generation of social centres to be set up in the mid-1980s. The founding of Forte Prenestino on 1 May 1986 by a group of local young people was part of a 'Festival of Non-Work' that harked back to Autonomia's vision of a work-free society. Today, the social centre continues to play an important role in the local community, still a relatively impoverished suburb of Rome. It offers spaces for a huge range of functions, including a bar and wine shop, library, exhibition space, practice rooms for musicians, a theatre, cinema, sports and leisure centre, and artists' performance space. Its range of activities was and still is widely varied, documented in the self-published book *Fortopia* (2016).[25] These include political activism, for example recent events supporting other social centres at risk of eviction or environmental campaigns like NO TAV, protesting the building of a high-speed railway line between Lyon and Turin. The centre also hosts a vast array of workshops and

Interior of one of the tunnels in Forte Prenestino, 2016

classes – from pilates, boxing, yoga to music production – and cultural events such as concerts and festivals. Forte Prenestino's reputation as a music venue was cemented by the creation of its own record label, featuring local rap and reggae bands. Most of the organization and staffing of events is done by volunteers, with income generated through the sale of food and drink on site. And, even as many of Rome's other social centres have been legalized, Forte Prenestino remains an illicit occupation – maintaining its long-standing commitment to be a fully self-financed and self-managed site of cultural production open to all.[26]

Historically, social centres have generally attracted niche audiences of young people interested in pursuing alternative lifestyles (Forte Prenestino has its origins in the punk movement). More recently, though, there are signs that their appeal has started to broaden. In 2011, some musicians and actors took over an 18th-century theatre in the centre of Rome after it was shut down due to government budget cuts for the arts in the wake of the 2007–08 financial crisis. In a similar vein, in 2012, a group of locals in the Trastevere district squatted a defunct cinema that was to be replaced with a car park, reanimating the spaces in the style of the classic era of cinema.[27] Meanwhile, the grounds of Forte Prenestino have been turned into an ecological garden that involves the participation of a diverse range of local people, as well as tapping into a broader movement establishing alternative ways of growing food on vacant land in cities across the world. Expanding its remit in this way, Forte Prenestino is a powerful counter to the private ownership of land and speculative property development that have come to dominate global urbanism, even in historic cities like Rome. As argued by Pierpaolo Mudu, this is 'radical in terms of reclaiming a change from the roots, literally, within a more general attempt to delink people from pervasive capitalist control'.[28]

Forte Prenestino, showing the extensive grounds in which it is located, 1986

Can Batlló, Barcelona, 2011–

The recent broadening of participation in social centres like Forte Prenestino came in the wake of the global financial crisis of 2007–08. Spain was hit particularly hard by the crisis because its economy was over-reliant on the construction industry, making up 11 per cent of the country's GDP as compared with the EU average of just 5.7 per cent. After the crisis, at least 400,000 people were evicted from their homes after defaulting on their mortgage payments, while around six million housing units across the country stood either empty or half-finished. In this context, squatting became both a necessity and also a political statement against austerity. This was particularly so after the 15–M movement in late spring 2011 saw thousands occupying the principal public squares in Spanish cities demanding that politicians address the basic housing needs of its growing precariat.[29] This led to the formation of the Podemos political party in January 2014, which, as of 2019, is in a coalition government with Spain's Socialist party.

In Barcelona, long-standing social centres, such as La Rimaia, Can Masdeu and Barrilonia, gave support during the 15–M occupations; while the PAH radical housing movement (Platform for Mortgage Victims) squatted empty buildings to house the homeless. At the same time, others have seized the opportunity to take control of sites left in limbo by the collapse of the construction industry. On 11 June 2011, a group of activists known as the Plataforma Can Batlló and hundreds of local residents gathered outside a former factory in the La Bordeta district of Barcelona, three km from the city centre, threatening to occupy it as a squatted community centre. Two days before, the Plataforma had been given the keys to a warehouse on the site, to allow them to take over its management. Since the late 1970s, the local community had been promised new public space on the site of the abandoned factory, but the complex had continued to operate privately as municipal administrators stalled on their pledges.

Part of the Can Batlló complex, showing both abandoned and renovated sections of the site in 2019

Former warehouse covered in street art at the Can Batlló, 2019

The 2007–08 financial crisis brought things to a head as development plans were stalled. This prompted a remarkable coming together of local people – a young architects' collective LaCol, the long-standing neighbourhood association based around a much older social centre, and the project organizing group, the Plataforma Can Batlló.[30]

Since 2011, the Plataforma has renovated some of the former industrial buildings that make up the Can Batlló; other parts of the site have remained abandoned or scheduled for demolition to make way for public space. The renovated buildings now house a library, auditorium, bar, artists' studios, indoor play area and even a climbing wall. As it has developed, more and more spaces have been turned over to community control and the complex now hosts a wide range of activities, including a wood and metal workshop, brewery, bicycle repair shop, community garden, dog park, sports facilities, social movement archive, circus arts facility, and indoor children's playground.[31] More recently, LaCol have completed the building of the city's first cooperative affordable housing complex, which is also the largest timber-framed building in Spain.

In early 2019, Barcelona's progressive mayor, Ada Colau, recognized the achievements of the Plataforma, awarding them 54 million euros to support the overall completion of the Can Batlló complex.[32] In 2019, the city agreed to maintain the buildings of the complex for 50 years, giving control of the programming to the Plataforma. This was Colau's way of demonstrating her commitment to the city's social movements (Colau was one of the founders of the PAH in 2009). However, a change in the political makeup of Barcelona's municipal authority in 2019 now threatens that agreement, with the budget for Can Batlló's continuing development yet to be allocated (as of spring 2020).

Although Can Batlló was never a squat, its broad social programme ties in with the recent diversification of squatting in Barcelona as a whole. In providing new affordable apartments, the site reflects the key role of housing in the political agenda of progressive politics in the city since the financial crisis – the mayor is also planning emergency housing on the site using shipping containers. After the 15–M occupations in 2011, activists began squatting empty bank premises to demand the rehousing of those made homeless by foreclosures, one example being the occupation in 2013 of three buildings owned by the public bank SAREB. Here, the 146 homeless people who participated in the occupation successfully lobbied the Catalan government to re-house them, as well as redevelop one of the bank's buildings into social housing.[33] In other examples, squatting bank-owned properties forced the owners to provide affordable rental contracts for housing. Solidarity has also grown between existing social centres and the 100 or so squats now scattered around the Barcelona metropolitan region. But, even as projects like Can Batlló are now supported by the municipal authorities, other social centres have been targeted for eviction. The attempted demolition of the nearby Can Vies social centre in May

2014 led to riots in Barcelona and protests all over Spain, with Can Batlló offering its support in the form of fund-raising events and helping to rebuild the social centre after the authorities relented.[34]

The way in which Barcelona's squatting initiatives are developing signals precisely the kind of unifying politics that is required to challenge the dominance of private-sector speculative urban development. Very gradually, public claims are being made by these small-scale tactical interventions, ones that are already having a profound effect on both the city's image and its municipal governance. The key is for those claims to always be open to challenge, particularly from marginalized groups, such as migrants, who are often excluded as members of this 'public'. And it involves a constant recognition that one person's choice is another's necessity – that there is never a clear line between what is needed and what is desired.

High-wire walker at a public event at the Can Batlló in 2019

Scaffolding

Necessity, it is said, is the mother of invention. In architecture, this is apparent in perhaps the most overlooked form of temporary structure – scaffolding. The *Scaffolding* exhibition held at New York's Center for Architecture in late 2017 showcased how the flexibility, cheapness and speed of construction of scaffolding might be exploited to build emergency shelters for refugees, temporary houses for squatters and the homeless, art spaces in city squares, and others kinds of 'open-source' designs that promote bottom-up participation in building.

Larger-scale uses of scaffolding as a building material can be seen in projects such as the architectural practice MVRDV's 2016 installation 'The Stairs' – a huge scaffolding staircase leading up to the rooftop of a 1950s office block in central Rotterdam; and German studio J Mayer H Architekten's temporary art gallery in Munich in 2013 – a three-storey scaffolding structure covered in plastic sheeting and timber-plank walkways. By opening up the upper layers of the city more fully to inhabitation, both of these projects used the spectacular views gained from elevated platforms as a way of imbuing scaffolding with more than mere utility. Yet, despite their suggestion of radical openness, and their undoubted spectacular constructional aesthetics, these large-scale scaffolding structures don't provide much in the way of a progressive social agenda; rather they simply add to the general trend of urban architecture that views sociability and connectedness as just another pretext for consumption.

More radical in its intent is the use of scaffolding as a tool of protest. Because of its cheapness, ubiquity and ease of construction, scaffolding has become a commonly used building material in the variety of protest camps that have proliferated in recent years – from the 'tripods' used to mark the Camps for Climate Action at various locations from 2006–2010 to the observation tower built at Grow Heathrow. An early example – and still one of the most powerful – was the scaffolding erected by anti-roads protestors who occupied a terrace of 35 houses in Claremont Road in Leytonstone, east London, for eight months in 1994 in their campaign against the extension of the M11 motorway. The houses stood in the path of the new road and were to be demolished. Knowing full well that the terrace was doomed, the squatters nevertheless turned the street into a site of extraordinary creativity – both street and houses were painted with murals, junk sculptures were made in one of the houses, while a gallery, two cafes, an information centre and a bicycle workshop provided a social hub for the wider community.

Most spectacular of all was the 100ft-high 'Dolly' tower that the protestors constructed from hundreds of pieces of salvaged scaffolding. They bolted it together in a haphazard fashion and connected the resulting tower to the rooftops of the houses with tensile netting. The tower became a prominent local landmark and was also the site of the final holdout of one of the protestors, Phil

Scaffolding, Claremont Road anti-roads protest, London, 1994

MVRDV's installation 'The Stairs' in central Rotterdam, June 2016

McLeish, who resisted eviction by scaling its heights. A site of carnivalesque festivity, the scaffolding tower at Claremont Road offered a powerful spectacle of its own, but one imbued with radical political intent – a counter-spectacle to the ones offered by neoliberal capitalism. According to one activist, the very temporary nature of the structure imbued it with additional power. Borrowing terminology from anarchist Hakim Bey, Claremont Road was called a 'Temporary Autonomous Zone' – a site of anarchist freedom that actively sought to remake the world anew in both its radical embracing of communal life and its decision to inhabit what is temporary, what is doomed to destruction.

In this reading, the temporary isn't a weakness; rather, the opposite – it precludes the possibility of failure because the ideas of the site can simply move elsewhere and begin again anew. In an urban world that is increasingly threatened by multiple forces of destruction, the embracing of the temporary as a strength rather than a weakness may be an important way in which radical change can be both embraced and enacted. As the Claremont Road protest demonstrates, scaffolding offers opportunities for all of us to create new kinds of architectures that grow out of the old – parasitic architectures of temporary defiance in the face of their inevitable destruction.

The 'Dolly' tower and aerial netting at the M11 Link Road protest, Claremont Road, 1994

IV. PROTEST

Your camp is not just a piece of natural heritage that you are defending, it's your home. You know every bit intimately, you've watched it change, you know how it runs day to day …. It's where you live. And it's your work, you labour hard to make things happen here, that's what you spend most days doing. You become familiar, attached—John Merrick, *Battle for the Trees* (1996), p. 90

In England in 1649, a radical political group led by Gerard Winstanley and calling themselves the 'True Levellers' occupied St George's Hill in Surrey and began digging the land for cultivation, as well as building rudimentary shelters. Known popularly as 'The Diggers', the group wanted to see the return of common land to the people, advocating its collective cultivation. Although the movement only lasted a few years, it has resonated down the centuries as a formative instance of squatting and self-building as a way of protest. Their more recent namesakes, the San Francisco Diggers of the 1960s, used a mixture of direct action and street theatre to advocate a free lifestyle; while The Land in Ours campaigning group in the UK referenced The Diggers in their call for free access to land and the saving of common spaces from development.

This section explores how protest camps, at heart, are about much more than simply mounting a form of resistance. Whether they are ostensibly challenging institutionalized racism (Resurrection City); nuclear proliferation (Greenham Common); environmental destruction (Grow Heathrow and Extinction Rebellion); or the erosion of democracy (Tahrir Square, Occupy Wall Street and the Umbrella Revolution), protest camps are always about building new societies. They are, in effect, micro-utopias. They may be short-lived or long-lasting, small or large scale, but wherever there is a protest camp, there is a powerful attempt to build anew.

Out of all the sites examined in this book, protest camps demand the highest levels of commitment and sacrifice from their participants. They are often dangerous places to live: many hundreds died in the encampment in Cairo's Tahrir Square in the spring of 2011; residents of Resurrection City and Occupy Wall Street were subject to police brutality; the women of Greenham Common had to endure constant evictions and often appalling living conditions; while the British anti-roads protestors of the 1990s were literally dragged out of their treehouses by police and private security forces. Moreover, after widespread changes in squatting law in many European countries in 2011, protestors now face the constant threat of eviction – those at Grow Heathrow in London continue at present to hold out against the odds. Even members of Extinction Rebellion are regarded as potential terrorists in many countries. And, after the Umbrella Revolution in Hong Kong in 2014 spawned a much larger wave of protests in 2019, both police and protestors' tactics hardened in a spiral of violence. Protest camps shows that taking a stand against authority is never without a cost.

Toilets constructed at Oxford Circus for Extinction Rebellion protestors in April 2019

Resurrection City, Washington DC, May–June 1968

Although the origins of protest camps are multiple – from the Diggers of the seventeenth century to indigenous resistances to colonial land grabs – the first of any scale was Resurrection City, a planned camp of nearly 3,000 of America's poorest people in the heart of Washington DC in May and June of 1968. A product – and culmination – of the Poor People's Campaign, an initiative of Martin Luther King Jr that married the aims of the Civil Rights Movement with those of anti-poverty activists, Resurrection City was a short-lived community of blacks, Native Americans, Hispanics and poor whites from the Appalachians. It was remarkable for both its scale and also for the fact that the project was permitted by the authorities, located, as it was, in direct view of the White House. By the end of its six-week life, the City had dwindled to just a few hundred residents, the rest ground down by incessant rain, poor organization and lack of hope in the prospect of genuine welfare reform.[1]

Yet, in its early weeks, Resurrection City provided a powerful model of building from the bottom up. Residents marched to the site in nine separate 'caravans' from all parts of the United States, organized by the leaders of the Poor People's Campaign, with Reverend Ralph Abernathy taking over from King when he was assassinated on 4 April 1968. The hundreds of shelters in Resurrection City were built by the residents themselves. A committee consulted architects for prototypes and decided on triangular tent-shaped structures made of a mixture of plywood panels and plastic sheeting. Assembled quickly by both individuals and small teams, they were some of the first architect-designed structures that could be built by anyone: harbingers of Walter Segal's self-build method in that the architects provided simple instructions for assembly. Over time, the structures were personalized by their residents – most often in the form of painted decoration, names and other identifiers. Some were even able to customize their builds – adding an extra storey to the modular design or, more commonly,

Plywood shelters built at Resurrection City, May 1968

Resurrection City after heavy rain, June 1968

a door or window in place of the flimsy canvas openings. The shelters were built for both individual families and small groups of singles and they were grouped together in compounds of nine units, with larger compounds of four centred on a leader's shack – a feature borrowed directly from the layout of military camps. These larger compounds were arranged either side of a Main Street that housed all the communal facilities, including dining and meeting spaces, medical tents, a bakery set up by the San Francisco Diggers, toilets, a child-care facility and a security base. A fence surrounded Resurrection City, keeping public, press and police out; the site had its own self-organized security force.[2]

Once building was completed, the problems began. First, it became a mud-bath after it rained heavily on day 28 of the City's 42–day existence, with photographs by resident Jill Freedman showing shelters half-submerged by water and hastily constructed timber boardwalks surrounded by impassable mud.[3] In addition, effective organization of such a large group of people was hampered by a conflicted approach. On the one hand, residents themselves participated in building the city; on the other, they had only limited opportunities to join in with other aspects of its organization, other than the regular protest marches that were a critical part of life there. And the leaders, including Ralph Abernathy himself, never lived in Resurrection City, preferring to base themselves in a nearby hotel. There were also problems with a poorly organized police force that often made security problems worse. But most damaging of all was the loss of hope: the assassination of Senator Robert F Kennedy on 6 June 1968 was an enormous blow to the City's residents, especially since it came so soon after the killing of Martin Luther King in April. In addition, the agenda of the Poor People's Campaign never garnered the support of middle-class white progressives that the early Civil Rights Movement had. Placing the issue of financial inequality before race, Resurrection City explicitly challenged the economic basis of American capitalism rather than just civil rights.[4]

By the end, Resurrection City had descended into a chaos of mud and despair, its last few days marred by rioting and police brutality, the disassembling of the camp on 24 June mostly greeted with a sigh of relief by the US left-leaning press. It was felt by many that the more hopeful life the City had promised its impoverished residents had not been realised: that it had become an urban ghetto just like any other and that the demands of the Poor People's Campaign had been completely rebuffed. But, for resident Jill Freedman, the fact that it became just like any other city wasn't surprising or indeed part of her despair; rather it was that its temporary success in forging hope only served to flag up just how intractable inequality had become under a capitalist regime and that, in the end, the issue of civic rights had merely served to conceal a much deeper and more universal crisis at the heart of American life.[5]

Plywood panel from a mural created at Resurrection City

Greenham Common Women's Peace Camp, UK, 1981–2000

In contrast to the short lifespan of Resurrection City, camps established during the Cold War to resist the proliferation of nuclear weapons were sometimes very long-lasting, their targets secretive and implacable objects buried in silos. The Faslane Peace Camp on the banks of the River Clyde in Scotland where the UK's Trident nuclear warheads are stored is still going after nearly four decades; while the longest-running anti-nuclear protest in American history (32 years) – a permanent camp across the road from the White House – only came to an end when its leader and sole occupant Connie Picciotto died in 2013. But perhaps the most widely known was the Women's Peace Camp set up around the fence of the US air base on Greenham Common, Berkshire, which existed for 19 years

Benders constructed next to the fence of the Greenham Common airbase, c. 1984

Constructing a bender at the Greenham Common Women's Peace Camp in 1983

from 1981 to 2000. At times, the numbers of protestors at the women-only site reached tens of thousands: a vigil in December 1982 involved 35,000 linking arms around the nine-mile perimeter fence; while another a year later drew 50,000.[6]

The Women's Peace Camp began as a result of a spontaneous decision by a group of 35 women from south Wales. Responding to the 1979 decision to house US nuclear-armed missiles in air bases across Europe, in August 1981 the group marched to Greenham Common from Cardiff to demand a face-to-face meeting with the British Defence Secretary, John Nott. When this was refused, the women decided to stay put, with local residents providing some initial provisions, such as caravans, tents and food. From very small beginnings – just a few

campers – the protest grew to encompass nearly all of the land around the air base – nine distinct camps, seven of which were named after the colours of the rainbow and mostly grouped around the entrance gates. Within the first six months, it was decided that the camp was to be women-only and gradually the site developed a worldwide reputation as a bastion for feminist practice, particularly as one of the gates (Green) was strictly lesbian. It was also recognized as distinctly anarchist in its politics: decision-making was consensual and, although long-term residents ('campers') had some additional status, it didn't prevent most Greenham veterans acknowledging that all who took part were 'Greenham Women' – whether the 'stayers' who came for shorter periods, the 'visitors' who just came for a few hours, or the thousands of supporters

Improvised bathroom at the Greenham Common Women's Peace Camp, c. 1984

outside who provided help with funding, communications and provisions. Significant donations included specially designed 'Getaway' tents – simple triple-hooped tents with an internal groundsheet that could be rapidly disassembled when the bailiffs arrived to evict protestors.[7]

In the mid-1980s, evictions were commonplace – police brutality often accompanied by that from Newbury residents unhappy at the presence of so many 'dirty' women nearby. For the protestors, living conditions were indeed extremely basic: latrines had to be hand dug into the earth and early structures like the numerous benders built in the woods were easy targets for bailiffs. The women at Greenham had been taught how to build benders by a group of travellers who visited the camp during a 1982 peace caravan – they're made from flexible tree branches that are forced into the ground and woven together to produce a rigid domed structure which is

then covered in textiles or tarpaulin for shelter. Repeated dawn raids by bailiffs meant that most of the camps at Greenham had a highly makeshift character as a result of the constant threat of displacement. However, the camp as a whole endured – well beyond the critical decision in 1987 by the world's then two superpowers to reduce their nuclear arsenals, which saw Greenham's 96 cruise missiles taken back to the US for destruction.

By the mid-1990s, the protest had dwindled to just one site – the main Yellow Gate. Here, Greenham Women continued to push for the return of the Common to public ownership in alliance now with Newbury residents who had formerly resented their presence. A critical event in this later period was the 1991 overturning of the conviction of two protestors for trespass (they were actually convicted in 1985 after breaking into the air base). With extraordinary tenacity, Jean Hutchinson and Georgina

Smith used the UK's ancient rights of commons to prove that they were not guilty of trespass and, subsequently, that the Ministry of Defence had actually acted illegally in building the air base in the first place, because they had not overturned these rights of commons.[8] The discovery of this legal oddity energized a wide group of people to push for the return of Greenham Common to public ownership; and, in alliance with Newbury Borough Council, a community land trust did just this – in 2000, the military fence was torn down and the public (and cattle) were free to roam the common once again, with a parliamentary Act passed in 2001 as a final stamp of authority.

Some of the Greenham Women went on to protest the building of new roads, such as the nearby Newbury Bypass in the mid-1990s; others continued to protest against nuclear weapons, helping actions coordinated by the Faslane Peace Camp. At least a few of the many hundreds of Extinction Rebellion members who set up the protest sites that badly disrupted life in London for a few days in April 2019 were Greenham Women – veterans who passed on their own experience to a new generation of activists. This coming together of generations was a powerful way in which Extinction Rebellion has garnered wide public support and a significant global presence. It's clear that the influence of protest camps like Greenham Common, through ideas lived out in practice over a long period of time, has extended far beyond their individual lifespans and specific targets of protest.

Newbury bypass protests, UK, 1995–96

Just as the Greenham Common Women's Peace Camp was winding down in the mid-1990s, another surge of protests was galvanized by the UK Conservative government's aggressive road-building plans. In an ironic turn of events, some of the concrete dug up from the decommissioned Greenham air-base runway was used to build the dual carriageway that bypassed nearby Newbury. Just as before, the new protestors were not supported by the town's residents, who were fed up with chronic traffic congestion in their town.

With the anti-roads protests came a new tactic of building structures in trees to give protestors some measure of added protection that the Greenham Women simply didn't have. Building a treehouse was simply a more sophisticated way of imposing a barrier between protestors and contractors or police. One of the first was a 'hut village' built in 1980 to protest the building of a new runway at Frankfurt airport.[9] Yet it was only in the UK anti-roads protests of the 1990s that the tree camp emerged as a commonplace and often powerful tool against the destruction of the natural environment.

Many of these protests were ultimately unsuccessful – the planned bypasses around Newcastle, Bath and Newbury were eventually built after tree protests set up in 1993, 1994 and 1995–96 respectively. Yet, the tactics employed were such that evicting protestors became so expensive and time-consuming that the UK government roads policy changed in the late 1990s – the incoming Labour administration of 1997 abandoning the roads-building programme it had inherited from the Conservatives.[10] Protestor Kate Evans, who had lived at Greenham Common in the 1980s, published *Copse* (1998), a book of cartoons that chronicled her life in some of the treehouses built on these sites. With one page offering step-by-step instructions on how to construct a treehouse, this book keyed into the radical DIY culture that was emerging at the time.[11]

Kate Evans's cartoon 'How to build a treehouse' in her book *Copse* (1998), p. 174

Many of the treehouses built in the 1990s were elevated benders – the stick-supported dome secured to a level timber platform lashed between branches. Occupied from just a few days to many years, these structures were sometimes 'fortified' by tunnels dug around the tree base (to prevent heavy vehicles from approaching), and barbed wire and razor fencing strung around greased trunks (to stop professional climbers hired by the police). Many protestors 'locked on' to the tree with an array of brackets, harnesses, clips, rope and tape. Some of these tree camps housed large structures: the 'Mothership', at one of the 30 separate protest camps set up along the route of the Newbury bypass, sleeping up to 30 people, including Kate Evans, who illustrated it in *Copse*.

More recent treehouses were built for much longer periods of occupation – the trio of structures erected at Stanton Moor protesting the excavation of a quarry in England's Peak District National Park remaining in situ for 10 years from 1999 until the planned quarry was eventually re-sited. Featuring pitched roofs and salvaged windows, these treehouses effectively became places of permanent occupation – a whole infrastructure of tree-based life emerging in the process, including rope and wire walkways between the individual houses.

The sense of heroic resistance that imbues many protestors' accounts of life in tree camps can be linked back to a children's pastime that became a national craze in the US in the early 1930s, when endurance contests were held to see how long children could occupy their self-built treehouses (an astonishing 107 days being the reputed record).[12] Yet, when living in trees, heroism is always accompanied by intense vulnerability, powerfully realised in a semi-fictional tree protest that forms part of Richard Powers's magisterial novel *The Overstory* (2018). Cut off from the ground, life is sustained by a constant

Eviction of the Tot Hill encampment in February 1996

One of the treehouses built by protestors at Stanton Moor, June 2007

interaction between the tree dweller and a network of support – whether the food or fuel that is hoisted up or waste materials that are lowered down.[13] These support networks demonstrate how our survival as a human species is predicated on a horizontal existence even though, presumably at some point in the distant past, our primate ancestors were fully at home in the forest heights.

Yet, the dream of an autonomous existence fuels the desire to live in a treehouse. In Andy Griffiths and Terry Denton's bestselling series of children's books, an imaginary treehouse grows from 13 to an extraordinary 104 storeys during the course of eight separate books, and is set in an alternative world of fantasy structures, improbable functions and bizarre accretions.[14] The practical, hands-on defence strategy of the treehouse as protest camp might seem a far cry from the skyward fantasy of a child's imagination; yet, both share a sense of utopian striving that relishes the isolation of vertical living as a potent incubator of new possibilities.

Grow Heathrow, London, 2010–

The anti-roads protests of the 1990s were harbingers of a more wide-ranging and mainstream environmental movement that is now centred on the dangers posed by climate change and mass extinction. The targets of climate-change protests are many and varied, from fossil-fuel based industries such as global aviation and shipping, to energy producers and corporations that unsustainably exploit the planet's resources.

Grow Heathrow is an off-grid community and protest site that has, since 2010, occupied a few acres of vacant land in the village of Sipson, just north of London's Heathrow Airport.[15] An attempt at evicting the community in early 2019 led to an extended standoff as protestors retreated to the areas of the site that could not be reached by security vehicles. Grow Heathrow was established in opposition to the UK Government's plan to build a third runway at the airport. A group of around 20 activists, local residents and people already living off-grid squatted on vacant land where three dilapidated greenhouses stood – remnants of a long-abandoned market garden.[16] The camp brought together two earlier political groups – the Transition Network (2005–) and Camps for Climate Action (2006–11) – to create an eco-community committed to sustainable ends that would operate outside the world of commodity capitalism.

Even though Heathrow's new runway was finally approved by Parliament in June 2018, Grow Heathrow has quickly transcended its function as a protest site so that, today, just like the much larger ZAD in northwest France, it presents a radical alternative to urban life that is based on autonomous, consensus-based communal living and sustainable ways of sourcing food and energy and disposing of wastes. A major boost for the site came with the UK Court of Appeal's ruling in February 2020 that the plan to build the new runway contravenes the UK's commitment

Compost toilets built by protestors at Grow Heathrow, December 2018

The 'Dump Starz' at Grow Heathrow, filled to overflowing
with salvaged materials, December 2018

to reduce its greenhouse gas emissions to net zero by 2050. In effect, it's the runway and not the protest camp that has now been deemed illegal.

On the four–acre site, residents have, over time, built their own homes out of salvaged materials – a mixture of recycled timber, pvc windows, tarpaulins and other plastics; each dwelling also has a fire pit connected to an improvised metal chimney. Houses constructed before the partial eviction in 2019 included a rectangular-plan shack, mostly built out of wood; a yurt, resting on piles of scavenged palettes; a bender – a tarpaulin-shrouded stick-framed ovoid that barely emerges from the ground; and a more conventional two-storey house complete with a porch. Each house also features a conventional wooden door, acting as both a place marker and structural support, the doors themselves sourced from skips – discarded remnants of other, far more conventional, homes and other buildings. No one person or family owns any of the houses – they are built for occupation for a limited time only (a maximum of four years) and then passed on to others when that occupation ends. In this way, each house develops incrementally – new features are added when it changes hands; stewardship taking the place of ownership.[17]

In between these dwellings was a network of other structures built for communal living: a shipping container repurposed as a guest house; a striking shower block supported by scaffolding found in a skip and powered by a wood-burning heater built out of discarded oil tanks; a timber-clad compost toilet raised high above the ground; a communal library of alternative literature and zines contained within a meeting place warmed by an efficient scavenged stove; and a salvage area enclosed in the remains of one of the existing greenhouses. Overflowing with scraps of timber, plastic and metal, the 'Dump Starz' testified not only to the ingenuity of the community in sourcing its building materials, but also to the extraordinary quantities of waste generated by urban living that usually ends up being dumped in landfill sites. At Grow Heathrow, materials were sorted into constituent piles for future usage.

Despite this abundance of materials sourced for re-use, the community was mostly reliant on donations, whether solar panels that provided half of its electricity, or battery units that ensured a reliable supply, and drinking water supplied for a reduced fee by the local water company. Although Grow Heathrow offers a frank demonstration of a kind of urban living that takes the idea of sustainability seriously, it also shows that a truly self-sufficient lifestyle is impossible – indeed, the very effort of achieving this only serves to reveal how dependent we are on resources from outside.

Self-built communities like Grow Heathrow are vital in cities because they demonstrate how to actually construct something radically 'other' to an urban life based on gargantuan consumption of non-renewable fuels, excessively authoritarian planning regimes, rigid social hierarchies, and building practices that are completely out of the hands of users. Yet in maintaining the community for so many years, and in spite of eviction attempts, the residents of Grow Heathrow have also shown how connections must be maintained between the subversive and the conventional, between autonomy and cooperation, and between starkly different urban communities. It may be very small in its extent, but Grow Heathrow is very big in its radical ambition.

Self-built house at Grow Heathrow with the Heathrow Airport Holiday Inn
in the background, December 2018

Tahrir Square, Cairo, 2011

For many, climate-change protestors are demanding the impossible, namely, the complete transformation of global society towards sustainable ends. Yet, since the 2000s, when mass popular protests led to the downfall of several autocratic regimes, the seemingly impossible has in fact been realised. In 2000, the Otpor! movement in Serbia succeeded in deposing president Milošević, leading to his trial for war crimes in The Hague; the 'rose revolution' in Georgia in 2003 led to the removal of the country's Russian-backed president; while the Orange Revolution in Ukraine in 2005 did the same in that country. But it was in the first half of 2011 that urban protests and occupations demanding regime change gathered extraordinary momentum in the Arab Spring movement, when cities in Tunisia, Libya, Egypt, Syria, Bahrain, and Yemen erupted in mass protests.[18] The ousting of Tunisia's longtime president Zine El Abidine Ben Ali in January 2011 inspired Egyptians to take to the streets of the country's major cities, with 21,000 protestors converging on Cairo's Tahrir Square on the morning of 25 January. Initially repelled by the security forces, 100,000 people returned to take the Square by force; and they remained there for 18 days before the resignation of president Mubarak on 11 February.[19]

Over those 18 days, an extraordinary community emerged, one that received sustained global attention, as a result of social media platforms like Facebook and Twitter. Forming a miniature city, the protest camp was home to a rapidly shifting population of hundreds of thousands of Egyptians from every conceivable social spectrum. Although often held up as an example of the success of peaceful mass protest in achieving democracy, the Tahrir Square occupation was in fact a place of violent confrontation between protestors and security forces, whether hired thugs, snipers, or plainclothes policemen. Aerial photographs of the encampment revealed how it functioned: a central circular space of tents and other temporary

Memorial to Mina Daniel, one of the hundreds of protestors killed at Tahrir Square. The Arabic texts read: 'Together in memory of the martyr Mina Daniel', November 2011

The encampment at Tahrir Square on 9 February 2011

structures was protected by a vast ring of people and makeshift barricades. The outer edges of the encampment were a perpetual battleground: hundreds died in the violence, mostly young people from poor areas of Cairo who brought both extraordinary courage and some previous experience fighting pro-state militia groups. Paving slabs were torn up around the Square and used as weapons, while molotov cocktails were made from flammable liquids such as petrol. This perpetually dangerous outer zone protected more vulnerable protestors within, including many children, who slept in tents in the centre of the circle. Improvised field hospitals run by volunteers treated the wounded, while pharmacies provided remedies for the effects of tear gas and medication for people with chronic diseases.[20]

Night-time image of the Tahrir Square encampment, 11 February 2011

Despite the constant threat of violence and the obvious uncertainty over the outcome of the occupation, many Tahrir Square protestors viewed it as a utopia – a liberated space in the city where everyone was equal and where a unified purpose – to resist and bring down a ruthless dictator and the state's violent machinery of oppression – governed every waking moment. It had a flat organizational structure in which no single group or movement dominated, something which allowed and encouraged inclusive participation. And far from being a place of anxiety, the encampment was full of creativity, with an improvised stage the setting for nightly protest songs, speeches, debates, news broadcasts, and entertainments.[21] This coming together of violence and festival might seem paradoxical; yet, according to writer and activist Rebecca Solnit, it is characteristic of human responses to disasters, whether natural or human-made.[22] Evidenced from her first-hand research of responses to 9/11 and Hurricane Katrina in 2005, Solnit has argued that, in times of great upheaval, people generally rise to the occasion – the disaster temporarily suspending the hierarchical organization of everyday life, releasing a capacity for self-organization that is latent within every one of us. This idea of a hidden anarchism – a universal human faculty that is normally not called upon or allowed to be utilized – presupposes the essential goodness of human nature. In this reading, the power of the panicking mob that every authority fears in times of upheaval is a myth generated to justify state oppression and the continuation of the hierarchies it requires.

Whether or not we subscribe to Solnit's optimism about human nature, it is clear that the effect of the Tahrir Square occupation was seismic, but not principally in terms of Egyptian politics which, after a period of turbulence, has seen the return of autocracy in the form of president Sisi who, since 2014, has clamped down once again on opposition. The principal reason why the impossible was achieved in Tahrir Square was that its egalitarian basis ensured that there was no command structure or official representatives that Mubarak's authorities could negotiate with. The impossible demand required an equally impossible society to develop – a genuine urban utopia. The fact that this society lasted only 18 days by no means discredits it. Rather, it shows us that such a society is always already present, waiting for the unthinkable to happen so that it might once again flourish.

Occupy Wall Street, New York, 2011

The global Occupy movement in the autumn of 2011 saw the occupation of public spaces in 951 cities in over half the countries of the world.[23] Directly inspired by the Arab Spring movement as well as anti-austerity protests like the 15M movement in Spain earlier in the same year, Occupy was key in harnessing the relatively new power of social media and digital communication to mobilize a vast network of protestors and financial support. In the US, the centrepiece protest was Occupy Wall Street, located in Zuccotti Park close to Wall Street, heartland of the US financial markets. This was the epicentre of the crisis that saw the country's sub-prime mortgage market collapse in 2007 and a massive taxpayer-funded $700 billion bailout by the Obama administration in 2008. The occupation in Zuccotti Park, which began on 17 September and lasted almost two months with up to 15,000 participants, was the culmination of a wave of protests in light of the financial crisis, which included the establishment of encampments – Walkerville in Wisconsin and Bloombergville in New York – that directly confronted the austerity policies of city mayors Scott Walker and Michael Bloomberg. These temporary tent cities got their names from the numerous Hoovervilles – shanty-towns for the homeless – that sprang up in American cities after the economic collapse of 1929.[24]

Although the initial call by *Adbusters* magazine for Occupy Wall Street urged Americans to make their own 'Tahrir moment', the two protests had very different intentions. Instead of the 'impossible demand' of regime change made by Egyptian protestors, a more nebulous appeal to redress inequality was made by Occupy. Citing the increasing gap between rich and poor – a result of a 30–year–old politics of economic liberalization that had concentrated huge amounts of wealth in the hands of the 1% – Occupy Wall Street made no clear demands; rather its slogan was 'We are the 99%'; its mantra was that 'this is a process not a protest'.[25] The process was to engage in

Protestors at Occupy Wall Street, 30 September 2011

a form of direct democracy that was seen as redundant in mainstream American politics, where money bought influence.

The central purpose of the Zuccotti Park encampment was to foster new ways of living together in cities based on governance by consensus rather than majority voting, and a thoroughly anti-capitalist sharing of resources – the mutual aid celebrated by Peter Kropotkin in the early twentieth century. To organize their camps, Occupy used a mixture of general assemblies and working parties.[26] Although the hundreds of encampments were short-lived, they nevertheless had a global influence that has inspired countless other protests, including the largest Occupy-related encampment in the summer of 2013 in Gezi Park in Istanbul, when over a million people protested against an authoritarian government that responded with extreme violence – 22 protestors were killed and 8,000 injured.

The People's Library at Occupy Wall Street, November 2011

Like many of the Occupy encampments, and in common with Tahrir Square, Zuccotti Park in those two months was likened to a utopian city-within-a-city. Generous financial and other donations allowed the site to maintain itself and support was also offered by leading leftwing intellectuals such as David Graeber, Naomi Klein, Noam Chomsky and Slavoj Žižek, who gave speeches and conducted 'teach-ins' at the site. Hundreds of tents were supplemented by makeshift libraries (thousands of volumes in Zuccotti Park), bicycle-powered generators, toilets in a nearby McDonalds, and an ingenious way of getting around the city authority's ban on amplification devices – participants themselves amplifying the words of presenters by repeating them in unison.

Occupy has been lauded by architectural theorist Stavros Stavrides as a means by which space in cities is 'commoned', that is wrenched back into true public governance.[27] That this was achieved only temporarily by thousands in Zuccotti Park, and many hundreds of thousands in smaller groups worldwide, is not to diminish its significance. For Occupy has inspired countless place-based occupations since 2011, with many hundreds of protestors using its tactics to address more specific issues: for example, in New York alone, racial discrimination in Occupy the Hood; a failing education system in Occupy the DOE (Department of Education); and greedy corporate elites in Occupy the Boardroom.

Seeing Occupy as a form of 'commoning' is important given the recent rise of so-called pseudo-public spaces in cities across the world. Responding to central government cutbacks in the wake of the 2007–08 financial crisis, many municipal authorities have sold off genuine public space to corporations (Zuccotti Park was, from its inception, a privately owned space). Future protestors will have to negotiate this dwindling of genuinely public space, as more and more cash-strapped municipal authorities sell it to private corporations. As the stakes become higher, protestors will need to be bolder, braver and even more persistent than their Occupy predecessors. But there is clearly an urgent need for such action, lest our cities lose altogether their precious common spaces.

Bicycle-powered generators at Occupy Wall Street, 2 November 2011

Umbrella Movement, Hong Kong, 2014

The city of Hong Kong is exemplary in its almost total privatization of once public spaces. Long before the hand-over of Hong Kong by its British colonial rulers to China in 1997, the city's public spaces had all but disappeared. Most had been incorporated into the footprints of high-rise commercial buildings, as shopping malls or other retail spaces. Even Hong Kong's vast network of elevated walkways – designed to provide traffic-free thoroughfares for pedestrians – are intimately wed to corporate space, managed as they are by the Jardines, one of Hong Kong's largest conglomerates.[28] When the Umbrella Movement brought the centre of the city to a virtual standstill for 79 days from September to December 2014, it effectively created entirely new public spaces in the absence of almost any existing ones. The protest occupied three main sites: first, a former civic square and seven-lane highway at the Admiralty, directly outside Hong Kong's legislative council; second, a heavily built-up site in Causeway Bay; and, third, a road in the Mong Kok area of Kowloon. The occupations were a largely student-led response to the lack of democratic accountability of Hong Kong's government, and the failure of attempts to bring in universal suffrage since the British first started to plan for such moves in the mid-1980s. Protestors numbered in the tens of thousands, with as many as 100,000 at times; and one of their first actions was to reclaim public spaces, when the Admiralty site was renamed Umbrella Square.

The initial student protests that began outside the government buildings on 23 September 2014 had aligned themselves closely with Occupy, taking up their call to reclaim public spaces. The police responded with tear gas and pepper spray, a counterproductive move that brought out thousands more on to the streets and a rapid escalation of the occupations in the following days. Over time, thousands of tents filled the occupied sites and, as with Occupy Wall Street, an improvised city-within-a-city

Improvised work-spaces below the canopy of umbrellas at Umbrella Square, 18 October 2014

Looking up at the canopy of umbrellas above Umbrella Square, October 2014

Tents on Harcourt Road outside Hong Kong's Admiralty, 27 November 2014

developed. Easy-to-erect gazebos and marquees became food stalls, first-aid tents, spaces for public meetings and study areas. Salvaged building materials such as wooden palettes and discarded tables and chairs were used to construct barricades, makeshift toilets and showers, desks for a temporary university, and stairs that overcame the concrete barriers that lined the road. A recycling station was even built on Harcourt Road in order to keep the site scrupulously free from waste. But the most prominent objects used in the occupation were the tens of thousands of umbrellas carried by the protestors, ostensibly as protection against tear gas and pepper spray, but also as a powerful symbol of political vulnerability – the cry of a disenfranchized youth against a future that promised little hope. The yellow ribbons worn by the protestors and tied to every available surface explicitly referenced the British suffrage movement a century before; they also gave this revolution a strongly visual identity that Occupy tended to lack.

Indeed, the Umbrella Movement became widely celebrated for the extraordinary creativity that flourished during its three-month lifespan. The occupation produced not only new kinds of public space but also public art. Umbrellas were used in many of these art works, including a vast multi-coloured canopy erected over Umbrella Square to shelter the protestors, and another structure in the same space named *Happy Gadfly*, made from discarded umbrellas, plastic bottles and other waste materials. Most spectacular of all was the Umbrella

Man, a 10ft-high wood-and-metal statue clasping a yellow umbrella. In Mong Kok, a shrine to Guan Yu was built from salvaged materials, while an enormous notice board, named 'Lennon's Wall' after Prague's anti-communist murals of the 1980s, featured thousands of multi-coloured post-it notes offering messages of solidarity and hope. In addition, the surfaces of occupied roads were covered in chalk drawings – a literal reworking of the street into a vast canvas for personal expression, rather than the regimented movement of traffic.[29]

The success of the Umbrella Movement should be read more in terms of its actualization of direct democracy rather than in changing the existing systems of power, which remained largely unaltered after the occupations were cleared in December 2014.[30] Like Occupy, the protests became a way in which citizens could act out their hopeful vision of a more democratic future. In those 79 days, Hong Kong became a different city – its air cleared of chronic pollution from automobiles, its streets turned into homes, its official borders and nomenclature repurposed and renamed from below. In effect, the occupations normalized dissent, something that has directly fed into the even larger waves of protests that convulsed Hong Kong in 2019. For many months, millions marched through the city's streets on an almost weekly basis, with much shorter-term but no less disruptive occupations a key tactic. With a subsequent tightening of control by Beijing, genuine electoral reform in the near future now looks unlikely.

Extinction Rebellion, London, 2018–

The Occupy movement has directly informed the evolution of a new kind of environmental protest against the lack of governmental action on mitigating climate disaster and preventing ecological collapse. In October 2018, the Intergovernmental Panel on Climate Change warned that we then had only just over a decade in which to act to avoid the unprecedented disaster of runaway global warming. In light of this dire prediction, the nascent Extinction Rebellion (XR) group, established in Britain by 15 academics in May 2018, suddenly galvanized the public imagination.[31] Together with the School Strikes for Climate, begun in Sweden by Greta Thunberg in August 2018, the actions of XR have been key in raising public awareness of the likely effects of climate change and confronting governments with their responsibility to act decisively and quickly, which they have mostly so far failed to do.

The tactics of XR are simple but spectacularly effective: in well-organized groups they 'retake' urban spaces normally given over to petrol-guzzling vehicles and transform them into temporary encampments open to all. Like the Umbrella Movement, XR engage in multiple, simultaneous occupations. One of their first large-scale actions, on 17 November 2018, was to block the five main road bridges over the River Thames in London for several hours, causing major disruption. Their most significant UK actions to date have been a 10–day occupation of four key sites in central London from 15 to 25 April 2019, a four-day occupation in central Manchester in September 2019, and a week-long campaign of actions in London in early October 2019 and a similar series of protests and blockades in August 2020.

In the April 2019 protests, activists blockaded Waterloo Bridge, Parliament Square, Oxford Circus and Marble Arch, as well as engaging in other smaller-scale actions. During the 10–day occupations, over 1,000

Extinction Rebellion's pink boat moored at Oxford Circus in April 2019

A free shop constructed at Marble Arch in April 2019

activists were arrested by the Metropolitan Police – a move that mainly served to bring more protestors to the sites where arrests had been made. This tactic of multiple occupations was made possible by instantaneous online communications through social media and it created a highly fluid protest that was very difficult to police effectively. It also powerfully disrupted the conventional everyday flows of traffic, people and goods that modern cities take for granted as normal – something that anticipated the much larger-scale disruption of the Coronavirus pandemic in 2020. For a brief period, significant areas of central London were largely car-free, the city's air seemed cleaner, its streets dominated by the noise of people rather than vehicles.

At the same time, XR protestors brought with them a range of structures to sustain the occupations. A pink boat was 'moored' in the centre of Oxford Circus, around which a sea of protestors gathered, some gluing themselves to the boat. Potted plants and small trees were brought to Waterloo Bridge, while coloured chalks enabled people to transform the surface of roads into a canvas for art. Tents dominated in the pedestrianized space at Marble Arch – barricades made from traffic cones, canvas banners and wooden palettes marking the edges of the zone of occupation. The protestors' everyday needs were met by a variety of ad-hoc structures: a small raised platform balanced on used car tyres supporting a sink on Waterloo Bridge, a place to wash dirty cups and dishes; toilets at Oxford Circus constructed from salvaged wooden panels and doors; a free shop made from similar materials at Marble Arch. In addition, structures were built simply for pleasure: an improvised stage made with pallets in the heart of Parliament Square hosting musicians and other performers; a skateboard ramp, one of the first things to be installed on Waterloo Bridge; sculptures and assemblages at all four sites melding protest and art in the mode of the Umbrella Movement. Finally, in a similar way to the Occupy movement, the day-to-day organization of the protest sites was facilitated by easy-to-erect gazebos and other inexpensive demountable structures. As with Occupy, a consensus-based politics emerged: small groups of protestors took responsibility for different tasks assigned to them. Indeed, one of the three key demands of XR – that a citizens' assembly be created to hold governments accountable for the transition to a zero-carbon society – came directly from anarchist practice, namely to make political representation a truly bottom-up process.

Since the April 2019 occupations, there has been much celebration within the XR movement, particularly after the UK became the first government in the world to declare a climate emergency shortly after the end of the London occupations on 1 May 2019. But its breezy optimism has been tempered by criticism of the movement as overly concerned with generating a spectacle (arrests seen as a status symbol) at the expense of the hard graft of long-term negotiation for concrete results.[32] XR has also been criticized for paying little attention to wider anti-capitalist struggles which are inextricably linked with climate change and ecological collapse, as well as focusing attention on developed-world communities that probably already have enough resources to escape the very worst effects of environmental breakdown.[33] And, despite bringing together young and old in XR occupations, the movement still lacks a broader social basis, particularly in relation to minority groups, the old working class and the new precariat. In the more recent October 2019 actions, XR protestors came into direct conflict with a hostile public. Two protestors who occupied the roof of a Tube train were forcibly removed by commuters, who were angered by what they saw as XR's counterproductive targeting of public transport.

It remains to be seen how the movement will develop in response to these criticisms, and also to an increasingly draconian approach by the police; but what it has undoubtedly achieved is a spectacular demonstration of the power of occupations to transform the nature of urban space, even if this is only temporary. When streets become places to live, when the dominance of cars is powerfully challenged, when politics grows directly from full participation, when everyday life itself merges with art and festival – then, the city is truly transformed into a new kind of space that prefigures more sustainable, emancipatory and hopeful futures.

Washing-up station on Waterloo Bridge, April 2019

V. ECOLOGY

We need to recreate everything along ecological lines ....
Here, humanity would neither give nor take; it would
actually *participate* with nature in creating the new levels
of diversity and form that are part of a more heightened sense
of humanness and naturalness—Murray Bookchin, *The Ecology
of Freedom* (1985), p. 367

To be ecological is generally assumed to mean to adopt a certain stance against the human world – to reject its destructive ways, its wastefulness, its exploitation of rather than care for nature. In a contrasting argument, Murray Bookchin invests ecological action with a profoundly positive intent. In his reading, to be ecological is to transform one's attitude towards what is human and what is not, to see that the two are always intertwined. Recognizing this – and living it – results in a diversity that grows as we grow together *with* nature. In this understanding, how we build is critically important because it, more than anything else, has the potential to create a world where the human and non-human are allowed to coexist.

This may seem an impossibly utopian proposition, given the current ways in which the human world is constructed with utter disregard for the rest of the biosphere, but it's been a key tenet in the development of alternative forms of building that date back at least to the early 1970s. This section begins in that period, charting an evolving awareness of the relationship between ecology and architecture in London, northern New Mexico, and southern Chile. In these contexts what counts as ecological building is highly varied: it's simultaneously about infrastructure (Street Farmhouse), spirituality (Lama Foundation), energy (Earthships), and poetry (Open City).

More recent eco-communities tend to be more unified in their approaches to building. The two UK-based projects explored here – Landmatters and Lammas – are both, in their own way, trying to engage with existing planning regulations. Small-scale and mostly rural, these eco-communities are actively trying to win support from the mainstream rather than escape from it. In an urban context, Prinzessinnengärten in Berlin provides a model for changing the way in which we engage with food in cities, offering an approach that grounds this specific and essential form of nature in communal participation.

The final piece moves to the hyper-urban context of Taipei. Here, the Ruin Academy asks provocative questions about just what kind of nature we deem acceptable within our buildings. There's always a tendency with ecological architecture to stress nature as a harmonious and balancing force. The Ruin Academy sees things differently: nature as disruptive, and the inorganic as subject to forces beyond our control – the ruination that is ever-present in the material world.

Street Farmhouse, London, 1972–75

The early 1970s witnessed the first widespread stirrings of unease about the ecological consequences of consumer capitalism and unchecked population growth, before its momentum was checked by the oil crisis of 1973. Growing out of the countercultural explosion of the 1960s, this ecological movement spawned some radical alternatives to industrialised production and mass consumption. One of these was what can arguably lay claim to be the world's first eco-house, built in 1972 by architectural student Graham Caine and his friends Bruce Haggart and Peter Crump from the collective Street Farm.[1]

Formed in 1971 in the febrile atmosphere of London's Architectural Association – still the world's only fully independent architecture school – Street Farm speculated about a new urban ecology that would see capitalist societies replaced with anarchist collectives. In two editions of their homespun magazine *Street Farmer*, the group presented a startling vision of tractors literally ploughing up streets, concrete high-rises overtaken by crops seeded from the sky, and bourgeois semi-detached houses 'transmogrified' into outsized cabbages.[2] Mixing absurdist humour with genuine outrage at the sterile uniformity imposed by architectural modernism, Street Farm also critiqued the better-known output of their contemporaries in Archigram – another radical architectural collective spawned from the Architectural Association. Although both groups shared a passion for liberation and a focus on the home as the site of radical transformation, Street Farm were highly critical of what they saw as Archigram's unequivocal celebration of technology and its failure to take capitalist economics to task for producing social alienation and environmental deterioration.[3] Street Farm argued that human liberation could only be realised through social and political transformation and not simply by technology alone.

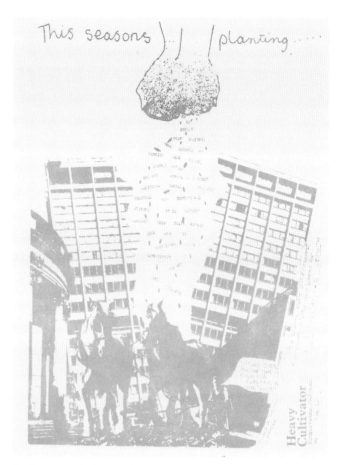

Seeding concrete high-rises in *Street Farmer* 2, c. 1972

Graham Caine's eco-house – Street Farmhouse – built in 1972
in Eltham, Surrey, and demolished in 1975

Caine's eco-house – Street Farmhouse – was the centrepiece of his final-year project as a 26–year–old student at the Architectural Association and, under the enlightened chairmanship of Alvin Boyarsky, was given generous funding so it could be realised. With the help of friends and his Street Farm colleagues, Caine built the house in four months from September 1972, having been given temporary occupation of a piece of land on the campus of Thames Polytechnic in southeast London. Divided into two principal structures – a timber-framed living unit resembling a chalet joined to a large polyhedral greenhouse made from transparent acrylic panels – Street Farmhouse became the home of Caine and his young family for two years until it was demolished in 1975. Widely illustrated in the national and architectural press, and even the subject of a BBC documentary *Clearings in the Concrete Jungle* in 1973, Street Farmhouse preceded better-known prototype eco-houses, such as Brenda and Robert Vale's Autonomous House of 1975 and the Integral Urban House built at Berkeley University in the late 1970s.[4] The motto of the structure as 'a house that grows' was featured on a banner hung from the living space. This was directly borrowed from Murray Bookchin's 1972 book *Post-Scarcity Anarchism*, with its central argument that technology could play an important role in liberating people to live self-sufficiently. It also came from Caine's previous

Graham Caine's drawing of the infrastructure of Street Farmhouse,
showing his body connected to all parts of the house, c. 1972

projects, particularly a proposal for a house that would literally be grown using giant bamboo, published in *Garden News* in May 1972.[5]

Despite Street Farmhouse's bricolage aesthetics – most of the building materials were salvaged locally – it became the site of a highly sophisticated experiment by Caine and his family in autonomous living – an off-grid house at its most radical. In addition to rudimentary structures for generating power – solar collectors and heat sinks – Caine also experimented ceaselessly with ways of turning waste material, including his own faeces, into energy. A series of tanks and digesters transformed human and vegetable waste into methane gas for cooking and compost for cultivation, while an invisible cellophane wall membrane purified rain water and condensation. In his own drawing of the house, Caine portrayed himself as a machine for generating electricity, his body connected to all parts of the house – a vital component of its sustenance.[6] During his two years of occupation, Caine hardly ever left the structure lest the body-centred systems he set up should malfunction. Indeed, when Caine was forced to leave for a few weeks due to a family emergency, his student replacement contracted flu, the antibiotics prescribed to him eventually poisoning the life-support systems of the house itself.[7]

This derailing of the ecological systems of the Street Farmhouse flags up the central problem of autonomous living spaces. Even though Caine intended the house to be a model for a new kind of society that embraced self-determination as a fundamental tenet in all aspects of life, it nevertheless failed because of its vulnerability to disorder. The ways in which humans occupy houses is fundamentally unpredictable and thus any regenerative system put in place is at risk of failing. Caine himself recognised this when he stated in 1973 that he and his family had never actually tried to attain self-sufficiency, viewing this isolationist approach as 'socially undesirable'.[8] In the end, it was precisely what was outside that corrupted the closed-system of the eco-house.

Lama Foundation, New Mexico, USA, 1967–

As many countercultural figures recognised in the 1960s, spirituality was also an important element in ecological practices. Among the tens of thousands of communes founded in the United States in the late 1960s and early 1970s, many had an overtly spiritual basis stemming from a rejection of conventional organized religion (mostly Protestant Christianity in the US) and an embracing of other traditions, including Buddhism and Hinduism.[9] In 1962, Steve and Barbara Durkee went on a road trip in the American southwest, intent on founding a community grounded in spiritual education. Later, under the influence of Meher Baba, an Indian spiritual master who inspired many countercultural figures in the 1960s, the Durkees renounced the pleasures of LSD, marijuana and alcohol and set up the Lama Foundation on land they purchased in the Sangre de Cristo mountains north of Taos in New Mexico. Although the strict prohibition of intoxicating substances would soon be relaxed, the daily meditation practice that began when the Durkees and their friend and funder Jonathan Altman started living there in May 1967 would continue to this day, making the Lama Foundation one of the longest-lasting countercultural communities in the United States.[10]

The siting of the Lama Foundation in New Mexico was significant, for it joined a venerable lineage of alternative communities in that state, from Mormon settlements established in the 1870s, cooperative communities like Cedar Grove, founded on Ba'hai principles in 1962, to the first hippie communes of the 1960s, such as Hog Farm and New Buffalo.[11] The Lama Foundation also drew on the experience of Drop City, and particularly its key builder Steve Baer, who first developed his 'zomes' – polyhedral alternatives to geodesic domes – in that community. When Baer left Drop City in 1967, he relocated to New Mexico, where he would build more zomes at the Manera Nueva commune in Placitas near Albuquerque and assist in the

The central 'zome' at the Lama Foundation, the roof structure designed by Steve Baer and completed in 1968

Communal kitchen at the Lama Foundation, built in the late 1960s

design of the first permanent buildings constructed at the Lama Foundation in 1968.[12] Still used today for communal meditation, the original dome at the site was designed by Baer after the Durkees and others had started building an octagonal structure from adobe bricks, only to falter with the roof. Using timber struts covered in glass and supported on adobe walls, Baer's zome looks quite different from those he built at Drop City, with their multi-coloured car-top panels. Rather, the natural materials seem to merge into the landscape in which they sit, the mud of the adobe directly borrowed from Pueblo Native American practices that had been in place for centuries in northeast New Mexico. Perhaps in return for Baer's assistance, the Lama Foundation published his series of *Dome Cookbooks* from 1968 – DIY handbooks for anyone who wanted to follow his lead in building zomes.[13]

This 'open-source' design book was a pioneer in its field, directly influencing Stewart Brand's bestselling *Whole Earth Catalog*, first published in 1968. With a focus on self-sufficiency, ecology, alternative education, DIY construction and holism, the *Whole Earth Catalog* became a touchstone of what has subsequently been termed 'systems-thinking' in design and ecology that tackled the world's social and ecological imbalances through a holistic approach. Brand later argued that computers were the ultimate tool for creating alternative networks, an intimation of the kind of optimism that surrounded the early days of the World Wide Web in the 1990s.[14]

What the Lama Foundation took from Brand's system-thinking is its grounding of holistic ways of living in spiritual practices. While Brand became more and more preoccupied with cybernetics, residents at the Lama Foundation maintained a broader and more open-minded sense of what might be needed to develop a fully rounded ecology of freedom. Only a dozen or so people live there permanently (and only for a maximum of seven years), the hundreds of summer visitors coming for spiritual retreats or education in ecological building. A devastating fire in 1996 nearly destroyed the community – many of the self-built homes were burnt to the ground, the original domed structure and kitchen miraculously survived. What has been rebuilt since then are a host of ecological houses and hermitages for visitors constructed from natural materials, including timber salvaged from structures destroyed by the fire.[15] The result is a community continuing to evolve, one that responds to events on the ground with the kind of acceptance that characterises their longstanding spiritual practice. Here, buildings develop as a result of their being embedded in a distinct environment rather than through the generalised imposition of technological systems, an ecology of freedom that is paradoxically achieved by accepting and working with local constraints.

Adobe building at the Lama Foundation, constructed after the 1996 fire that destroyed many of the community's structures

Earthships, global, 1970s–

The wild lands of northern New Mexico hosted many countercultural communities in the early 1970s, as well as entrepreneurs developing new ways of building outside of the constraints of formal planning regulations. Architect Mike Reynolds moved to the area in the early 1970s to develop self-sufficient houses known as earthships – now overseen by his successful company Earthship Biotecture.[16] Reacting against the huge volumes of waste generated by a burgeoning consumer culture in the USA, Reynolds started using discarded tin cans in 1970 as infill for walls and, shortly after that, discarded automobile tyres as basic building blocks. Filled with earth that is compacted by the repeated blows of sledgehammers, these tyres are stacked to form walls, infilled with glass bottles and cans and rendered with cob, mud or cement. Timber frames are then attached to the walls to support roof structures, with mud also used to make domes and other roof coverings. A hodgepodge of the vernacular and the industrial, earthships have a very distinct visual identity that has proved immensely popular.

Earthship near Brighton, completed in 2007, which hosts workshops and public tours

To date, many hundreds have been built in the USA, concentrated around Taos – close to the Lama Foundation – where the Greater World Earthship Community now comprises over 100 houses. Since the 1990s, earthships have been built all over the world, the largest grouping to date – 12 – in the Aardehuis (Earth House) Project Olst in the Netherlands. In many cases, Reynolds acts as a consultant. For example, in 2000, he inspired a group to build a prototype earthship just outside of Brighton in the UK. Completed in 2007, the site now hosts regular workshops and public tours, even as the larger 16–home scheme it was meant to kickstart in the town has yet to materialise.[17]

The way in which earthships work as buildings is as important as the materials they're constructed from. In 1973, when global oil prices skyrocketed, Reynolds became concerned about the long-term viability of fossil fuels and he began to experiment with self-sufficient energy systems in his earthships. Since then, every aspect of their design has been developed to make them autonomous buildings: the thick tyre walls provide effective thermal insulation while passive solar gain (south-facing windows and sophisticated ventilation) generates comfortable interior temperatures without the need for any additional energy use. Battery packs store electricity generated by solar panels, wind turbines and hydro-pumps; while all rainwater and 'grey' waste water is recycled – in part to nourish indoor plants grown for food. Hybrid structures in every sense of the word, earthships are easily adapted to different climates: from the hot desert of New Mexico where they originated to the tropical climate of Puerto Rico and the temperate downland of southern England.

Earthships are often visually striking buildings: mud or cob construction allows for sensuous curved walls, while coloured-glass bottles embedded in those walls produces a rich visual effect. Inside, earthships are generally luxurious by the standards of most eco-friendly

An earthship home built near Taos, New Mexico, 2012

buildings, with large bathrooms that contrast sharply with the spartan compost toilets and communal showers of eco-communities like Lammas. Indeed, much of the press coverage on these buildings (and there's a great deal) emphasises the beauty of their materials, sensuous forms and self-sufficiency – the earthships themselves seemingly doing the work of harvesting and recycling resources at no cost to their human occupants. This tends to play down the work involved in building earthships (by all accounts backbreaking and time-consuming) and also the ways in which they might connect with anything outside of them, including fellow earthship inhabitants. In this reading, earthships are really just glorified bunkers that tap into romantic notions of self-sufficiency that are the bedrock of libertarian politics in the US – an individualist survivalist ideology that forgoes any connections with the outside world. Presented in this way, it's difficult to assess how earthships work in a communal setting, as they do in Taos and other eco-communities such as Olst in the Netherlands.

The notion that the waste products of industrial capitalism might be valid elements in a sustainable form of building is also problematic, and this has been drawn to the attention of some who are seeking to place more of an emphasis on the eco-credentials of earthships.[18] In claiming that materials like car tyres and tin cans are the truly 'natural' resources of our time, Reynolds challenges purist ideals of sustainable construction that tend to ignore or condemn such wastes.[19] As Drop City's builders recognised in their attempts to turn dead cars into living buildings in the late 1960s, there's a painful contradiction in condemning waste but also needing it. Yet perhaps this is a more honest, indeed more truly sustainable, way of thinking about the relationship between the natural and the human. This is what keeps earthships grounded, even as they seem to float in their bubbles of autonomy.

Earthship under construction near Taos, New Mexico, 2009

The Open City, Ritoque, Chile, 1971–

At the same time as tens of thousands of disillusioned North Americans were fleeing their apartments in cities for self-built homes in communes and alternative communities, another very different architectural utopia was being constructed at the other end of the continent. The Open City of Amereida occupies 670 acres of dune fields, wetlands and pine forests along the Pacific coast immediately south of Ritoque, a small seaside town in Chile. Purchased in 1970 by teachers at the Faculty of Architecture of the Catholic University in nearby Valparaiso, the Open City was founded in 1971 and was inspired by a radical approach to architectural research, teaching and practice that used poetry as an inspiration to build. This method grew out of a lifelong collaboration between Chilean architect Alberto Cruz and Argentinian poet Godofredo Iommi. Reacting against the post-Enlightenment grounding of architecture in reason and science, Cruz and Iommi instead wanted building to be a poetic act. They believed that architecture, just as much as the other arts, could express interior truths that were apprehended intuitively.

Hospedería de la Entrada (Entrance Lodge) at the edge of the Open City, completed in 1982

Hospedería del Errante (Wanderer's Lodge), constructed from
1981 to 1985 at the Open City

The Open City was founded after nearly two decades of experimentation at the Catholic University in Valparaiso, as Cruz and Iommi gathered around themselves a cohort of artists, poets, architects, and engineers who shared their vision. Remarkably, they were supported by the University, who funded their experimental approach for over half a century.[20] Today, the project is paid for by the Corporación Cultural Amereida, an independent organization set up to ensure the continuation of the initial vision. No-one who builds or lives in the Open City owns land or buildings and they live according to the anarchist principles of cooperation and mutual aid.

The poetry that generates the buildings in the Open City is heavily influenced by the French Symbolists and Surrealists; techniques they pioneered, such as automatic writing and the analysis of dreams, form an important part of the working method of the Valparaiso School of Architecture. First, a 'brief' is determined by a poem composed on site; then teachers and students work collaboratively to give structural form to the poem. Sometimes, this may result in a small-scale intervention: for example, the many 'agora' scattered around the Open City, marked in the sand by bricks, posts or sculptures. Other times, the poem will result in a habitable structure – a house or studio. Precisely what the end product will be is never known, as each project evolves in its own time. It's remarkable that such a radical approach has been supported for so long by a higher-education institution.

An early focus for building at the Open City were house-like structures named *hospedería* ('guesthouse' in English), the first being the Banquete Hospedería (Banquet Lodge), completed in 1974. The most prominent, the Hospedería de la Entrada (Entrance Lodge), built in 1982, is a five-bay wooden structure whose enclosed spaces step

Hospedería del Taller de Obras (Hanging Lodge) in the foreground, completed in 2006, with several other buildings behind

up from the sand as three staircases descend back down to the touch the ground. The slanting roofs are orientated towards the sun, not for the purposes of collecting solar energy, but rather as a poetic gesture of connection to the elements. The whole structure is raised high above the dunes on numerous wooden piles, allowing the sand to move under the building. Around this first 'house' lies a series of sculptural pipes that sing in the wind.

Many other extraordinary *hospedería* buildings followed, including the Hospedería del Errante (Wanderer's Lodge, 1981–95), the Hospedería del la Rosa de los Vientos o Las Celdas (Compass Card Lodge, 1998), and the Hospedería del Taller de Obras (Hanging Lodge, 2006).[21] These structures were built from a mixture of timber (usually the main structural element), brick and concrete; and many in their fragmented and angular forms resemble the salvaged buildings imagined by American architect Lebbeus Woods in his drawings from the 1990s. Yet, these are not entirely anarchic structures: teams of students work with skilled contractors in bringing the houses to realisation, so that habitable structures can at least be ensured.

Although the Open City superficially resembles many other off-grid communities, it operates under a very different rationale. Rather than being governed by political or ecological concerns, its autonomy is focused on the imagination. Just how this operates at a communal level is difficult to ascertain because it must always happen in the very moment of practice – a meld of subjective memory, sensory apprehension of the environment, and intuitive connection to building materials. This kind of improvised architecture was celebrated by Charles Jencks and Nathan Silver in their 1972 book *Adhocism*, a manifesto against the totalitarian approach to urban planning seen in post-war architectural modernism.[22] Arguing that *tabula rasa* urban planning should be replaced by incremental approaches that integrate re-use into the lives of buildings, *Adhocism* looked to anarchist ideas to inspire a new kind of architectural freedom. Rejecting any kind of determinism in building – whether by means of drawings, plans, models or briefs – the Open City provides a thoroughgoing experiment in precisely the kind of adhocism advocated by Jencks and Silver.

Landmatters, Devon, UK, 2003–

In a striking parallel with the early 1970s in the American southwest, the 1990s in Britain saw a new kind of grass-roots environmental awareness develop, one that led to the promotion of 'low impact development' in the country-side. This was not only an anti-capitalist strategy concerned with reversing the human exploitation of nature, but also a direct response to the need for low-cost housing and for developing more holistic ways of communal living. Landmatters is one such community, founded by a small group of friends in 2003, when they purchased 42 acres of land in southwest Devon. After a protracted series of negotiations with the local planning authority, during which time two temporary permissions were granted, the site was finally given permanent planning permission in April 2016.[23] In 2020, Landmatters comprised 10 adults and 10 children. The community is rooted in permaculture – a sustainable system of growing food that keys into a broader holistic, integrated practice that balances the needs of nature with those of humans.[24]

One of the original benders constructed at Landmatters in 2003

The majority of the eight dwellings that were originally constructed were benders, inspired by their earlier use in protest camps, such as Greenham Common Women's Peace Camp and the anti-roads protests of the 1990s. Energy is generated by a combination of photo-voltaic panels and wind turbines, while each bender is heated by a wood-burning stove. Since permanent planning permission was granted, more ambitious structures have been built alongside the original benders, including a cob roundhouse and a straw-bale home with a steeply pitched timber roof. All homes are built as low-impact dwellings, principally as a result of the terms of the planning permission granted. Benders, cob and straw-bale structures have both marginal visual presence in the landscape, compared with conventional buildings, and are also close to nature through the materials they're built from. Where possible, building materials have been sourced from renewable resources or salvaged from skips and other waste dumps.

Straw-bale house under construction at Landmatters in February 2019

Interior of a bender at Landmatters

Self-building with natural materials results in homes that are wedded to the needs and desires of their occupants: as one resident put it, her home is an extension of the self, rather like a second skin.[25] There's also a strongly didactic purpose in such architecture – it's meant to inspire others to do the same and education forms a key part of the work that occupies the residents of Landmatters. Linked via the Internet to a network of alternative communities, Landmatters ties in closely with the Transition Network movement that is based in the nearby town of Totnes. According to its founder, Rob Hopkins, the Transition Network seeks to scale up the idea of permaculture to the level of towns and cities by arguing for a much more joined-up way of thinking about urban development.[26] It does this by bringing the focus back to the local level, clawing back urban space for greater citizen control and common ownership from market forces and the state.

With thousands of initiatives in over 50 countries, Transition Network has grown exponentially from its humble origins but it has still yet to fully embrace cities – and particularly the rising number of global megacities – as part of its wider vision of permaculture. For that to happen, the local must be able to key into the global, without losing the holistic vision of permaculture. The challenge is to imagine how the micro-level permaculture of communities like Landmatters might be scaled up to the level of a city – not a literal translation of either their structures or lifestyles but rather a much broader application of their holistic 'green' vision to the sheer diversity of activities that go on in cities. If Landmatters show us how to build homes and grow food in sustainable ways, how might the same ideals be applied to the construction industry, banking, mass transit systems, catering, retail, schools, parks, libraries, religious life, culture, museums, digital communications, and so on?

Lammas, Wales, UK, 2009–

The Undercroft, an earth-sheltered roundhouse built by Simon Dale at Lammas in 2009

Lammas is a low-impact, off-grid eco-village at Tir-y-Gafel in Pembrokeshire in southwest Wales.[27] Consisting of 15 smallholdings on around 100 acres of land, the community was granted planning permission in 2009 after twice being refused by the local council, even though the group who purchased the land modelled their application closely on the council's own policies for low-impact development. Thus, unlike most eco-villages in the UK – including Tipi Valley, Landmatters and Tinker's Bubble – which were built illegally and then either remained invisible or tried to secure permission in retrospect, Lammas was a legitimate development from the start. This was a deliberate attempt by the five founding members to make otherwise alternative forms of development speak to the mainstream. And since 2009, Lammas has attracted thousands of visitors

An assemblage of structures comprising one of the homes at Lammas in 2019

Community hub building at Lammas, built by members of the community in 2009

every year – a purpose-built community hub showcases ecological design and also hosts events and workshops. Lammas has also featured regularly in the popular media, perhaps most notably in Channel 4's long-running series *Grand Designs* (1999–). It's also contributed to a change in Welsh planning law, the One Planet Development policy from 2011 making it possible for others in Wales to follow the example set by Lammas. But such permission comes with stringent caveats: to secure it, you have to be committed to make a sizeable proportion of your income come directly from the land (as much as two thirds); and also be prepared to rigorously monitor your ecological footprint in all parts of your life.

As of 2019, there were nine completed houses at Lammas, along with the community hub and a host of other buildings that met the needs of its residents, including greenhouses, workshops, sheds, toilets and a chalet for visitors. Little here is provided by the state: recyclable rubbish is collected but all energy is sourced from renewables (a hydro-powered electricity supply supplemented by solar panels); drinking water from a nearby spring; human waste dealt with in compost toilets.

In part the result of his appearance on *Grand Designs* in 2016, Lammas's most well-known self-builder is Simon Dale. Before joining the community in 2009, he and his wife Jasmine had already built a 'Hobbit House' for their family in 2003: an earth-sheltered roundhouse constructed from locally sourced timber (mostly tree stumps and branches) infilled with straw bales and cob. Tragically, a fire destroyed this house, which prompted the family to move to Lammas in 2009. Here, Simon used the same techniques to build a new home – the Undercroft – joined to a greenhouse to act as a thermal envelope as well as a place to grow food. Dale embarked on a larger house, Earthsea, in 2013, which took him four years to build with the help of over 400 friends and volunteers. For a second time, the Dales' home burnt to the ground, on New Year's Day 2018, leaving only the foundations and a few charred pieces of structural timber intact. The experience of losing two of his self-built homes to fire left Simon and his family broken and they were forced to leave Lammas to live with friends.[28]

The community will, of course, continue to evolve, but there's no doubt that it has been badly affected by the fire and left vulnerable by the departure of one of its most skilled members. Tragic though it was, the fire undermines the image of these 'Hobbit' houses as cosy retreats – homes that are more in tune with the natural world. Reinforced by the immense popularity of Tolkien's *Lord of the Rings* trilogy and Peter Jackson's film adaptations, the organic forms and semi-subterranean appearance of hobbit houses present a reassuring image of harmony – the houses aesthetically as much as functionally 'low-impact': half buried in the earth and often covered in turf to make them less visually obtrusive. And the houses at Lammas are by no means isolated examples – dozens more hobbit homes are scattered throughout Wales, mostly self-built out of the public eye because they were done so without planning permission.[29]

Hobbit homes create an architecture that is intimately bound to the landscape, whether through natural building materials or the local infrastructures that connect inhabitants with resources. The permaculture practised at Lammas is entirely at odds with conventional forms of farming that dominate the Welsh landscape – mostly meat and dairy production for a global market, underwritten by unsustainable consumption patterns and energy production. In replacing one type of farming for another that is seen as more sustainable and holistic, Lammas is attempting to create a new kind of place, one that is orientated towards an alternative future, where productivity is measured less in terms of financial profit than that of the individual and the local ecosystem. Indeed, during the long process of consultation before Lammas was established in 2009, existing local residents expressed concern that its eco-vision would eclipse their own problems, such as a a dwindling population and cuts to local services. Perhaps, in the long term, it is the wider connections that Lammas makes with its surroundings – and particularly the next generation of land workers – that will be its most important legacy, rather than the seductive aesthetics of its self-built houses.

The charred remains of Simon Dale's Undercroft home in 2019

Prinzessinnengärten, Berlin, 2009–

A relatively early example of an urban farm, Prinzessinnengärten was founded in 2009 on a brownfield site on Moritzplatz in the Kreuzberg district of Berlin. Abandoned for over half a century – a result of, first Allied bombs, then the nearby Berlin Wall, then a failed highway project and then deindustrialization – the 6,000 square metre site was leased by Berlin City Council to the company Nomadisch Grün (Nomadic Green, made up of Marco Clausen and Robert Shaw) as an experiment in alternative urban land use. Although only granted a temporary lease, Prinzessinnengärten has remained in place for over 10 years, mainly as a result of vigorous campaigning on the part of Clausen and Shaw, local residents and a veritable army of over 1,000 volunteers. What has resulted is a genuinely incremental form of urban development.[30]

Die Laube (The Arbour) in the Prinzessinnengärten, completed in 2017

Library and cafe in the Prinzessinnengärten, September 2018

View of the Prinzessinnengärten site from the top of
the Arbour structure, September 2018

Although the site's principal activities revolve around the urban farm – a tightly packed array of raised beds that can be easily transported elsewhere – many other structures have been added during the project's lifetime. These include shacks built from salvaged wood that house tiny retail units, a bicycle repair workshop, and an information centre, and also, more recently, a 10m-tall wooden structure called *Die Laube* (The Arbour), designed by Quest (Christian Buekhard and Florian Köhl) in collaboration with Clausen. With over 100 volunteers investing 10,000 hours from 2015–17, the structure has become the site's centrepiece, a scale model of it featuring in exhibitions in both Berlin and Seoul.[31]

Constructed almost entirely from reclaimed timber, The Arbour is a remarkable demonstration, albeit on a micro scale, of a genuinely flexible structure. Although it looks unfinished – the timber frame reminiscent of the bare-bones structure of a vernacular building – the open-frame is designed to be entirely demountable. There are no walls, but both the ground and first floors are effectively enclosed spaces: a canvas structure attached to metal stilts can be pulled over the ground-flood decking to protect it from the elements, while the first level is sandwiched between the two floors above and below. Fully demountable wooden stairwells link each of the three floors, the upper deck functioning as an open-air bar and restaurant.

The Arbour fully embodies the Prinzessinnengärten's ambition to foster and reinforce connections between local sites of resistance to gentrification (currently accelerating in Kreuzberg) and more official forms of urban planning. As Clausen has made very explicit, the goal of Prinzessinnengärten has always been to resist the privitization of public land in Berlin (and elsewhere), asserting through its open-door policy and participatory ethos that common spaces are at the heart of the future of urban development.[32] Hosting an array of workshops, conferences, literary events, concerts and discussions, The Arbour has brought architecture into the heart of Prinzessinnengärten's vision for more holistic future cities, whether in spanning the gap between the urban and the rural, or in creating free spaces where profit-making is less important than community development, and where participation of the broadest kind is invited to create buildings and spaces. Here, the structure's name mirrors that given to the many thousands of wooden sheds built on countless allotments in Berlin, first established in the mid-nineteenth century. Many of these self-built *Lauben* (arbours) were converted into dwellings during times of periodic housing shortages – after 50 percent of the city was destroyed by Allied bombs in the Second World War, more than 120,000 people lived in self-built sheds and other structures well into the 1950s until Berlin was reconstructed in a modernist idiom.[33]

Prinzessinnengärten is but one of a large number of similar sites in Berlin that are fostering an informal DIY-urbanism. In Kreuzberg alone, there are several other sites that have claimed temporary ownership of brownfield sites, including the tent-city of Teepee Land – a squat right on the banks of the River Spree opposite the Holzmarkt development; and a protest camp on waste-ground at the southern Kottbusser Tor, set up in 2012 by the Turkish tenant's initiative Kotti & Co in protest at rising rents. And just across the Spree in nearby Friedrichshain is the Young African Art Market (YAAM), a ramshackle collection of self-built structures that house eateries, an art market, bars, and clothes shops.[34]

These sites are staking a claim on land as 'commons' in order to challenge notions of private ownership that seem to be a perquisite for municipal authorities looking to redevelop vacant lots. They may encompass very different practices – in Berlin, urban farming, squatting, protest and retail – but they are all linked by a common desire to claim their right to the city, irrespective of nationality, ethnicity, gender, class, wealth, power or expertise. What is so powerful about sites like Prinzessinnengärten is how long it has maintained this level of openness in the face of an existing power that would rather see the land turn profit into the hands of a private elite.

Ruin Academy, Taipei, 2010–

Night-time view of an interior space in the Ruin Academy, one of the plant 'tenants' (bamboo) shown in the left foreground, 2010

Perhaps the most radical way to allow nature into architecture is to simply let buildings become ruins. Without human occupation, and the ceaseless maintenance this entails, buildings inevitably start to decay. Fluorescent light tubes are the first to go, after a couple of years, followed, in the next few, by all the other fixtures and fittings. After 25 years, suspended ceilings cave in, radiators clog up and leak their contents, elevators stop working, pipes burst and plasterboard disintegrates. After 50 years, precast concrete slabs begin to crumble from within, steel cables snap and anything made of iron collapses. After a century, steel-framed buildings come down, brickwork becomes unstable and internal timber finally falls victim to rot and the jaws of insects. After two centuries, not much would be left, save broken bits of plastic which may never disappear and the remains of what were once brick walls, foundations and hunks of stone. For anything built by humans, there is only one true and unrelenting form of anarchy: nature itself tearing away at what we create. Even

Interior of a room in the Ruin Academy showing the multiple holes in the walls and ceiling to allow rainwater to nourish the plants growing inside, 2010

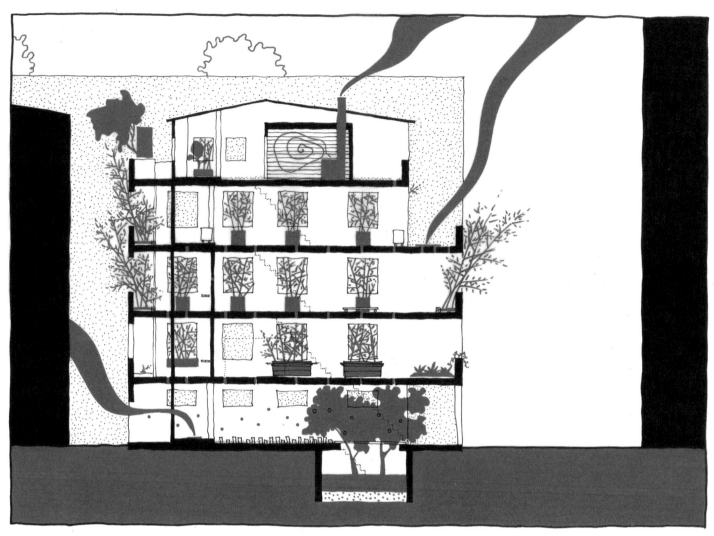

Sectional drawing of the Ruin Academy by Marco Casagrande, 2010

ancient ruins that we now treasure only survive because humans have intervened in this slow slide into chaos; their ruin 'value' held sacrosanct even as we stop the process of disintegration in its tracks.

To explore how ruin might enter more creatively into architecture, Finnish architect Marco Casagrande set up the Ruin Academy in 2010 in Taiwan's hyper-modern capital Taipei. It's an independent architectural research centre cooperatively run by the Finland-based Casagrande Laboratory and the Taiwanese JUT Foundation for Arts & Architecture. Occupying an abandoned five-storey apartment building in the centre of Taipei, the Ruin Academy embodies what Casagrande has called the Third Generation

City – a post-industrial urban landscape that reincorporates nature into its built fabric. Here, walls are punctured with holes and windows removed to let rainwater enter the building, ostensibly in order to nourish bamboo and vegetables growing in raised beds of soil (and out through the window spaces), but also creating an ad-hoc system of ventilation. All interior walls have been removed to allow for maximum flexibility of use. Sleeping areas have been created using movable mahogany panels, and a public sauna on the top floor brings an everyday Finnish practice into a tropical setting.[35]

The Ruin Academy offers a startling reversal of conventional ideas of ruination as a wholly negative process.

Casagrande wants the ecology of architecture to include non-human participants, even as that inevitably sacrifices the comfort that comes from keeping nature out of our buildings. In the Ruin Academy, it's an unruly nature that enters back in, one that makes the human-built world seem vulnerable. Casagrande has called this a 'weak' form of architecture – one that is designed to push humans towards a more submissive relationship with nature.[36] Using the image of a weed taking root in the smallest crack in an asphalt surface, Casagrande invites nature to 'turn the city into part of itself – [for] the city to produce life, resonating with the rest of nature'.[37] Remarkably like Street Farm's early 1970s intimations of seeds germinating and tearing apart concrete tower blocks, the Ruin Academy translates their wild collages into built reality.

The series of workshops held at the Ruin Academy since 2010 – on anarchist gardening, urban acupuncture, and river urbanism – have fleshed out more fully the kind of melding of the human and non-human realised in this single building. In this expansive remit, self-organized illegal occupations of land are the harbingers of a new bottom-up form of urban development; 'holes' in the official city – informal practices of all kinds – are like the pinpricks of needles used in acupuncture treatment of the human body; while re-wilded rivers, allowed to naturally flood once again, would demand an entirely new relationship between water and buildings.[38] This, in short, is an ecological urbanism that recognises the right of all life – human and non-human alike – to determine how a city should be built.

VI. ART

The bricoleur ... 'speaks' not only *with* things ... but also through the medium of things: giving an account of his personality and life by the choices he makes between limited possibilities. The bricoleur may not ever complete his purpose but he always puts something of himself into it—Claude Lévi-Strauss, *The Savage Mind* (1966), p. 21

In *The Savage Mind*, anthropologist Claude Lévi-Strauss focused on a figure he termed the *bricoleur* – an individual who is able to create his/her world through spontaneity, invention and creativity. Standing in opposition to the architect and engineer, the bricoleur improvises with what is at hand to make his or her world. Artists have long used techniques of bricolage to assemble their works – from traditional folk art to the abstract collages of Kurt Schwitters; the creative possibilities of ideas wedded to the materials the artist chooses to use.

This section explores how artists use building as a tool for creative expression. Unlike architects, who are usually forced to compromise their creative vision according to the dictates of a client, many artists have greater individual autonomy in their work and are therefore in a strong position to creatively crack open the often restrictive definitions of architecture itself. Beginning with the high-concept work of Gordon Matta-Clark and ending with the social housing built by Theaster Gates, this section navigates between the refined and the savage, the educated and the untutored.

Houses are a focus here. In Clarence Schmidt's House of Mirrors – a key work of 'outsider' architecture – creating a home is about giving expression to unconscious desires, the polar opposite of modernism's idea of the house as a machine for living in. Three other houses – Ben Cummins's Piano Raft, the NOLA art house in New Orleans, and Martin Kaltwasser and Folke Köbberling's *Hausbau* – each offer different notions of autonomous homemaking – respectively, a floating raft gradually turning into a musical artwork; a party-house in a post-disaster city; and a deliberate translation of informal settlements in the Global South to a fast-regenerating Berlin. The final two pieces on the Heidelberg Project in Detroit and the Dorchester Projects in Chicago show that artist-led architecture can be socially transformative in a way that architects' work so often fails to be, despite the high-minded rhetoric of socially conscious designers.

In these diverse projects, art interrogates architecture about its own status and how it should be practised. In early 1970s New York, the mercurial Anarchitecture group, a collective of artists including Gordon Matta-Clark, were more interested in the physical and metaphorical voids, gaps and leftover spaces in the city than in its physical buildings. Here, architecture is not about solving problems (as it so often is purported to be); rather, it attacks what is taken for granted – the law and authority of building as it is – so that something genuinely liberating can emerge in its place.

Gordon Matta-Clark, *Conical Intersect*, Paris, 1975

Conical Intersect and the condemned apartment building
in which it was installed, Les Halles, Paris, 1975

The first artist to explicitly bring together anarchism and architecture was Gordon Matta-Clark. His self-proclaimed 'anarchitecture' emerged out of his own traumatic experiences in 1970s New York. Living in the city's SoHo district, the young artist witnessed first hand how the city's descent into near bankruptcy left many of its buildings teetering on the edge of destruction. On 3 August 1973, during a telephone call to his mother, the ceiling of the apartment on Broadway in which his cousin lived collapsed and he was killed, likely the result of years of municipal neglect.[1] This personal encounter with architectural destruction must have seemed uncannily prescient to an artist who had just started to make what would become his iconic trademark: geometric cuts into buildings slated for demolition. These were rectangular holes cut into the floors of condemned tenement buildings in the Bronx, which Matta-Clark began in 1972. As he developed this unique form of art, the ambition of the works grew, culminating in *Conical Intersect*, completed in the summer of 1975 as part of the Paris Biennale.[2]

Together with a team of assistants, Matta-Clark cut a cone-shaped section through a soon-to-be-demolished seventeenth-century apartment building in the Les Halles/ Beaubourg district of inner-city Paris. Comprehensively redeveloped in the early 1970s, this area saw the construction of the high-tech Centre Pompidou, designed by Renzo Piano and Richard Rodgers, and which can be seen in many photographs of *Conical Intersect*, as it was built right next to the condemned apartments. As with all Matta-Clark's building cuts, *Conical Intersect* uses pure geometric forms in a highly subversive way. In place of the orthogonal geometries of conventional architectural drawings, in which the design is laid out in advance through abstract lines, Matta-Clark's hand-hewn cuts brutally and violently reassert the body of the user in space. Taking advantage of obsolescent buildings, Matta-Clark forged a radically new

One of Gordon Matta-Clark's photomontages of *Conical Intersect*, 1975

way of engaging with the built environment. In effect, he used violence to call attention to the inherently destructive nature of architectural modernism.

The building cuts were just one element of Matta-Clark's extraordinary range of work. He also made and collected photographs of graffiti in New York which, in the early 1970s, was barely known about. He researched and purchased tiny parcels of land in the city which had been requisitioned by the city authorities over the years. His photographs of the walls of condemned buildings in the Bronx speak powerfully of the specific material conditions of the city in a period of obvious decline. He was also a pioneer of socially engaged art, setting up the restaurant *Food* in 1971, and creating mobile public artworks like *Fresh Cart* (1972) and *Graffiti Truck* (1973).

Matta-Clark's most enigmatic work remains his contribution to the Anarchitecture Group, a short-lived collective of artist that met for a few months in New York in 1973 before setting up the group exhibition *Anarchitecture* at 112 Greene Street in March 1974.[3] Consisting solely of identically sized photographs – all of which were anonymous – the exhibits were highly provocative reformulations of what architecture might be: a building destroyed by a gas explosion; a derailed train; boats smashed together by a storm; the air between the twin towers of the newly built World Trade Center; holes in the ground; fallen monuments; crumbling walls. These were about as far away from conventional definitions of architecture as one might imagine. As Matta-Clark said of the group: 'we were thinking more about metaphoric voids, gaps, leftover spaces ... for example the place you stopped to tie your shoelace.'[4]

The images collected in *Anarchitecture* display an overt concern with how we think and the language we use to talk about architecture. This is anarchist architecture as concept: a bottom-up process that starts not with an actual building but rather with a radical reformulation of what it means to inhabit a chaotic city. Matta-Clark embraced the fecundity of chance events: for example, the rings left by a teacup on a sheet of paper suggesting the complex plan for the building cuts he made for his work *Office Baroque* in Antwerp in 1977. This opening up of architecture to much broader and richer understandings is his most powerful legacy, one that has inspired a wide range of artists engaging with architecture understood in this way, including Richard Wentworth's *Making Do and Getting By* series (1980s–) and Thomas Hirschhorn's *Gramsci Monument* (2013).

Martin Kaltwasser and Folke Köbberling, *Hausbau*, 2004–05

The work of Berlin-based artists Martin Kaltwasser and Folke Köbberling takes Matta-Clark's conceptual anarchitecture and turns it into something tangible. From 1998 onwards, the duo have used discarded materials to build structures which, although temporary, question why the construction industry generates so much building waste, most of it simply buried in landfill sites. They began their work in 1998 in the spartan apartment they rented in Berlin's Kreuzberg district. Creating interior fittings entirely from materials thrown out from other premises, they also initiated a 'free-cycle' scheme in the neighbourhood, where unwanted goods would be left outside homes for reuse by passers-by.[5] The artists have subsequently expanded their practice to include a whole series of prototype houses, exhibition pavilions, and bespoke structures for architectural festivals, such as their *Jellyfish Theatre* at the 2010 London Festival of Architecture, and the *Kraftwerk Lohberg* in Dinslaken, a prototype pavilion generating electricity from bicycles, completed in 2015 on the re-cultivated terrain of a former coal mine.

In their two *Hausbau* (House Building) projects from 2004 and 2005, Kaltwasser and Köbberling initiated a self-build scheme on a patch of open land near the Berlin

Martin Kaltwasser and Folke Köbberling's *Jellyfish Theatre*, installed at the 2010 London Festival of Architecture

Martin Kaltwasser and Folke Köbberling's first *Hausbau* project
on waste-ground on the edge of Berlin, 2004

suburb of Gropiusstadt, a high-rise estate built in the 1960s and home to many immigrants. The first project was just one house, built as quickly as possible and lived in by the artists for one week; the second an attempt to build a temporary informal community – a total of seven houses, a communal kitchen and other buildings lived in by the artists and architectural students for 10 days. With their junk aesthetic and absence of any formal planning, these informal structures could not have been more different from the ultra-rationalised high-rise housing nearby. Both *Hausbau* projects were inspired by the artists' interest in the informal settlements surrounding Istanbul, which they visited in 2004. Known in Turkish as *gecekondu* (literally 'built overnight'), these vast areas of self-built housing have mushroomed in the past half century as rural migrants have flocked to the city in search of new opportunities. They take their name from an Ottoman law

which ruled that a house could not be demolished if a roof had already been constructed (hence the extraordinary speed of construction).[6]

In taking inspiration from Istanbul's *gecekondus*, Kaltwasser and Köbberling draw on a long fascination with informal settlements in the developing world. Beginning with architect John Turner's celebration in the 1970s of the spontaneity, ingenuity and resourcefulness of the urban poor in South America, informal settlements have gone from being seen by architectural modernists as literally 'off-the-map' to being models of flexibility, resilience and adaptability in urban design, exemplified more recently in the practices of Urban Think Tank in Caracas and Elemental in Santiago-de-Chile. Kaltwasser and Köbberling's work intimates that this precarity will soon become more widespread. The *Hausbau* functions as

Night-time view of the first *Hausbau*, 2004

a prototype home for a future world of increased scarcity, states retreating from their social responsibilities, and a hostile environment that requires high levels of resourcefulness and resilience.

Kaltwasser and Köbberling's work also illustrates the concept of 'cradle-to-cradle' design probably first coined by Walter R. Stahel in the early 1980s but more fully developed by Michael Braungart and William McDonough in the late 1990s.[7] 'Cradle-to-cradle' models human industry on the life cycle of birth, death and rebirth in nature, the latter predicated on the return of nutrients to the earth through decay. It asks that designers take seriously the life of a product after its redundancy, ideally ensuring that it can be recycled endlessly so that no waste is ever produced. However, while claiming to offer a powerful critique of the throwaway culture of consumer capitalism, 'cradle-to-cradle' often fails to address just why so much waste is produced in the first place. It could be argued that those who salvage for reasons of necessity – the self-builders of Istanbul's *gecekondu*s for example – don't have the luxury of questioning its basis; but in giving salvage a more elevated meaning, Kaltwasser and Köbberling's work should do more than simply flag up the prolificacy of the industry from which it is born; it should aspire to change the conditions under which it is made.

Clarence Schmidt, House of Mirrors, 1940–68

Clarence Schmidt's House of Mirrors, which he built and lived in from 1940 onwards until it was destroyed by fire in 1968

Trash is often the medium of choice, if not necessity, for 'outsider' architects – untaught self-builders who have created thousands of idiosyncratic built environments around the world. Although self-building of this kind has no doubt existed for centuries, it has only gained significant attention since the 1960s, when attempts were first made in the USA to catalogue and preserve works of architecture created by those without any formal training. Within the earliest of these re-evaluations, Clarence Schmidt's House of Mirrors took pride of place. In 1940, the New York stonemason and plasterer built himself a log cabin on a steep hillside he'd purchased just outside Woodstock. Over the following two decades, Schmidt carved out a series of rough stone terraces and then constructed an extraordinary structure: a seven-storey assemblage of scrap materials, including innumerable mirrors (from which the house got its name), windows, and timber

panelling all stacked on top of one another. At the heart of this labyrinth, hewn into the rock itself, was what Schmidt called his 'Inner Sanctum' – the artist's home. The 35 additional rooms built around it were filled with a cornucopia of salvaged materials, including children's toys, bicycle wheels, deer antlers, and dried plants. A tangle of Christmas lights, mirrors and glass gave the structure a dream-like appearance at night. Above the house, Schmidt also built a roof garden using scrapped automobile parts, piles of stones, old bedsteads, farm tools, and other pieces of discarded machinery as well as defunct domestic objects like washing machines.[8]

Although the house was clearly a product of an intensely personal obsession, Schmidt welcomed numerous visitors, including celebrities such as Bob Dylan and Joan Baez and those wishing to document it, such as photographer Gregg Blasdel and filmmaker Beryl Sololoff, the latter releasing the short film *My Mirrored Hope* in 1973. But by then, the House of Mirrors was gone, destroyed by fire in 1968, probably started deliberately by a disgruntled neighbour offended by the anarchy of the project. As art historian Roger Cardinal has argued, outsider architecture is highly vulnerable to destruction: as well as being often structurally and materially fragile, it also attracts as much hostility as it does admiration.[9] Indeed, when Schmidt, undaunted, started building another house soon after, that too succumbed to fire in 1971. Broken by this second act of vandalism, Schmidt entered a nursing home and died seven years later.

In 1961, the House of Mirrors was appropriated as an important precursor to Assemblage art in the New York MOMA exhibition *The Art of Assemblage*. The exhibition explicitly elevated the project as part of a venerable lineage of autodidact architecture – from French postman Ferdinand Cheval's Palais Idéal (1879–1924), greatly admired by the Parisian Surrealists, to Simon Rodia's

Salvaged objects collected by Clarence Schmidt in the grounds
of his second house, 1970

Watts Towers (1921–54) in Los Angeles, one of the first US sites to be preserved and protected by the state.[10] In art critic Allan Kaprow's view, Schmidt's work could be linked to Assemblage because it adhered to what he called the 'form-principle' of change. Instead of being a static object that has a sense of completeness, the House of Mirrors was always in a state of becoming, a site in which 'space is slowly unwinding, rather than crisply delineated as in the usual house'.[11] This was an architecture of accretion rather than of design, a house that quite literally emerged over time as a direct material expression of the inner desires of its resident.

Despite his house being an intensely personal form of expression, Schmidt nevertheless asserted that it emphasized connection over isolation. He once hung a banner over a section of his garden which read 'My Mirrored Hope – One for All and All for One' – the call of an individual and his subjective world to be a focal point for a collective form

of liberation.[12] Indeed, the uncompromising subjectivity of Schmidt's house is actually outward facing, offering inspiration to anyone and everyone to free their imaginations. And, in the years following the Woodstock music festival in 1969, many anarchic houses were built in the area by those 'drop-outs' who had simply stayed on afterwards, inspired by Schmidt's example of self-building.[13]

The will to destroy works of outsider architecture (and many others besides Schmidt's end up vandalised, demolished or burnt down) comes from a rejection of the power of creativity manifest in these works. To hostile onlookers, the House of Mirrors disrupted conventional notions of order in the built environment. In seeing imaginative reuses of waste as meaningless piles of rubbish, or disorderly forms of construction as dangerously subversive, not to mention potentially damaging to property values, detractors cannot accept that the desires of autodidacts like Schmidt might also lie within themselves.

Ben Cummins, The Piano Raft, 2013–

Ben Cummins's Piano Raft, moored at Oddy Locks in Leeds in January 2019

Personal obsession has also driven artist Ben Cummins to build his home from salvaged materials. Since 2013, he's been living on a self-built canal boat that he is very slowly towing from Liverpool to London, where he hopes to deliver a piano he has on board. The project resembles fellow artist Simon Starling's 2005 work *Shedboatshed*, in which Starling turned an old wooden shed into a boat, sailed it down the River Rhine from Schweizerhalle to Basel, and then reassembled the shed for exhibition at the Museum für Gegenwartskunst, before reversing the process. It took Cummins six years to travel from Liverpool to Leeds and he hopes to arrive in London to deliver his piano within 25 years. Having been hounded for many years by the UK Canal & River Trust for his highly unconventional approach to canal-boat living, he's recently received approval from them largely on account of his community activities.

The boat itself is called the Piano Raft, reflecting Cummins's larger vision of the boat as a work of art that incorporates pieces of musical instruments into its structure, from the stops of an organ to the inner workings of a harp. The interior is filled with other instruments: guitars, a small organ and the piano itself. Cummins hopes that his house will evolve into a pubic project that offers novel ways of perceiving the environment. At the same time, it's also a place of retreat, being almost entirely off-grid: solar panels provide electricity; waste is composted; and mobility is by human power alone. It's also an incremental structure – the basic shell being a donated artwork *The Pride of Sefton* created out of discarded furniture by his artist friend Ben Parry for the Liverpool Biennale in 2009.[14] Over the years Cummins has made the boat habitable, adding a bedroom at the back and a living space in between. Most of the wood he gathers for fuel is gifted by loggers – the remains of trees cut down and left on towpaths for canal-boat owners to use. This salvage economy makes possible houses that minimize their inhabitants use of resources.

The Piano Raft received a good deal of media coverage in 2018 due to it winning the 'Unexpected' category of the Cuprinol-sponsored 'Shed of the Year' competition.[15] Celebrating eccentric or impressive examples of shed building, this competition has yielded some extraordinarily inventive forms of self-building on a small scale but only occasionally for structures that also become homes. UK planning regulations mean that houses rarely get built in Britain that are outside the norms of conventional building practice; yet, on water, those rules are more flexible and the Piano Raft is an example of how one might build a home entirely from waste materials and with only an improvised infrastructure.

When *The Pride of Sefton* was exhibited at the Liverpool Biennale in 2009, it was intended as a shelter

Exterior of the Piano Raft with its assemblage of fragments of different musical instruments, January 2019

after an imagined future apocalypse had destroyed conventional forms of infrastructure. In its reincarnation as the Piano Raft, Cummins has created a new kind of environment of making, where the final product isn't yet known. Cummins is reminiscent of the river dwellers in William Morris's utopian vision of London in *News From Nowhere* (1892), where a capitalist industrial economy has been succeeded by one based on the free exchange of goods and knowledge, with a focus on creativity rather than drudgery in making. In a similar way to the House of Mirrors, the Piano Raft makes the valueless wastes of neoliberal capitalism live again, their very dislocation from that system allowing them to become refreshed with new meanings. Engaging with waste in this way demonstrates an essential and hopeful truth (often hidden or suppressed) that everything can always become something else.

The Art House, New Orleans, 2005–11

A collapsed house in the Bologny neighbourhood in New Orleans, February 2006

Climate-related disasters are already affecting many cities in the world, providing a terrifying foretaste of the future for many more. Before the category five hurricane Katrina struck New Orleans in August 2005, between 80 and 90 percent of the city's residents were evacuated; those that remained were largely impoverished African-Americans who had no other option. An enormous storm surge breached the network of levees and flood walls that have traditionally defended the low-lying city from catastrophic flooding; after Katrina hit, 80 percent of New Orleans lay underwater, 1,464 people died (according to official statistics) and 275,000 buildings were damaged, many beyond repair.[16]

The rebuilding of the devastated city has divided opinion. Some have argued that New Orleans has become another victim of 'disaster capitalism', where the shock of a natural disaster enables free-market economics to flourish, as most people are too traumatised to resist it. Others offer a more hopeful picture of creativity and compassion flourishing among the ruins: Rebecca Solnit's book *A Paradise Built in Hell* (2010) being perhaps the most high-profile example. In her optimistic reading of urban disasters, art can provide a way of reinvigorating damaged communities by inspiring others to create and participate. One such project in New Orleans was The Art House, located at 1614 Esplanade Avenue in the Tremé district of the city, just northeast of the famous French Quarter.[17] Empty even before Katrina hit, the large nineteenth-century house was bought in 2005, only for the owner to see its value plummet in the aftermath of the disaster. In 2008, it was transferred to John Orgon, who started a scheme to provide affordable housing for artists.

The Art House was home to over 100 artists during its six-year life, some of whom constructed a vast four-storey treehouse in the backyard, the majority of its building materials were salvaged from other abandoned sites in New Orleans. Stairs were built to allow access to its improvised structures, which included a small timber house, a platform made from a reclaimed satellite dish, a 'spider' swing and numerous hammocks. The treehouse hosted many parties, with around 100 people filling its spaces for the New Year celebrations at the end of 2009.

The Art House was located in an historic African-American neighbourhood in New Orleans, yet all the artists who lived there were white incomers taking advantage of cheap rents – a picture repeated in many other blighted African-American areas of US cities, most notably Detroit. In occupying a house in an impoverished part of the city, these artists were implicit avant-garde gentrifiers. When the Art House was sold in 2014, it was put on the market for over $475,000 – over six times the price paid for the property in 2008.[18] Here, as in countless other examples across the world, artists had turned dereliction into profit, albeit at a cost to themselves. The Art House is now, unsurprisingly, a private residence for a wealthy

Makeshift treehouse in the grounds of The Art House in New Orleans, 2010

incomer. This cynical manipulation of creativity for personal or corporate financial gain puts pay to the idea that artists are innocent bystanders to neoliberal processes of gentrification. At the very least, they should be resisting this process by forming alliances with local people. In failing to make these connections, the residents of the Art House were guilty of seeing the post-disaster city as a 'blank canvas' for uninhibited creativity – their salvaging of materials for art was at the expense of more socially useful ways of remaking the city.

Yet salvage in the wake of disaster can be a more redemptive process. Katrina destroyed 275,000 homes in New Orleans, buildings that had to be either bulldozed and buried in landfill (or in situ in some cases); salvaged for use in other buildings; or renovated/rebuilt. The recent prohibition against exporting US waste abroad, together with a drive to treat this waste more sustainably, meant that, in New Orleans salvage rates were high – up to 75 percent in some cases. Thus, in the city today, a great deal of material from wrecked houses has been incorporated into new ones.[19]

Anthropologist Shannon Lee Dawdy spent three months in the immediate aftermath of Katrina studying how these remains were dealt with in different neighbourhoods of the city. In the months immediately after the disaster, she observed how residents dealt with their trauma by returning to their damaged homes to salvage what they could.[20] For these displaced residents, every single piece of detritus held within itself the memory of some individual or collective trauma. Seen in this way, The Art House seems grossly insensitive.

View of the slide installed in The Art House, 2009

Tyree Guyton, The Heidelberg Project, Detroit, 1986–

Artist-led regeneration has emerged from the ruins of another American city hit by disaster; but more a slow-motion hurricane of entirely human origin. Since the late 1960s, Detroit has seen a dramatic loss of population in its overwhelmingly African-American inner city (mostly a result of white flight to the wealthy suburbs), coupled with disinvestment of its principal industry – automobile production.[21] Although there's been a recent revitalization of the city's core, as of 2020 nearly one third of Detroit's sprawling 138 square miles is still vacant. There are also tens of thousands of abandoned properties, mostly houses and former factories outside of the greater downtown area. In recent years, Detroit, like New Orleans, has seen an influx of young, mostly white, artists attracted by low property prices and rents and a growing commercial market for art in the city.[22] In the last 15 years, abandoned houses have been variously painted orange, cut into pieces, salvaged and reassembled, covered in detritus, and turned into eco-homes or temporary exhibition spaces. Yet, one artwork – the Heidelberg Project – has, so far, outlived them all, despite the odds stacked against it.

Created by African-American artist Tyree Guyton from 1986 onwards, the Heidelberg Project spans an entire

Baby-doll house, Heidelberg Project, destroyed by arson in 2014

'Penny Car' outside polka-dot house made by Tyree Guyton
at the Heidelberg Project, Detroit

block in one of the most deprived black-majority neighbourhoods on Detroit's east side. Like Clarence Schmidt's
House of Mirrors, the Heidelberg Project is conventionally
described as 'outsider' architecture – an environmental
work created by a self-taught artist. Although Guyton's artwork has become a major tourist attraction in the city, it
has never been less than controversial, mainly because it
calls attention to conflicted issues of race, diversity and the
failure of the city authorities to tackle endemic crime and
abandonment in this area of Detroit. Collecting vast quantities of detritus – including children's toys, rusted metal,
charred bits of wood, even whole boats and cars – Guyton
has variously attached it to abandoned houses, defunct
streetlights, or reassembled it on sidewalks, vacant lots,
and in the burnt-out remains of arson attacks. The sum

of this is a visceral and disturbing historical record of the
violence suffered by the city's black population, including
murder, child abuse and exploitation, unemployment,
drug addiction and economic deprivation.

The Heidelberg Project's unflinching confrontation
with dark pasts has led various incarnations of Detroit's
municipal authorities to try and demolish it, and also local
residents to target it in arson attacks. Guyton has defied
all of this hostility, continuing to add to his work, for
example, by piling up new objects on top of the charred
remains of one of the decorated houses destroyed by a fire
in 2014. He's also been successful in expanding the remit
of the project to encompass social outreach programmes
in local schools, in hosting an arts academy and an annual
art-making camp that seeks to empower disadvantaged

Painted boat filled with abandoned soft toys, Heidelberg Project

residents.[23] Ever the contrary, in 2016, just when the project seemed finally to be recognised by the authorities as a genuine asset to the city, Guyton announced that he would be slowly dismantling his work, in order for it to travel to be shown in galleries. With areas on the edges of Detroit's urban core now on the brink of gentrification, it's a move typical of Guyton. He has, in effect, destroyed his work in order to save it – his community now transformed, in part by his own hand, into a new investment opportunity.[24]

Theaster Gates, Dorchester Projects, Chicago, 2009–

The first house Theaster Gates purchased and transformed on Dorchester Avenue, Chicago

African-American artist Theaster Gates uses the income generated by sales of his work to fund ambitious urban regeneration projects in black-majority areas of Chicago, St Louis and Omaha.[25] Fully embracing the contradiction of his socially conscious work being wedded to the global art market, he openly declares the amounts of money he acquires in lectures and talks; and is unapologetic in his turning of these financial gains into social ones.[26]

Gates began his career as a ceramicist. In 2009 he purchased a foreclosed house on Dorchester Avenue in the Grand Crossing area of Chicago's South Side – an impoverished black neighbourhood hit hard by the financial crisis. Renovating the house with materials salvaged from nearby defunct industrial premises – including

wooden boards from a Wrigley's chewing-gum factory – Gates's house was just the starting point in an ambitious programme of urban renewal, collectively known as the Dorchester Projects, that has seen the artist purchase and refurbish several other buildings in the area, including a former cinema, bank, and housing project. These buildings are transformed into centres for artistic production with Gates himself instigating banquets, concerts, exhibitions, workshops, talks, and ongoing residencies for artists. What Gates is attempting to do is to create a new economy of art, one that doesn't turn its back on an elitist market but rather uses it for more egalitarian ends.[27]

The influence of Gordon Matta-Clark looms large over Gates's practice, particularly in his challenging of architectural conventions.[28] For example, Gates calls the spaces he makes places of 'urban ecstasy'. This is architecture understood as a direct catalyst for the utopian transformation of urban life. So, in the original house he purchased on Dorchester Avenue, Gates created a rich archive of images of art and music, including 60,000 glass slides of Western art donated by the University of Chicago's art history department, 14,000 volumes of art books, and 8,000 vinyl records from local shops that were closing down. This has created a readymade treasure-trove for those that would normally be excluded from other repositories of culture, whether implicitly or otherwise. Gates fuses artistic practice with the spaces and structures in which that practice plays itself out. Thus, in the Dorchester Projects, there is no distinction made between architecture, art and everyday life.

Gates has been criticied for casting himself in a role that should really belong to the municipal authorities or others with the necessary power and money to redress inequalities.[29] He's also been taken to task for failing to challenge an art market that is thoroughly financialised, hierarchical and highly exclusionary.[30] But embroiling

Opening reception of a conference held at the Dorchester Projects in June 2011

himself in these bigger issues would undoubtedly take Gates out of the local contexts to which he has devoted himself, what he describes as a 'staying put' in the places and with the people he knows best. This is utopianism as 'method' rather than as a concept – of incremental moves towards something better, where the value of individual contributions ultimately lies in their ability to inspire others to work towards achieving the same ends.

VII. SPECULATION

It is only through the exercise of imaginative vision that one can see the potential for change in what otherwise might appear restrictive. Social or architectural reality, if viewed as a set of determinate rules or procedures, tends to shut down the imagination, because the apparent certainty leaves no gaps for vision to open up. However, the contingent, with its multiple but uncertain potentials, allows the imagination room to project new futures—Jeremy Till, *Architecture Depends* (2009), p. 192

To speculate is to imagine; it is to present something in your mind's eye that is absent. It's a conjuring act, a form of magic in which new images are revealed to the person who imagines. From the moment they enter architecture school, students work out how best to visualize the ideas they imagine; and they continue to do so even when they eventually get to build something concrete. But, even though the tools of the architect have the power to disclose transformative visions of imaginative possibility, the built environment rarely matches these; rather it follows a different path, driven by the dictates of cost, efficiency or simply inherited traditions.

This section explores how speculation can contribute to a reimagining of architecture as self-generated. It begins in the heady days of the 1960s, when architects were caught up in the seismic social and technological transformations that characterized that decade. Projects like New Babylon saw in the white heat of technology the potential for architecture to be reimagined from the bottom up – more process than product, guided by computers responding to human desires. At the same time, though, much more down-to-earth projects put forward very different kinds of futures: here, a pastoral vision of a mundane British terrace turned into an anarchist commune.

Wilder speculations resurfaced in the 1980s and 1990s, as writers and artists began to sense the transformative potential of digital technology. The science-fiction novels of William Gibson saw San Francisco's Bay Bridge reconstituted as an informal settlement; while architect Lebbeus Woods imagined the same city rebuilt from its own ruins after a future devastating earthquake. Rebuilding of a very different kind happens at every moment in the wildly popular video game *Minecraft* – a virtual playground where Lego has become a virtual tool for collaborative world-building. Essentially a digital form of open-source architecture, *Minecraft* has the capacity to make us question why we can't build similarly in the real world; and there are some architects who are now trying to facilitate that through digital platforms. The final piece considers how speculation informs projects by architecture students, in this case an ebullient mix of politics and art-making in an imagined future Hong Kong.

Imagination can never be shown to have a direct affect on decisions made in the real world; rather it acts to open up spaces of possibility that may or may not be taken up by others. But at heart, it's a fundamentally generous act – it is always excessive, always asking more from the built environment so that it can awaken rather than deaden our desires.

Constant Nieuwenhuys, New Babylon, 1958–74

One of Constant's numerous models of one of the sectors of New Babylon, c. 1958

In the immediate post-war period, there was a pervasive belief that machine production would soon remove drudgery from work and that more and more time would be freed up for leisure. Many modernist architects argued that a centralized socialist state was the best tool for achieving the kind of transformations they saw fit for the technological age of mass production – for example, the characteristic high-rise social housing of the 1950s and 1960s. But there were always dissenters within the modernist camp, the first stirrings of which were seen in 1953, when Team 10 broke away from the functionalist dogma of CIAM (Congrès Internationaux d'Architecture Moderne). Perhaps the most uncompromising of this new generation of renegade architects was Constant Nieuwenhuys. His involvement in a succession of radical art groups – COBRA, the Situationist International and Provo – fed

the development of his gigantic New Babylon project – effectively a vision of a future city of liberated inhabitants.[1] Constant worked on New Babylon from around 1958 until 1974, when his vast collection of models, drawings, paintings, photographs and collages were acquired by the Haags Gemeentemuseum in The Hague, after a retrospective exhibition of the project was held there.[2]

How to describe the bewildering scope of New Babylon? One might start with the models. They take many different forms but metal and plexiglass predominate, often photographed from low angles to suggest inhabitation and to magnify their scale. Although the structure of the city would continuously evolve, its fixed elements were glass floors suspended within a metal-framed megastructure. The spaces within would be self-assembled by the New Babylonians themselves, enhanced by myriad technological devices drawn from the evolving field of cybernetics. Freed from work by machine production, citizens of the city would be engaged in constant creativity, assembling and disassembling partition walls to make rooms for such varied pleasures as water play, erotic games, dancing, and light and sound shows. The distinct 'sectors' of the city (often the subject of Constant's individual models and drawings) would link up in a continuous chain of urban development that would eventually straddle the entire planet. Raised up on enormous columns, the new city would literally be built on top of existing ones. In a move characteristic of earlier modernist visions, all traffic would flow beneath the structure, meaning that inhabitation would be undisturbed and focused almost entirely around the pursuit of pleasure.

Although Constant never prescribed just how his city would be built, let alone who would finance it, he insisted that its architectural forms would be inseparable from the lives of its inhabitants. This had the effect of

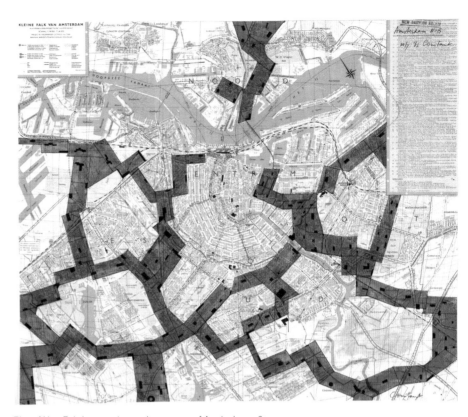

Plan of New Babylon superimposed over a map of Amsterdam, 1963

drawing attention to the lack of genuine radical transformation that had come in the wake of modernist experiments in the immediate post-war period. Indeed, the freedoms then anticipated in machine production and new technology had been betrayed by an increasing fetishization of efficiency that sidelined social emancipation in favour of rationalized control. Of course, Constant was far from alone in his condemnation of this betrayal but he was perhaps unique in holding onto a radical vision of technology as a force for liberation.

The imagined inhabitants of New Babylon were sometimes represented in Constant's drawings, but mostly as indeterminate blobs or smudges – a far cry from the overly realistic, if generic, images of people one tends to find in conventional architectural renderings. But perhaps this isn't surprising given Constant's assertion that a new kind of society would need to come into being before New Babylon could be realised. There's an assumption here about the nature of human desire: that people would, if allowed, fully embrace their own creativity and freedom. This is, in effect, the long-standing problem of the ethos of the avant-garde: that lone pioneers will eventually draw everyone else into their radical orbit. The principle

of disorientation that Constant saw as paramount in releasing the creativity of the city's inhabitants would surely be exhausting if it were unrelenting. The lack of differentiation here is key: the future inhabitants remain as indeterminate smudges because their very individuality would disrupt the transformative 'unitary urbanism' that Constant envisages.

Today, we're confronted once again with the prospect of a future world without work, when technologies that Constant could only have dreamt about have already become a reality.[3] Whether this freedom will result in a surge of creativity, or just simply more spectacular – and passive – forms of entertainment is still uncertain. Indeed, perhaps the most visceral reimagining of New Babylon has been in science-fiction cinema – the 2012 remake of *Total Recall* set in a future London with exactly the kind of vertiginous space frame envisaged by Constant. But here, the spectacle doesn't transform or disorientate in the way New Babylon was supposed to. Rather, it merely serves as a backdrop for spectacular action. Radical visions are perhaps most successful when their uncomfortable tensions are ignored, their anti-spectacle stance reversed to serve the very thing they despise.

Perspective view of the connecting units of New Babylon, 1960

Clifford Harper, 'Autonomous Terrace', 1976

The fascination with cybernetics evidenced in New Babylon was grounded in the idea that, through computers, one could exert some measure of control over the environment. This was American maverick engineer Richard Buckminster Fuller's notion of a 'spaceship Earth' – an all-encompassing approach to design that saw the application of high technology as the most viable path to sustainability. This gained widespread acceptance through Stewart Brand's *Whole Earth Catalog*, first published in 1968, which took Fuller's top-down approach and transformed it into a DIY movement among countercultural entrepreneurs.[4] Yet, in this period, there was another, very different, kind of environmental utopianism that was much more down-to-earth. Published in 1976 by a group of British technologists, environmentalists and scholars, *Radical Technology* was a direct response to the *Whole Earth Catalog*, offering a similar format, presenting various DIY technologies as tools to democratize design.[5] But, in contrast to the futuristic domes and high-tech wizardry of Fuller and Brand, *Radical Technology* presented a communitarian approach to design with a pastoral vision that had a distinctively British lineage dating back to the the utopian visions of William Morris in *News From Nowhere* (1892).

The most celebrated parts of *Radical Technology* were Clifford Harper's illustrations. Comprising six 'Visions' of alternative forms of social life, these drawings were grounded in localized social contexts: a collectivized garden; a community workshop in the basement of a house; a small rural housing estate; a workshop and media centre; and an 'autonomous terrace'. As the authors of *Radical Technology* pointed out, in the mid-1970s, there were many hundreds of Victorian terraces in British towns and cities that were condemned and awaiting demolition, but with their infrastructures still intact.[6] Harper imagined one of these terraces repurposed as a communal dwelling, with partition walls and garden fences removed to create

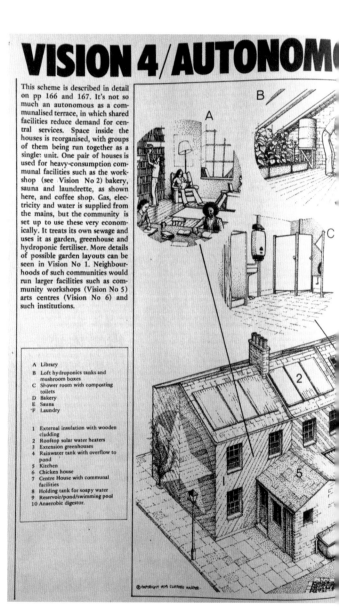

Clifford Harper's illustration of an 'Autonomous Terrace' published in *Radical Technology* (1976), pp. 168–69

a co-operatively owned space that would function as an alternative micro-community within an existing town or city. Individual rooms would remain private, but the rest of the space would accommodate playrooms, a pottery, darkroom, library and music and games rooms. One pair of houses would be transformed into the Centre House – a community hub housing a bakery, sauna, workshop and laundry. In the gardens, food would be grown, as on a traditional urban allotment, but with more sophisticated means of cultivation, such as hydroponics. For their energy needs, the community would tap into the existing networks of water supply, electricity and gas, although using considerably less of these resources than a conventional terrace.

In stark contrast to the spectacular high-tech visions offered by New Babylon, the Autonomous Terrace is decidedly homespun and pastoral. This is very much a vision of subversion from within, a tactic that chimes with Colin Ward's writings and the British tradition of a more gentle and everyday form of anarchism. The freedom-in-community promoted in the Autonomous Terrace is starkly different from the individualized libertarianism of Constant and Brand.[7] Its social vision is embedded in the local, in the already-existing pathways towards greater autonomy. Indeed, as Harper acknowledged, the terrace is not so much autonomous as communalized.

This vision has produced many real-life examples such as the Fireside Housing Co-op in Sheffield. In 1996, a group of friends formed a small housing co-operative and purchased a house in a terrace in the deprived Burngreave area of the city. Over time, four adjoining houses were acquired, with a fifth bought in 2018, with 12 people living there in 2020.[8] The gardens were made communal and, more recently, the old kitchens knocked down and replaced with a two-storey, timber-frame structure that joined all of the houses.

Communal structure built on the back of a Victorian terrace
cooperatively owned by the Fireside community, Sheffield, 2020

Fireside is a fully mutual housing co-op, meaning
that all the members are tenants – there is no ownership,
other than as a whole group. Although the co-op doesn't
possess the full range of communal facilities envisaged
in the Autonomous Terrace, it nevertheless demonstrates
that its basic premise – that housing and other assets can
be shared rather than owned – is a pragmatic solution to
the tendency of privately owned housing to become un-
affordable. By emphasizing speculative social situations
rather than technological hardware or innovative structures and forms, the Autonomous Terrace demonstrates
that anarchist architecture can never be isolated from the
life that goes on within it. Indeed, just like New Babylon,
but in a very different way, it confirms that social transformation must always go hand-in-hand with spatial and
architectural transformation.

William Gibson, The Bridge, 1990s

As personal computers first reached a mass market in the 1980s, the emancipatory promise of cybernetics in an earlier generation suddenly gained wider potency. The emergence of cyberpunk as a recognized cultural genre – in music, film, fiction and graphic novels – centred on speculative visions of how human life would be transformed in a media-dominated and information-saturated age. With a distinct future-noir aesthetic fusing high-technology and punk counterculture, bodies with machines (usually computers), and the virtual and the material, cyberpunk injected the rather dry technocratic vision of cybernetics with a sense of sublime beauty and radical new social and cultural possibilities. Perhaps nowhere was this more so than in William Gibson's 'Bridge' trilogy of novels: *Virtual Light* (1993), *Idoru* (1996) and *All Tomorrow's Parties* (1999), in which the Bay Bridge in San Francisco, left unstable after a future earthquake, is taken over by thousands of squatters and mutates into a fantastic bricolage of salvaged materials:

Hodgetts + Fung's rendering of an inhabited Bay Bridge in William Gibson's science fiction writing, 1989

> The integrity of [the Bridge's] span was rigorous as the modern program itself, yet around this had grown another reality, intent upon its own agenda. This had occurred piecemeal, to no set plan, employing every imaginable technique and material. The result was something amorphous, startlingly organic. At night, illuminated by Christmas bulbs, by recycled neon, by torchlight, it possessed a queer medieval energy. By day, seen from a distance, it reminded him of the ruin of England's Brighton Pier, as though viewed through some cracked kaleidoscope of vernacular style.[9]

Throughout the course of the three novels, the social life and practical infrastructure of the Bridge is fleshed out in extraordinary detail. We are immersed in the everyday lives of those who live in the shack-like rooms; we learn about the improvised sewage and electricity supply networks; and we inhabit the heady micro-worlds of the Bridge's countless bars, shops, and clubs that fill its interstitial spaces. Gibson is not describing an urban environment that can be planned. Rather, there is no agenda, no underlying structure to the formation of the Bridge community: 'the place had just *grown*; it looked like one thing patched into the next, until the whole space was wrapped in this formless mass of *stuff*, no two pieces of it matched.'[10] Gibson contrasts this anarchic form of urban growth with that envisaged by the mega-corporations who are seeking to remake San Francisco into a self-sufficient luxury enclave for the super-wealthy. Gibson asks us whether we truly do prefer to have our cities made for us by others, or whether we'd be willing to take matters into our own hands, joining with those who are already forced by necessity to do so.

Another drawing by Hodgetts + Fung of the Bay Bridge
imagined by William Gibson, 1989

For architect Jonathan Gales, architectural salvage begins in a very different place from Gibson's damaged or derelict structures, namely in an imagined future when all architecture is in a state of incompletion. In his short film *Megalomania* (2014), made by Gales's animation studio Factory Fifteen, the whole of London has become a vast construction site, with all of its buildings caught in arrested development that could result in either future decay or development.[11] In this seemingly abandoned city, the London Eye has grown informal appendages very much like those seen constructed on Gibson's Bridge, while a giant skyscraper structure pictured at the end of the film is in fact an enormous assemblage of different construction elements: scaffolding, cranes, panels, and a concrete frame. Inspired by the sudden collapse of the global construction industry in the wake of the 2007—08 financial crisis, which temporarily halted the building of now iconic buildings like London's Shard and Dubai's Burj Khalifa, not to mention countless areas of new housing across Europe, *Megalomania* exaggerates the time-lag between a building's construction and completion in order to flag up how vulnerable architecture is to fluctuations in the flow of global capital.[12] In visualizing an entire city as a petrified construction site, the film asks if unfinished buildings might become the norm rather than the exception in our future cities and how, like Gibson's Bridge, they might be salvaged to become something entirely different.

Still from Jonathan Gales's short film *Megalomania* (2014) showing the London Eye repurposed for informal dwellings

Lebbeus Woods, various, 1980s–

A drawing from Lebbeus Woods's *Aerial Paris* series, 1989

Construction based on salvage characterized the work of American architect Lebbeus Woods. In the 1980s and 1990s, he took Gordon Matta-Clark's term 'anarchitecture' and turned it into an entire speculative practice. In hundreds of exquisite drawings and models, Woods built up a portfolio of imagined structures that took to task the tendency within certain strands of post-modernist architecture to neglect the social and political.

In several essays and pamphlets published in the 1990s, Woods argued for the development of a new kind of 'heterarchichal' architecture, one that would abolish the existing hierarchies in cities. This radical anarchist vision grew out a sense of optimism following the fall of the Berlin Wall in 1989 and the collapse of the Soviet bloc in 1991 as well as in rapturous anticipation of the coming freedoms to be offered by personal computers and a future global information network. The highly fragmented forms and machine-like growth of his proposals after 1985, such as *Aerial Paris* (1989), were predicated on the creation of genuine 'freespaces' in existing cities that would facilitate the formation of a new anarchist society.[13] In *Aerial Paris*, the free-floating structures challenged the museum-like city of Paris beneath as being unfit for purpose in a society where everything else was in ceaseless flux. Anticipating the global sea of flows of the digital age we are now immersed in, Woods's flying city imagines an architecture that is entirely provisional and responsive to the flux around it and to the individual desires and needs of its inhabitants.

In the mid-1990s, Woods's work became focused on the destructive elements of both nature and human society. After witnessing the deliberate targeting of cities during the Bosnian War (1992–95), he turned his attention to the role of design in reconstruction. His 1993 publication *War and Architecture* was a manifesto for the reconstruction of Sarajevo. Woods envisaged the bomb-damaged

Lebbeus Woods's drawing of the collision of new construction and damaged buildings from a series of proposals for the reconstruction of Sarajevo made during the Bosnian War, 1993

buildings of the city being reconstructed from their ruined fragments. This was counter to conventional ways of rebuilding war-damaged cities: namely, the careful restoration of damaged or destroyed structures, or the modernist idea of the *tabula rasa* – starting afresh from a blank slate.

In the mid-1990s, Woods turned his attention to a different kind of destructive force in his series of projects intended to prepare the city of San Francisco for the 'Big One' – a hypothetical earthquake of magnitude 8+ that will almost certainly strike the city sometime in the near future. In absolute opposition to the conventional policy of strengthening existing structures, Woods imagined a whole series of buildings that were constructed, transformed or even completed by earthquakes themselves – 'an architecture that uses earthquakes, converting to a human purpose the energies they release ... an architecture that inhabits earthquakes, existing in their space and time'.

Model of a Horizon House (2000), one of many structures that formed part of Lebbeus Woods's post-earthquake project for San Francisco

Lebbeus Woods, *Quake City*, from *San Francisco: Inhabiting the Quake*, 1995

In *Quake City* – a gigantic structure that Woods imagined straddling a redundant industrial dock – architecture simply accumulates over the years, with each successive earthquake shifting its 'fragmented, irregular mass, reshuffling the plates that once might have been called floors, walls, or ceilings'.[14] The whole of the new city would be built from scavenged materials, whether discarded timber, corrugated iron and other sheet metal, or piping and plastics. For Woods, architectural salvage wasn't just about creating a certain kind of aesthetic – a grandiose form of upcycling; rather, it deliberately shifted the power to build into the hands of users rather than architects.

Of course, just like Constant's New Babylon, Woods's vision of a self-built city emerging from the ruins of the old depends upon a radical reshaping of human desire. Woods might imagine his structures as 'freespaces' built by citizens liberated from the shackles of authoritarian control; yet, he presupposes that people would choose a nomadic and free-spirited urban existence in favour of the comfort and security offered by the conventional home.

Minecraft, 2009–

At the same time that Woods was developing his imagined 'freespaces', a libertarian culture of entrepreneurship was coalescing in California's Silicon Valley. When the World Wide Web finally arrived in mass culture in the mid-1990s, it promised unfettered new freedoms for its users and a utopian culture of sharing that would be completely un-regulated. Today, we are so embedded within digital culture, and so aware of its dangers, that such dreams now seem at best naive, at worst duplicitous. Yet there are many places where the empowering vision of the digital world still holds true, perhaps most notably in the rise of open-platform games such as Minecraft.

Designed by Swedish developer Markus Persson in 2009 and released by Mojang in 2011, Minecraft is one of the most popular video games ever made: in its first 10 years, it sold over 176 million copies and such was its success that it was purchased by Microsoft for $2.5 billion in 2014. Minecraft is an open-ended 'sandbox' game where players build constructions of textured cubes in an almost infinitely varied world. With no instructions or tutorials provided by the designers, players – as their self-chosen avatars – are free to negotiate the many worlds (called 'biomes') in any way they see fit. They can choose three different playing modes: Creative Mode (which is basically

Still from Minecraft showing a characteristic house built by game players in 2019

Still from Minecraft showing a modernist-style house built by a game-player in 2020

just building); Survival Mode (in which you gather resources and build shelters to escape nocturnal monsters); and Adventure Mode (navigating a world and rules created by someone else). Players can also choose to operate on their own or, through servers, in collaboration or competition with others. Skill-sharing in Minecraft has become a whole industry in itself, with many gamers posting on-line tutorials on video platforms such as YouTube (and becoming Minecraft celebrities in their own right).

Just like its pre-digital precursor LEGO, Minecraft has proved especially popular with children. It's one of the ways in which younger children first engage with on-line communities before they're exposed to other social media platforms. Some have argued that Minecraft is an ideal educational tool in this respect, but also a means by which children can learn about the built environment. Alexandra Overby and Brian Jones believe that Minecraft 'reframes the player's identity as an architect and developer', thus allowing children to learn how to build simple struc-tures, to pay attention to scale and perspective in design, and to plan ahead and manage the resources they have gleaned.[15]

Architects have also seen potential in Minecraft to radically change the culture of design and planning, opening it up to a much wider range of participants.[16] The company Blockworks, founded in 2013, uses Minecraft as a design tool: in 2015 they ran a Brutalist Build workshop at the RIBA's *Day of Play* event in London, in which 120 young people were assigned a plot in Minecraft and asked to build a Brutalist-inspired structure. Blockworks have also used Minecraft to envisage future sustainable cities: an alternative 'green' London for the *Guardian* newspaper in 2015 and a vision of Dublin in 2066 for Ireland's 200th anniversary celebrations in June 2016.[17] Going further, Danish architect Bjarke Ingels, founder of design firm BIG, has argued that real-life buildings should be more like those in Minecraft. His concept of 'Worldcraft', the sub-ject of a film he presented in 2014, is an impassioned call to democratize design by making it more participatory and populist.[18] Arguing that the fictional worlds created in Minecraft 'empower people with the tools to trans-form their own environments', he sees the wider potential of design professionals to mirror the game in how they operate in the world.

Open-Source Architecture, 2011–

Prototype WikiHouse exhibited at the University of Westminster in June 2012

Minecraft is just one example of how the internet has led to a radically new form of collaborative knowledge generation, what Charles Leadbeater has called 'we-think'.[19] Software like YouTube, Wikipedia and Linux allow participation from anyone who has an internet connection; and, since its launch in 2011, Wikipedia in particular has proven to be an immensely successful example of the crowd-sourcing of vast pools of knowledge, much to the chagrin of educators at all levels. But, as architect Carlo Ratti has argued, architects have been very slow to catch up, even as they've always known that the overwhelming majority of the built environment isn't actually designed by architects.[20] In response, John Habraken suggests that 'we should recognize that the built environment is an autonomous entity that has its own ways, and the architect should study that and explain how and why he can participate in a largely autonomous process.'[21]

Ratti, Habraken and many others collaborated to produce a manifesto for open-source architecture and, appropriately enough, they were able to publish this on Wikipedia in 2011.[22] Generated by a participatory process that saw hundreds contribute to its content, this manifesto continues to evolve – just like any other Wikipedia entry, it remains open to modification.

Open-source architecture claims that, in the digital age, all aspects of design can be thoroughly decentralized. Using platforms like the Open Architecture Network and OpenStructures, anyone can contribute and modify architectural plans and specifications. Some building projects are now funded by crowd-sourcing platforms like Sponsume and Kickstarter, breaking down the traditional architect/client hierarchy. In open-source architecture, standards would be devised by open collaboration rather than imposed top-down – a move pioneered by Wikipedia. At the same time, construction would exploit the open-source hardware movement pioneered by MIT's Fab Lab in the early 2000s. Here, tools like CNC machines and 3D printers are shared to enable users to produce and manipulate materials themselves, bypassing inefficient and expensive middlemen. Finally, the built spaces themselves would be fully networked, allowing constant feedback on their performance as they 'intelligently recognize and respond to individual occupants'.[23]

Even as digital technologies increasingly envelop our lives, this vision of buildings and cities as 'computers to live in' largely remains a utopian speculation. Attempts to build in this open-source way have, to date, been small scale and largely experimental. The best known is WikiHouse, set up by Alistair Parvin and the London design practice oo:/ in 2011. WikiHouse enables

The Urban Village Project, shown at IKEA's Democratic Design Day in 2019, using modular building systems derived from open-source platforms like WikiHouse

users to download Creative Commons-licensed building plans from its online library, customize them using free software like SketchUp, and then use the plans to create jigsaw puzzle-like pieces of plywood with a CNC machine. Like a scaled-up piece of IKEA furniture, WikiHouses built to date include the Gantry Studios (2018) in London, a farmhouse in Warwickshire (2017), and a pilot scheme for affordable houses in Sheffield in 2018. WikiHouses have also been used by architects Space Craft Systems as a quick and low-cost way of rebuilding after the 2011 earthquake in Christchurch, New Zealand.[24] More ambitious plans put forward in 2019 include the Urban Village Project, showcased in IKEA's Democratic Design Day annual event, which proposes a modular building system for an entire urban neighbourhood that could be disassembled, replaced, reused and recycled when needed.[25] Scaling-up further, the Xinqiao Open Source City in Shenzhen envisages a new urban corridor that would be self-built by residents in collaboration with Hassell Studio.[26]

Although there is great potential for open-source platforms and technologies to radically transform architecture, Open Source has yet to produce the kind of diversity it imagines will result when users choose everything rather than architects, developers and planners. Existing WikiHouses tend in the other direction, towards a dull uniformity that comes with prioritizing efficiency and cost-effectiveness. In addition, as demonstrated in most of the projects realised through WikiHouse, it is architects and not users who are generally taking advantage of open source to actually build. As much as it is celebrated for allowing users to more effectively channel their needs and desires, open-source architecture doesn't address such fundamentals as acquiring land, the provision of infrastructure and secure foundations, or how to shape a different kind of imagination of architecture. Its overt faith in the transformative power of technology is, in fact, an unhelpful residue of the top-down thinking of the past.

Anthony Ko, An Activist Artefact, 2017

Towards the end of every academic year, architecture schools around the world put on their degree shows. For final year students, this is often in the context of fierce competition for prizes and also to garner attention from the architectural press and maybe even secure employment. Anthony Ko's final year project 'An Activist Artefact' formed just one of the hundreds of speculative proposals exhibited at the 2017 Summer Show at the Bartlett School of Architecture in London, one of the world's largest and most prestigious architecture schools.[27]

Ko, who grew up in Hong Kong, proposed a politically charged architecture in the sensitive border of Hong Kong in 2047 – 30 years after the end of the 'Normalization' period, that is, the process agreed between the Chinese and British governments in 1997. In Ko's project, an autonomous fortress-like artists' commune will have emerged on the no-man's-land between Hong Kong and Shenzhen. In visualizations ranging from long sections to a colourful axonometric with contextual photographic collages, Ko depicts a veritable cacophony of architectural forms. Four towers shield a vast open square and artists' working and living spaces. This creative commune would be funded entirely by the production and selling of subversive artworks. Comprising a hybrid assemblage of materials – striped awnings, movable partitions, brick, concrete and bamboo scaffolding, the whole structure is an agglomeration of kits of parts, from the towers to an array of mobile devices, such as vending machines, futuristic vehicles and outdoor theatres.

Even as the project presents the future built environment as one dominated by ecstatic artistic energy – Ko's imagined occupants variously jump, dance and wildly gesture inside this mini-city – there's an underlying seriousness to the work that explicitly references the wave of pro-democracy protests in Hong Kong that have convulsed the city since the Umbrella Revolution in 2014. The riotous aesthetic of An Activist Artefact reflects the look and feel of the Umbrella Revolution, which saw improvised artworks playing a key role in the occupation of urban spaces by protestors.

Since graduating from the Bartlett, Ko has returned to his native Hong Kong to practise as an architect. In 2017 he founded the Dilemma Studio, which brings together both speculative and real-world projects in its diverse portfolio.[28] To date, the Studio has built the 'Nostalgists' pavilion, exhibited in both Morse Park and Kowloon Tsai Park, as well as mobile street furniture in the Oil Street Art Space, which curates and presents sketches made by local people in community workshops. Both projects are small-scale realisations of the mobile structures that populate An Activist Artefact. The Nostalgists pavilion is effectively a down-scaled version of the 'Indexical Tower' envisaged in An Activist Artefact, a repository of artworks and collective social memories that would be a bastion of resistance against a presumed oppressive Chinese regime after 2047. The pavilion is designed to foster resistance to the increasingly authoritarian government of Hong Kong. By collecting and preserving everyday collective memories of the city, it provides a space for individual desires to be valued. It embodies anarchism as 'a perpetually evolving process of geographical prefiguration' that builds a new society in the shell of the old right here and now.

Anthony Ko's isometric drawing of the Indexical Tower, 'An Activist Artefact', June 2017

Perspective view of 'An Activist Artefact' by Anthony Ko, exhibited
at the Bartlett School of Architecture in its 2017 Summer Show

VIII. PARTICIPATION

In reality, architecture has become too important to be left to architects ... all barriers between builders and users must be abolished, so that building and using become two different parts of the same planning process—Giancarlo de Carlo, a lecture given in Liège in 1969

Architects only design a tiny fraction of the built environment (no more than five percent globally); the rest is put together by planners, developers and contractors according to a mixture of standard models, inherited traditions and structural know-how. Ordinary people are excluded from this process, even if they are sometimes entitled to raise objections. Experts continue to assume that they know what is best for the masses. In architectural circles at least, this institutionalized arrogance has begun to be challenged, as alternative practices have broadened the remit of design and, with it, those who are asked to participate.

This final section explores how participation might work in designing and making buildings. First, there is indirect participation, as seen in the work of Giancarlo de Carlo and Lucien Kroll, two modernist renegades working from the 1960s onwards. This is when architects maintain control of the design process but build in flexibility to their plans so that users can have some say in the process. Second is direct participation, pioneered by architects like Walter Segal and the Bauhäusle project in Stuttgart, where inhabitants actually build for themselves. Yet, even in these direct models, the architect remains a figure of authority, architecture a product rather than a social process.

An expanded mode of design is characteristic of recent practices like Raumlaborberlin, Assemble and atelier d'architecture autogérée. Although these practices do produce buildings, they are usually temporary structures that explore radical ways of involving people in the design process itself. In Raumlaborberlin's Utopia Station in Milton Keynes, visitors were encouraged to explore their own imaginations to generate design ideas; while in the Granby Four Streets project in Liverpool and the Agrocité in Paris, buildings form only one part of a holistic approach to design that embraces everything from food production to leisure and culture.

The final piece explores the work of Spanish architect Santiago Cirugeda. In his practice, Cirugeda combines design with activism – he builds but also advises communities on how to get around planning regulations to achieve what they want. This reveals the central paradox of anarchist architecture – there is no such thing as building without a community; and there is no freedom for oneself without, at the same time, there equally being freedom for others.

Spanish architectural collective Recetas Urbanas engaged in building a structure in an empty lot in Barcelona, 2005

Giancarlo de Carlo, Villaggio Matteotti, Terni, Italy, 1969–74

Modernist architecture – that developed in the many meetings of the Congrès Internationaux d'Architecture Moderne (CIAM), founded in 1928 and disbanded in 1959 – only began to be questioned in any sustained way in the 1950s. Italian architect Giancarlo de Carlo was just one of a group of architects who attended the later CIAM meetings with increasing frustration at their rigid and authoritarian attitudes towards 'users'.[1] Together with a group of dissident architects, including Peter and Alison Smithson, Ralph Erskine and Aldo Van Eyck, de Carlo formed a rival organization – Team X or Team 10 – which sought to re-invigorate links between design and the society it professed to serve.[2]

In a lecture in 1969, de Carlo presented a powerful manifesto for a more participatory approach to design.[3]

Villaggio Matteotti, Terni, built from 1969–74, showing the variegated approach and multiple setbacks and overhangs of the apartments

First-floor pedestrian walkway in the Villaggio Matteotti, Terni

He argued that architecture was not about implementing a plan but a process that required participation at every stage: from the assessment of what people actually want, the putting forward of a design proposal, to the inhabitation of the built structure itself. Projects must therefore be subject to revision at any stage in this process: a feedback loop between the expertise of the architect/planner and the multiple and divergent responses from those directly affected by the project. In arguing for the 'disorder' of the real world to burst the bubble of modernist autonomy, de Carlo explicitly rejected architecture as an ordering project; instead, he argued that architects must use the inherent complexity of the world as a generative force, opening up the opportunity for those without power to become the 'bearers of new values which already exist potentially and are already manifested sporadically in the margins which are not controlled by institutional power'.[4]

In the same year that he presented his manifesto for participation, de Carlo was invited to design new social housing in Terni, an industrial city 100km northwest of Rome. He was brought in to mediate a dispute between the state-owned steelworks and its workers: the former wanted to sell properties to tenants to avoid paying for their renovation; while the workers wanted new houses. De Carlo persuaded the government to fund a participatory approach, eventually building 240 dwellings. In consultation with future residents, de Carlo tested out his threefold process-based approach to design, conducting interviews with over 100 residents with the help of a sociologist. He opened up the conventions of modernism to embrace a range of options for residents to choose from: a total of 45 possible permutations of five basic building types, each containing three dwellings. The result was a variegated approach with multiple set-backs and over-hangs that suggests that each of the three storeys has been designed independently.[5] Over time, the concrete terraces and walkways have become softened by vegetation. This compositional strategy of variations on a theme was also taken up by de Carlo's Team X colleague Aldo Van Eyck, and it represents the partial liberation of architectural form from the stringencies of the standardized elements so beloved of modernists.

Without residents actually building their own houses, these permutations are inevitably limited to what the architect deems appropriate and, with hindsight, there are clearly limitations to de Carlo's participatory approach, even as his original definition remains remarkably prescient. In his later works – particularly his decades-long series of interventions in the historical Italian hill city of Urbino – de Carlo widened his definition of participation to embrace much more than future users alone.[6] He thoroughly researched the wide array of factors that feed into urban identity, such as residents' feelings about where they live, historical developments, the materiality of landscape and the built environment, and local building traditions that have evolved over time. Here, participation embraces both material and immaterial things, the human and non-human environment alike, and imagination and concrete reality. The role of the architect is not to impose his/her imagination on the existing environment but rather to listen to the multitude of things that already make that environment what it is. This is participation conceived in its broadest possible sense – the art of design being an art of full engagement, planning as an unending dialogue, the building a form that 'percolates' rather than 'explodes' into the context in which it is embedded.[7]

Lucien Kroll, La Mémé, Brussels, 1970–76

There were only a few architects of the 1960s and 1970s who took Giancarlo de Carlo's call for greater participation seriously. One of these was a Belgian friend, Lucien Kroll, who criticized mass production and standardization of building components as producing sterile urban environments that were completely inflexible to individual needs and desires. Instead, with painstaking precision, Kroll developed an alternative approach that aimed for maximum diversity through the manipulation of simple arrangements of modular components.[8]

For his most ambitious project – the new medical faculty of Louvain's Catholic University at Woluwé-Saint Lambert on the outskirts of Brussels, largely built from 1970 to 1976 – Kroll used a modified version of architect John Habraken's SAR system developed in the early 1960s.[9]

Apartment complex of the medical faculty of Louvain's Catholic University
(La Mémé) at Woluwé-Saint Lambert, Brussels, built from 1970–76

Variegated windows and cladding of the apartment complex of La Mémé

This was a modular structural component made up of columns and a horizontal brace that could be used as a building block for any kind of structure. It would produce an incremental approach to construction, where the support structure acts as a frame for diversity, rather than imposing the rigid kind of rationality seen in mass-housing blocks of the 1960s.

The medical faculty (or La Mémé as it is usually referred to) is comprised of 11 separate buildings totalling 40,000 square metres of floor space. It remains one of the most ambitious attempts in modern architecture to wed mass production with creative diversity. Kroll's involvement in the project came about after the students of the Catholic University, no doubt influenced by the revolutionary ferment of 1968, rejected a conventional low-grade

modernist design put forward by the University. Instead, the students themselves approached Kroll to produce an alternative proposal, and his strikingly organic assemblage of apartment blocks, restaurants, administration buildings, theatre, parsonage and chapel, sports facility, school and nursery, were realised in no small part due to the influence of student opinion in this febrile period.

La Mémé is a jumble of variegated materials and forms that creates a strong mosaic effect. The shapes and dimensions of windows vary wildly – each tailored to suit the temperament of individual students. The supporting structure is infilled with wood, aluminium and iron panels; and many of the buildings employ set-backs to create a ziggurat-like effect. In the accommodation building, Kroll even allowed students to design their own customized spaces in the loft areas, acting as a facilitator rather than director of design.[10] In between the buildings are ad-hoc gardens and sculptures made from leftover materials (often built by the construction workers themselves); while the remarkable Alma Metro station – a later addition to serve the university and built from 1979 to 1982 – is almost Gaudíesque in its sinuous, flowing forms and sculptural approach.

Key to the achievement of this extraordinary level of diversity was Kroll's use of an irregular grid of columns as the foundational structural element. In conventional construction, particularly large-scale projects, supporting columns are arranged rationally in gridded lines so that structural uniformity is achieved. The result is modular spaces that can only accommodate minimal if any variation. Instead, Kroll's 'wandering columns' are arranged in a loose grid that allows them to be spaced at irregular intervals. This enables an immensely flexible floor plan that accommodates variation on each of the different storeys.

The professional contractors who built La Mémé worked very differently than usual, being moved around by Kroll to build different parts of the project. In declaring that 'repetition is a crime!', Kroll vehemently rejected the idea that mass production inevitably led to standardization and the erasure of difference.[11] Even as his original plan for La Mémé has been altered over the years by the controlling instincts of the University's officials, it nevertheless remains a testament to a counter-modernism that is borne out of a popular welling of desire for the liberation that technology always promises but so rarely ever delivers.

Walter Segal, Walters Way and Segal Close, London, 1977–87

Roughly contemporaneous with Lucien Kroll, architect Walter Segal developed a method of building that was revolutionary in allowing users to fully participate in its realisation.[12] Having moved from Berlin to London in 1936, Segal taught at the Architectural Association and began his architectural practice. In 1963, he decided to demolish and rebuild his home in Highgate, creating a temporary structure – the 'Little House in the Garden' – to accommodate himself and his then wife during the rebuilding process. Taking only two weeks to build and costing just £800, the house comprised a simple post-and-beam timber frame infilled with plasterboard with no 'wet' processes involved – the timber and cladding secured with bolts and screws alone. The foundations were simply paving slabs laid on the ground.

Segal compared this method of assembly to Meccano, the model construction system created in 1898 by Frank Hornby. Also similar to Habraken and Kroll's flexible 'supports', Segal's method subverted the tendency of ready-made mass-produced materials to result in standardized architectural forms. Instead, just like Meccano, Segal's approach allowed users themselves to mediate the transition from design to use, placing in their hands a much greater range of possible design options. In a different vein, Colin Ward compared Segal's approach to that of vernacular traditions in architecture, such as medieval English houses, American timber-frame buildings and Japanese houses, emphasizing the fact that many of these structures were self-built.[13]

After building the 'Little House', Segal mainly worked on small-scale commissions that derived from his own self-built project, until, in the mid-1970s, he found an unusual ally in the London Borough of Lewisham, through a mutual chain of connections with friends. Segal knew Colin Ward who knew Brian Richardson, an assistant Borough Architect in Lewisham. He, in turn, approached Ron Pepper and Nick Taylor who chaired the Housing and Planning committees and it is they who backed the idea and persuaded the council to support the proposal and make sites available for self-built social housing using Segal's method. Although the project was beset with problems – mostly delays caused by the inflexible ways of funding and controlling buildings in the UK – the first phase (seven properties on what is now Segal Close) was completed in 1982. A further 13 houses were finished in 1987, after Segal's death, and named Walters Way in his honour. Financed entirely by public funds, each plot was allocated to their respective builders by means of a ballot. Nearly 200 people applied for the original scheme of only seven houses, but no-one was excluded from applying on the basis of their income, gender, age, or ethnicity.

The original residents described the building process as simultaneously empowering and alarming, both communal and solitary. Up to 30 people were needed to lift the wooden frames of each house – the first element to be built; but many of the jobs thereafter could be done single-handed; each house-builder constructed at their own rate, with most of the homes taking between one and two years to complete. Throughout this time, the community cohered organically, a process that has been cemented over the years by continuing responsibility for the private roads, communal outdoor spaces and regular social gatherings, such as annual street parties.[14] The houses too have evolved: extensions have been added, internal walls moved around; one resident even enveloping his house with glass in order for it to become more energy efficient. What the community cannot do, however, is keep their homes affordable: most were bought by their original residents and then sold on at a profit – in 2019, a three-bedroom house in Walters Way went on the market for £810,000, a price which, although in keeping with London's grossly

Self-built house on Segal Close, Lewisham, in the early 1980s

Self-built house on Walters Way, Lewisham, in the mid-1980s
with a later extension and treehouse

Perspective view of the proposed new housing at Church Grove,
Ladywell, designed by Architype, 2019

overinflated housing market, hardly counts as affordable. And expensive housing inevitably means a loss of social diversity, directly threatening the egalitarian basis of the original project.

Together with Segal, the architect Jon Broome supervised most of the work on Walters Way, taking over full control of both developments after Segal's death in 1985. Broome now lives in a house he designed and built close to the one he originally constructed on Segal Close with his sister. With his architectural practices Architype and Jon Broome Architects, Broome has become a leading proponent of self-build housing, updating Segal's method to encompass issues of affordability and sustainability.[15] In the early 1990s, he initiated many co-operative housing schemes in London, including one directly across the road from Segal Close. In addition, three projects in Brighton, and others in Birmingham, Sheffield, Colchester, and Glasgow were facilitated by Architype. In 2019, Broome was involved in the Rural Urban Synthesis Project (RUSS), a community land trust in Ladywell, another district in Lewisham, set up in 2009 by Kareem Dayes, the son of

Dave Dayes and Barbara Hicks, who built their house in Walters Way in the 1980s.

Striving for affordability, sustainability, self-governance and community engagement, RUSS is developing a scheme of 33 homes to be built on Church Grove in Ladywell. This was granted planning permission in 2018, as well as a crowd-funded Community Hub that will be built according to Segal's methods but with sustainable building materials.[16] In addition, the affordability of the homes will be protected by preventing them from being sold onto the open market in the future, with nine different options being put forward for buying into the scheme. Just like the projects for Segal Close and Walters Way, residents have been chosen by ballot. However, the trade off is that only 20 percent of the project will be self-built and this will be confined to interior fixtures and fittings only – the actual percentage will vary from person to person, depending on how much 'sweat equity' they want to earn, as well as how much aptitude, time and appetite for self-building they have.

Peter Sulzer and Peter Hübner, Bauhäusle, Stuttgart, 1980–83

In the late 1970s, two architecture professors at the University of Stuttgart, Peter Sulzer and Peter Hübner, invited Walter Segal to lecture at the University, with the intention of using his method to build some experimental structures on the campus. In 1980, they began work on a new student dormitory that would eventually become known as the Bauhäusle, literally the 'little Bauhaus', an ironic take on the iconic German design school that flourished in the 1920s.[17]

With approval granted by the University, together with a small amount of state funding, Sulzer and Hübner began to integrate the design and building of the Bauhäusle

Reconfigured communal space in the Bauhäusle, built by students and contractors in 2019

One of the more unusual student rooms built as part of the Bauhäusle from 1980–88

The informal aesthetic of the Bauhäusle, University of Stuttgart, built from 1980–83

into their teaching programme. Over three years, 200 students were involved in the process; the design and building of each of the 30 planned rooms of the dormitory assigned to individual groups. Although these groups had relative autonomy in their decision-making, they were all constrained by the need to source free building materials. The architects provided other constraints: a modular system in which room sizes were standardized and an insistence that interconnecting corridors be enclosed. The ten 'houses' that comprise the completed structure were formed from groups of three or four bedrooms – the gaps in between the houses infilled with common spaces, corridors, and passageways. Seen from the air, the completed structure appears strikingly organic – as if everything had been improvised on site. Roof-lines slant at different angles; windows face all directions; roofs are covered in a hodgepodge of turf, tiles, ashlar and

plasterboard. However, as Sulzer made clear, this improvised appearance belies the presence of a complex order behind it. The design process was, in fact, a painstaking interchange between drawings, models and buildings. Drawings provided ways of indicating spaces where one group needed to negotiate with another; models allowed the students to work out how their individual designs would interconnect; while the use of Segal's flexible timber-frame construction for all of the houses allowed changes to be made as building proceeded.[18]

Sulzer and Hübner's model of participation was rooted in the pragmatics of the building process itself. The architects provided a clear 'ordering structure' to the design, but they also left room for changes. At times, design expertise came to the fore (for example, in obtaining planning permission and developing a sound and durable structure);

at others, the process was mutual, professors and students alike learning through making. The latter allowed for contingency to enter into the design process itself, resulting in architecture that was grounded in everyday life rather than the hierarchies of institutionalized expertise.

Originally planned as a temporary building, the Bauhäusle's 15-year planning permission has been renewed twice since its completion in 1983 and it continues to house around 30 students each year. Maintained by the *Studierendenwerk* (Student Services) of Stuttgart University, its long life has been secured mostly on account of deep loyalty to the communal values the building promotes. Students who are selected to live there are expected to undertake repairs themselves, the University supplying raw materials and some external help for bigger projects, such as the recent replacement of one of the rooms which involved designing and building a completely new structure.[19] Students are also able to customize their rooms as well as their external terraces. All around the Bauhäusle is evidence of this: a window blind made from a piece of fabric attached to hooks; shelves fashioned from cast-off pieces of wood; chairs from discarded pallets.

What the Bauhäusle exhibits most strongly is the value of a form of education that is focused on making rather than the acquisition of knowledge through academic study. This keys in with a central tenet in anarchist notions of education – that learning should not be based on hierarchical systems of knowledge valuation – academic prowess at the top; practical skills at the bottom – as is generally the case in most state-funded education in the Global North. Rather, practice-based approaches enable students to follow their creative bents by doing and making.[20] As confirmed by students who live in the Bauhäusle today, the building itself stimulates this, because it was born from a form of creative thinking that is not distinct from doing.[21]

Raumlaborberlin, Utopia Station, Milton Keynes, 2019

In autumn 2019, German collective Raumlaborberlin transformed the central street of Milton Keynes – Midsummer Boulevard – into a setting for a free festival of creative urban living.[22] They built, among other things, the Utopia Station, which combined steel scaffolding, metal staircases, striped awnings and a bricolage of salvaged windows to create a three-storey structure. Visitors were welcomed in the Idea Kitchen on the second floor, where members of the design team made tea and provided a questionnaire which visitors used to sketch their own planning proposals for Milton Keynes. Afterwards, they engaged in a game of chance: they spun a wheel of fortune to see if their ideas would be taken to the production stage. If they were lucky, their ideas were taken down to the first level of the structure, where Teleinternetcafe – a Berlin-based team of architects and urban planners – translated the ideas into models. These models were then brought together to form an evolving exhibition on the ground floor.

Such playful subversion is characteristic of Raumlaborberlin – a group of a dozen or so artists, architects and urban planners. Although they've worked all over the world since their formation in 1999, many of their projects are based in Berlin, finding in its post-unification spaces opportunities for ways of challenging conventional models of neoliberal urban regeneration. One of their first projects was a proposal for an artificial mountain to be created in Moritzplatz, an under-utilized former industrial space in the city's Kreuzberg district (never built, the site has subsequently become home to the Prinzessinnengärten). With a defiantly optimistic vision of a bottom-up urbanism developing from architects and planners responding directly to people's needs and desires, Raumlaborberlin have instigated a huge range of projects in their 20–year existence, the most well-known probably being the Küchen-monument (Kitchen Monument) in 2006, a 20m-long inflatable sculpture built to house up to 80 participants, the programme changing according to the sculpture's location (for example, in Berlin, it has functioned as both a communal kitchen/dining room and a ballroom for dancing).

Their most ambitious project to date was the Floating University, first built on the site of Berlin's abandoned Templehof airport in the summer of 2018. This project created a gathering place for visiting students and scientists, the result of 25 international universities 'plugging in' to the site as an alternative platform for education outside traditional institutions. Built by a large group of students and teachers from universities across Europe, the campus was a remarkable bricolage of materials and functions. Combining steel scaffolding, metal staircases, simple timber-frame structures and inflatable roof canopies, it housed learning spaces, a modular kitchen, workshops, a 100–seat auditorium for public events, gardens and open-air floating platforms for socializing. The

Members of Teleinternetcafe creating models of urban planning proposals suggested by visitors to the Utopia Station, September 2019

Raumlaborberlin's Utopia Station on Midsummer Boulevard
in Milton Keynes, September 2019

artist-in-residence Katherine Bell created the project's most innovative structure: a water filtration system that used a wheel to draw rainwater through a series of interconnected bathtubs containing biological filters such as sand-biofilm, mushroom mycelium and zebra mussels.[23]

Constantly testing the boundaries between public and private space and the legal and the illicit, Raumlaborberlin's projects are primarily interested in using urban space to incubate radical alternatives – a method of urban planning that is rooted in encounter rather than problem-solving from a distance. Thus, the group might spend many weeks engaging with a proposed site by talking to local people in order to assess their desires and needs. And the result of this may not be a building or structure; it could just as easily be a piece of writing – a graphic novel for example – or online forums for discussion or education. In stressing architecture as an event or 'happening', Raumlaborberlin drew on the work of the Situationists in 1960s Paris, where public space was re-imagined as a site of action derived from individual and collective desires.

Raumlaborberlin's projects are mainly supported by public arts funding rather than private clients – for example, their Milton Keynes project was paid for by the town council. This reliance on arts funding clearly limits the scope and permanence of their projects (nearly all are temporary interventions), but it also gives the collective a freedom that most architects and urban planners often lack. The discussions and events that went on at the Utopia Station – on climate change and cities, shortages of resources, hyper-accelerated urban development and population growth – may be familiar ones in urban planning and architectural education and practice; yet, the fact that they took place in structures created in response to those very questions gave them added potency.[24] With the Utopia Station, Raumlaborberlin demonstrated that architecture can contribute to a participatory urbanism by being an incubator for it, its very conception and construction embodying the principles that are being nurtured in those that use it.

Assemble, Granby Four Streets, Liverpool, 2013–

Many of the volunteers who helped build Raumlaborberlin's early projects were architecture students. Some of these would be inspired to form their own collaborative and participatory practices, such as Assemble, founded in 2010 by 16 architecture graduates from the University of Cambridge. Their first project together was the Cineroleum – a temporary cinema housed in a derelict petrol station in the Clerkenwell district of inner London. Built by more than 50 volunteers using reclaimed or donated materials, this project was clearly indebted to Raumlaborberlin in its fusion of participatory building and a playful form of salvage. Assemble would replicate this method with their Folly for a Flyover, transforming another disused urban space in London (a motorway undercroft) into a new

General view of the Granby Four Streets, Liverpool, in July 2019

Interior of the winter garden on Cairns Street, completed in 2019 by Assemble

public space that was hand-built by 200 volunteers and disassembled after nine weeks, the materials being reused for a play area and garden at a local primary school. Yet, it was Assemble's involvement in the Granby Four Streets urban regeneration project in Liverpool that brought them international acclaim. Their work there was awarded the 2015 Turner Prize – the first architectural practice to win this prestigious art competition.[25]

The Granby Four Streets are the last remaining Victorian terraced houses in one of the UK's most deprived inner-city areas. Before Assemble were asked to become involved by HD Social Investments in 2013, residents of these streets had been actively resisting their slated demolition by Liverpool City Council. With a long history of systematic disinvestment and municipal neglect, particularly after the 1981 riots that protested police treatment of black residents, the Granby Four Streets saw the emergence of a grass-roots occupation of the terraces to prevent their demolition and the displacement of the community. This protest produced a melding of art and everyday life, in a similar way to the Claremont Road anti-roads protests in London in 1994. Boarded-up houses were painted with murals and adorned with ad-hoc sculptures, poems, and memorials to past residents, while 'guerrilla' gardens were created on the streets – planters and furniture blurring the boundaries between public and private space. The culmination of this was the creation of a community land trust in 2011, an attempt to secure the future of the area within this vision of an incremental, self-sustaining and community-led approach to the rehabilitation of housing, public space and the high street. The creation of the land trust also saw the widening of participation beyond the geographical borders of the community itself, drawing in both funds and new interest groups – a process that has not been without conflict.[26]

Ducie Street, one of the Granby Four Streets, in September 2019. Currently awaiting renovation, the houses still retain evidence of their occupation by local activists in the 1990s

As design consultants, Assemble have overseen the creation of a ceramics workshop in one building designated as a new community-owned space, the renovation of ten derelict houses on Cairns Street, and the completion of a winter garden within a terrace on the same street in 2019. Furnished with ceramics made in the workshop, the winter garden functions as a community space, artist's studio and cafe, the first artist-in-residence Nina Edge creating a striking glass chandelier that hangs from the roof. Prior to their intervention, the floors of the existing houses had collapsed, leaving behind interiors with exposed masonry. Instead of rebuilding these decayed floors, Assemble instead chose to leave them open, allowing the trees planted inside to grow eventually to full height. As stated by founding member of Assemble Anthony Egri, the garden is designed to 'nurture creative practice in the area' through both its spaces and its metaphorical associations with the abundance and fecundity of nature – a long-standing symbolism of winter gardens dating back to the late eighteenth century.[27]

Assemble embody an inherent contradiction in contemporary urbanism, namely that 'creative' forms of DIY urbanism tend to fill the gap left by the retreating state and the wealth of resources it potentially has to offer.[28] There's a strong sense of stasis in the Granby Four Streets, the deliberately incremental approach to redevelopment inevitably being a very slow process that seems so inefficient compared with the speed of privately led speculative building. In addition, the involvement of Assemble in the project was the result of private money coming from an enlightened 'mystery millionaire' – a former stockbroker from Jersey who formed HD Social Investments and actively sought out socially worthwhile projects to channel his capital into. These contradictions demonstrate that, however well-meaning participatory forms of building are and however much they grow out of grass-roots initiatives, they are nevertheless still dependent on funding from sources that are clearly embedded in the current system of speculative capitalism.

atelier d'achitecture autogérée, Agrocité, Gennevilliers, Paris, 2016–

Getting around the contradictions of capitalism is central to the work of Paris-based collective atelier d'achitecture autogérée (Studio for Self-Managed Architecture). Since 2001, this ever-changing group of architects, artists, urban planners, landscape designers, sociologists, students and residents have instigated a wide range of projects in Paris and other European cities, where the goal is to create a 'network of self-managed places' that build urban resilience in the light of threats such as climate change and ecological breakdown.[29]

In their first projects – the ECObox (2001–) and Passage 56 – abandoned spaces in Paris were repurposed for use by local residents. ECObox was first a temporary garden in La Chapelle, assembled from discarded wooden pallets and designed to be moved around to serve local needs, while Passage 56 has evolved into a community garden and informal meeting place for residents on the edge of the 20th *arrondissement*. Supplemented by other mobile facilities, such as a kitchen, library, media lab and DIY workshop, both projects embody aaa's ambitious strategy of creating a new kind of city based on a local circular economy and entirely built and maintained by residents themselves.[30]

The more recent Agrocité project, sited in Colombes, another suburb of Paris, from 2011 until its eviction in 2016, and more recently on a former car park in nearby Gennevilliers, is even more ambitious in its aims. Intended as just one element in a larger network of new forms of urban living, including self-built cooperative housing and recycling facilities for building materials, Agrocité embodies the hope that unsustainable patterns of consumption might be broken by a return to localized ways of growing food and handling wastes.[31] With around 200 volunteers and just one paid employee building and maintaining the project, Agrocité is currently a very

small-scale attempt at urban transformation and it sits in between the vast concrete tower blocks housing thousands that characterize the stigmatized suburban areas of Paris. Its principal building is a space for meetings, workshops and administration; its colourful salvaged windows and raw timber could not be more different from the monolithic concrete buildings that surround it. With work underway in 2019 to build an underground reservoir to collect grey water, Agrocité intends to become a waste-free site of production – a circular process that embodies the principles of the three 'R's – Reduce, Reuse, Recycle – that are widely used in urban waste management rhetoric but rarely implemented in a genuinely holistic way.

atelier d'achitecture autogérée (aaa) have been canny in finding loopholes in French planning law to get their projects off the ground. Moreover, by registering as a non-profit organization, they've been able to access public funds rather than relying on money from private clients. This has allowed them to implement a radical agenda of participatory design under the noses and with the sanction of officialdom. In contrast to more conventional forms of participation, where 'users' are consulted in a planning process that remains top-down in orientation, all the projects devised by aaa are, from the outset, self-managed by users. They are thus involved in every part of the planning and implementation of the projects, with designs evolving as decision-making negotiates a multiplicity of divergent opinions and desires.

Although Agrocité was initially welcomed and part-funded by the municipal authorities in Colombes, an election in 2014 brought in an unsympathetic mayor, who opposed citizen participation on the grounds that it sowed 'disorder' in the city – a clear attempt to stigmatize the project as anarchist. It was replaced with a car park in 2016 and Agrocité was forced to relocate to a much smaller site in Gennevilliers, when its mayor agreed to support the project.[32] Despite the ambitious transformative aims of R-Urban, small-scale projects like Agrocité are still dependent on the support of the hierarchical institutions and networks they are trying to replace.

However, at root, the tactics of aaa are not primarily concerned with winning over those in power; rather, they're about inspiring others to act in similar ways. In Paris, there are examples of recent attempts to reclaim spaces as urban commons, such as the currently illegal occupation of a patch of waste-ground outside the Père Lachaise cemetery. Opposing municipal plans to build more social housing, residents have occupied the land since November 2018, installing a range of makeshift structures that suggest, in embryonic form, a new kind of public use – for sport, gathering and food production – but which are still to be clearly defined.[33] And, on Sunday 22 September 2019, on the same weekend that a large area of central Paris was shut down by police in anticipation of yet another *Gilet Jaunes* march as well as a large-scale environmental protest, the city's fourth car-free day saw usually traffic-congested streets transformed into impromptu places of gathering – for music, cooking and place-making grounded in direct action. Employing tactics of surprise – quickly assembling mobile structures and barricades – activists were able to produce impromptu public spaces in just a few hours. These tactics may be temporary, and mostly small-scale, but brought together they suggest a growing movement of people that are willing to take back spaces for common purposes that may yet prove transformative.

Rear view of the community building at Agrocité in September 2019, designed by atelier d'achitecture autogérée

Agrocité, Gennevilliers, in September 2019, relocated here in 2016
after it was evicted from its original site in Colombes

Santiago Cirugeda, Recetas Urbanas, Seville, 2003–

Photograph of Santiago Cirugeda's Scaffolding project in Seville, illustrated in *Andalucía*, 22 June 1998

The Spanish architecture practice Recetas Urbanas (Urban Prescriptions), established by Santiago Cirugeda in 2003, believe that anyone can build. Straddling the often imprecise border between the legal and illegal, Recetas Urbanas combine architecture with activism, both designing and building structures and also advising community groups on how to get around planning regulations and raise money for their projects.[34] Although Recetas Urbanas was established before the global financial crisis of 2007–08, much of their work is a direct response to the catastrophic effects of that crisis in Spain. The collapse of the country's construction industry resulted in over half a million empty or unfinished buildings and a political regime of austerity that has seen the retreat of the state and very high youth unemployment. Like many other workers post-2008, architects in Spain have been forced to improvise in order to survive – with Recetas Urbanas leading a new drive to form a national (and, increasingly international) network of architectural collectives that can practise independently of the state and the neoliberal economy it supports.[35]

An early project, Scaffolding, from 1998, is indicative of Cirugeda's approach before he formed Recetas Urbanas. In a series of written instructions to residents of Seville, Cirugeda provided clear advice on how to build an additional room on a house without official permission. Using the pretext of cleaning up graffiti or some other disfigurement on a building, one could apply for permission to construct a temporary scaffold. Once this had been signed off by a willing architect, one could then build an extension illicitly before the official licence expired. And if the authorities forced you to remove it, one could simply repeat the process on another part of the building.[36] With the crisis of 2008 came an overtly political motive for such subversive activity – to fill the gap left by a retreating state. Since then, Recetas Urbanas's projects have become larger

Photomontage of one of Recetas Urbanas's Spider projects,
installed in a vacant plot in Seville in 2012

and much more wide ranging, including the provision of new school buildings in Barcelona and Madrid, the rescue of a dilapidated historic building neglected by the authorities in Seville, and the preservation of a cement factory in Los Santos de Maimon for use by artists. Their most eye-catching project was a group of spider-like structures built from 2009 onwards on vacant plots in the practice's home city of Seville.[37]

Most Recetas Urbanas projects depend on self-building in order to realise them – not only to save money in times of national austerity but also because community groups such as schools, artists' collectives, and charities want to be empowered to build for themselves. Operating at the very edge of legality – self-building isn't actually permitted anywhere in Spain – Recetas Urbanas work more like activists than professionals, studying the law as a pretext for getting around it. For example, in self-building

school buildings, otherwise illegal architectural projects can be justified for their educational value, thus putting them in a legal limbo that allows construction to go ahead. And building is usually very fast – materials like metal and timber beams and panels are easy and quick to assemble.

Rather than imposing design from above, Cirugeda and his colleagues make themselves available as facilitators for community-led projects, with design just one element in a host of processes that allow the projects to come to fruition. And although many have been developed against a background of continuing economic hardship and social crisis, they remain grounded in a playful subversion of existing codes and practices. This approach embodies the Situationists' practice of *détournement* (literally 'rerouting' or 'hijacking') that undermines a capitalist system from within. Recetas Urbanas do this precisely with planning laws and economic hardship that seem to place a stranglehold on subversive practices. Rather than waiting for the overturning of these oppressive conditions, Recetas Urbanas either simply ignore or subvert them, offering up their own solutions that make use of their expertise but also pass it on as a free resource to others. This is anarchist practice at its most radical – rooted in the here and now.

Constructing the School Grows project in Madrid in 2015, a self-built extension to the Madrid School of Design

STOP PRESS!
Antepavilion Police Raid No.2

At exactly 11 am on 25 June 2021, just as this book was going to press, around 100 police officers – spearheaded by the notorious strong arm of London's Metropolitan Police, the Territorial Support Group – stormed the premises of Antepavilion. It was the second such raid in a year. They broke through all locked doors and handcuffed everyone they found there, including White Cube artist Michael Armitage. Russell Gray, Company Secretary of the building owner, Shiva Ltd, one of his sons and two tenants of the building were arrested and taken to Kentish Town Police Station, where they were questioned and held overnight.

Gray was dragged from his stationary motorcycle and arrested for 'dangerous driving' as he arrived at Hoxton Docks. Those detained had their mobile phones confiscated, while back on site the police went through the building seizing bamboo poles, rigging wire, papers and a seemingly random selection of other items. The raid was nominally targeted at Extinction Rebellion activists, some of whom had attended tensegrity construction workshops at the Hoxton Docks site in the few weeks previously. These had focused on building lightweight mobile structures made from bamboo poles and steel wire cables. On the rooftop of the building were several linked towers rising through a 'cloud' of the same materials and construction techniques – an art installation titled *All Along the Watchtower*, designed by collective Project Bunny Rabbit. The installation echoed towers that Extinction Rebellion built at their protest sites in September 2020, particularly to blockade Broxbourne print-works in Hertfordshire. This was a protest at what Extinction Rebellion activists see as climate-change disinformation propagated through publications controlled by media mogul Rupert Murdoch.

The raid on the Antepavilion premises was part of a larger pre-emptive crackdown on Extinction Rebellion protesters; on the same day police also seized equipment and made arrests at two other sites in London, ahead of

CCTV footage of the police raid of Antepavilion's premises at Hoxton Docks, 25 June 2021

All Along the Watchtower – tensegrity structures made by Project Bunny Rabbit and installed on the rooftop of Hoxton Docks in June 2021

237

Police vehicles parked on Laburnum Street with *All Along the Watchtower* visible on the rooftop behind, 25 June 2021

Police officer guarding the entrance to Antepavilion's premises at Hoxton Docks, 25 June 2021

what they mistakenly feared would be disruptive protests in the capital. Extinction Rebellion said the raids were focused on people making art – an absurd overreaction on the part of the police. But it was an alarming one, reflecting the increasingly draconian approach towards activism involving public protest.

As for the raid on Antepavilion's premises, Gray emphasized that their hosting of the *All Along the Watchtower* project said nothing about the Extinction Rebellion cause. The tensegrity structure built on the roof of Hoxton Docks was just a striking example of the kind of installation that Antepavilion is all about – art meeting architecture. It demonstrates hands-on construction, craftsmanship and artistic freedom of expression that is the essence of the Antepavilion commission. The earlier towers built on the same principles were widely praised in the UK design press, being described by *Dezeen* columnist Phineas Harper as 'worthy contenders for the Stirling Prize', the UK's most prestigious annual architecture award.

That Antepavilion has been the target of two large-scale police raids in just one year demonstrates how high the stakes are becoming for those brave enough to challenge governmental control. 'Pro-active policing' means the authorities shutting-down anything they regard as even potentially capable of publicly challenging them – by extra-judicial means if necessary. To governments there is nothing sacred about art. The tensegrity towers built at the Antepavilion site were clearly an art installation, not weapons; the authorities' indifference to the distinction should worry us all.

Art and design have always had the potential to be a threat to those in power – to be suppressed should it become insubordinate. These events remind us how a liberal democracy like the post-Brexit Britain of Boris Johnson and Priti Patel is closer to embracing the concept of 'degenerate' art, evolved in Nazi Germany, than we all like to think. This book has celebrated those who do what they can to resist such creeping authoritarianism.

NOTES

PREFACE

1   See https://www.redbull.com/gb-en/theredbulletin/distdancing-dance-group.
2   See Bill Heine, *The Hunting of the Shark* (Oxford, 2011).
3   Quoted in Christopher Gray, 'The long hard fight to save the Headington shark', *Oxford Mail*, 24 August 2011, available at https://www.oxfordmail.co.uk/news/9213524.long-hard-fight-save-headington-shark/.
4   See http://www.headington.org.uk/shark/.
5   See https://antepavilion.org.
6   Correspondence and legal documents relating to Antepavilion can be accessed at https://antepavilion.org/hackney-fight.html.
7   The full judgement can be read at https://www.bailii.org/ew/cases/EWHC/QB/2020/2489.html.

INTRODUCTION

1   https://www.theguardian.com/commentisfree/2020/sep/22/donald-trump-has-a-grievance-against-new-york-and-it-tells-you-a-lot-about-his-presidency.
2   David Graeber, *Fragments of an Anarchist Anthropology* (Chicago, 2004). See also Robert Graham, ed., *Anarchism: A Documentary History of Libertarian Ideas*, 3 vols. (Montreal, 2005–12), vol. 1. Much of this thinking originated in Marcel Mauss's 1925 essay, 'The gift: forms and functions of exchange in archaic societies'.
3   See Pierre Joseph Proudhon, *What is Property? An Inquiry into the Principle of Right and of Government* (Scotts Valley, CA, 2015; original, 1840).
4   On Marxism and anarchism, see Paul Thomas, *Karl Marx and the Anarchists* (London, 1980).
5   See Marie Fleming, 'Propaganda by the deed: terrorism and anarchism in late nineteenth-century Europe', *Terrorism* 4 (1980), pp. 1–23.
6   See Leo Tolstoy, *The Kingdom of God is Within You* (London, 1894), a text which later had a profound impact on Mohandas K. Gandhi.
7   The most comprehensive guide to the range of practices associated with anarchism is Ruth Kinna, *The Government of No One: The Theory and Practice of Anarchism* (London, 2019).
8   Graeber, *Fragments of an Anarchist Anthropology*, p. 4.
9   As discussed in Simon Springer, *The Anarchist Roots of Geography: Toward Spatial Emancipation* (Minneapolis, MN, 2013), pp. 75–85.
10 On anarchism in Spain, see Frank Mintz, *Anarchism and Workers' Self-management in Revolutionary Spain* (AK Press, 2012).
11 Kinna, *Government of No One*, pp. 144–9.
12 See https://transitionnetwork.org.
13 Kinna, *Government of No One*, pp. 246–7. On the Rojava experiment, see Michael Knapp, Anja Flach and Ercan Ayboga, *Revolution in Rojava: Democratic Autonomy and Women's Liberation in Syrian Kurdistan* (London, 2016).
14 See Springer, *Anarchist Roots of Geography*.
15 Elisée Reclus, 'The history of cities' (1905), in John Clark and Camille Martin, eds., *Anarchy, Geography, Modernity: Selected Writings of Elisée Reclus* (Oakland, CA, 2013), pp. 163–85.
16 See Peter Kropotkin, *Fields, Factories and Workshops* (London, 1899).
17 See Patrick Geddes, *Cities in Evolution* (London, 1915). Geddes' 'biological' conception of cities is examined in Volker Welter, *Biopolis: Patrick Geddes and the City of Life* (Cambridge, MA, 2000).
18 Jane Jacobs, *The Death and Life of Great American Cities* (London, 2020; original, 1961), p. 12.
19 Richard Sennett, *The Uses of Disorder* (New York, 1970).
20 Charles Jencks and Nathan Silver, *Adhocism: the Case for Improvisation* (Cambridge, MA, 2013; original, 1972), p. 70.
21 See https://99percentinvisible.org/book/.
22 Paul Goodman, *Communitas: Means of Livelihood and Ways of Life* (Chicago, 1947).
23 A useful introduction to the wide range of Ward's writings can be found in Chris Wilbert and Damian F. White, eds., *Autonomy, Solidarity, Possibility: The Colin Ward Reader* (Chico, CA, 2011). See also Ward's own book *Anarchy in Action* (London, 1973) which brings together his abiding concerns.
24 Wilbert and White, *Autonomy, Solidarity, Possibility*, p. 84.
25 Colin Ward, *Cotters and Squatters: Housing's Hidden History* (Nottingham, 2002).
26 Dennis Hardy and Colin Ward, *Arcadia for All: The Legacy of a Makeshift Landscape* (Newton Abbott, 1984).
27 Colin Ward, *When we Build Again: Let's have the Housing that Works!* (London, 1985), pp. 27–45.
28 Springer, *Anarchist Roots of Geography*, pp. 85–6.
29 See Alfredo M. Bonanno, *Insurrectionalist Anarchism* (Trieste, 2007), available at http://theanarchistlibrary.org/library/alfredo-m-bonanno-insurrectionalist-anarchism.
30 See Murray N. Rothbard, *The Ethics of Liberty* (New York, 2003; original, 1982); and Robert Nozick, *Anarchy, State and Utopia* (Oxford, 2001).
31 See Kinna, *Government of No One*, p. 268.
32 The book is Jeremy Till, Nishwat Awan and Tatjana Schneider, *Spatial Agency: Other Ways of Doing Architecture* (Abingdon, 2011); the website is at https://www.spatialagency.net.
33 See Peter Blundell Jones, ed., *Architecture and Participation* (Abingdon, 2005).
34 Till, Awan and Schneider, *Spatial Agency*, p. 33.
35 Ibid., p. 32.
36 David Crouch and Colin Ward, *The Allotment: Its Landscape and Culture* (London, 1988).
37 Ruth Levitas, *Utopia as Method: The Imaginary Reconstitution of Society* (London, 2013).
38 Paul Dobraszczyk, *Future Cities: Architecture and the Imagination* (London, 2019), pp. 13–14.
39 Graeber, *Fragments of an Anarchist Anthropology*, p. 40.
40 Murray Bookchin, *The Ecology of Freedom: The Emergence and Dissolution of Hierarchy* (Chico, CA, 2005; original, 1985).
41 See also Murray Bookchin, *The Limits of the City* (New York, 1974).
42 Author's conversation with Tao Wimbush at Lammas in May 2019.
43 See https://www.london.gov.uk/sites/default/files/ecological_footprint.pdf.
44 David Harvey, *Rebel Cities: From the Right to the City to the Urban Revolution* (London, 2012), pp. 69–70.
45 Springer, *Anarchist Roots of Geography*, p. 165.
46 Murray Bookchin, *Urbanization without Cities: Rise and Fall of Citizenship* (Montreal, 1993).
47 Published as *Le Droit à La Ville* (Paris, 1968).

48 Harvey, *Rebel Cities*, pp. 22–3; and Peter Marcuse, 'From critical urban theory to the right to the city', *City* 13: 2–3 (2009), pp. 185–97.
49 Lefevbre, *Le Droit à La Ville*, p. 156.
50 See Kurt Iveson, 'Cities within the city: Do-it-yourself urbanism and the right to the city', *International Journal of Urban and Regional Research* 37: 3 (2013), pp. 941–56.
51 See Jeffrey Hou, 'Guerilla urbanism: urban design and the practices of resistance', *URBAN DESIGN International* 25 (2020), pp. 117–25.
52 Harvey, *Rebel Cities*, p. xvii.
53 See https://www.theguardian.com/housing-network/2015/dec/15/almere-dutch-city-alternative-housing-custom-build.
54 See https://www.mvrdv.nl/projects/32/almere-oosterwold.
55 Ursula K. Le Guin, *The Dispossessed* (London, 2000; original, 1974), p. 247.
56 David Harvey, 'The insurgent architect at work', in *Spaces of Hope* (Edinburgh, 2000), pp. 231–8.
57 Jeremy Till, *Architecture Depends* (Cambridge, MA, 2009), p. 192.

I. LIBERTY

1 The most extensive source on Christiania is H. Thoârn, C. Wasshede, and T. Nilson (eds), *Space for Urban Alternatives? Christiania, 1971–2011* (Gothenburg, 2013). See also the tourist leaflet *Christiania Guide*, available at https://www.christiania.org/wp-content/uploads/2013/02/Guideeng2.pdf.
2 This slogan was made popular after its use in the song 'I kan ikke slå os ihjel', composed by Tom Lundén and recorded by the group *Bifrost* for the compilation album *Christianiapladen* released in 1976 in support of the town.
3 See K. H. Koller, *Hundertwasserhaus, Wien* (Vienna, 1996); and Friedensreich Hundertwasser, *Hundertwasser Architecture: For a More Human Architecture in Harmony with Nature* (Cologne, 2018), pp. 190–214.
4 See Hundertwasser, *Hundertwasser Architecture,* and W. Schmied and A. Fuerst, *Hundertwasser's Complete Works: Collector's Edition* (Cologne, 2003) for the artists' other architectural projects.
5 See Hundertwasser, *Hundertwasser Architecture*, p. 36, for his remarks on modernist architecture.
6 Ibid., p. 198.
7 Peter Kraftl, 'Living in an artwork: the extraordinary geographies of the Hundertwasser-Haus, Vienna', *Cultural Geographies* 16 (2009), pp. 111–34; and 'Architectural movements, utopian moments: (in)coherent renderings of the Hundertwasser-Haus, Vienna', *Geografiska Annaler: Series B, Human Geography*, 92:4 (2010), pp. 327–35.
8 Kraftl, 'Architectural movements', p. 335.
9 See Robert Minor, *The Religious, the Spiritual,*

and the Secular: Auroville and Secular India* (Albany, NY, 1999); and the city's website at www.auroville.org.
10 On the architecture of Auroville, see Anapuma Kundoo, 'Auroville: an architectural laboratory', *Architectural Design* 2007, pp. 50–55; and John Mandeen, *Auroville Architecture: Towards New Forms for a New Consciousness* (Auroville, 2004).
11 Kundoo, 'Auroville: an architectural laboratory'.
12 Maddy Cowell, 'Trouble in Utopia', *Slate*, 24 July 2015, available at http://www.slate.com/articles/news_and_politics/roads/2015/07/auroville_india_s_famed_utopian_community_struggles_with_crime_and_corruption.html?via=gdpr-consent.
13 See Jennifer Raiser, *Burning Man: Art on Fire* (New York, 2016) for a lavishly illustrated overview of many of the artworks at Black Rock City.
14 On the history of Burning Man and its evolution, see Katherine K. Chen, *Enabling Creative Chaos: The Organisation Behind the Burning Man* (Chicago, 2009).
15 Nate Berg, 'Burning man and the metropolis: the public works of Black Rock City', *Places*, January 2011, https://placesjournal.org/article/burning-man-and-the-metropolis/.
16 On the philosophy of Burning Man and its global influence, see Neil Shister, *Radical Ritual: How Burning Man Changed the World* (Counterpoint, 2019); and Caveat Magister, *The Scene that Became Cities: What Burning Man Philosophy Can Teach Us About Building Better Communities* (New York, 2019). The ten principles can be found at the website of Burning Man at https://burningman.org/culture/philosophical-center/10-principles/.
17 Two excellent sources on Rainbow Gatherings are Chelsea Schely, *Crafting Collectivity: American Rainbow Gatherings and Alternative Forms of Community* (New York, 2014); and Michael Niman, *People of the Rainbows: A Nomadic Utopia* (New York, 1997).
18 See the website of the Rainbow Gatherings at http://www.welcomehome.org/rainbow/sites/0r97/rb097/basic2.html.
19 Schely, *Crafting Collectivity*, p. 8.
20 Kirsten C. Blinne and Tenali Hrenak, 'How Rainbow Gatherings work: (Dis)organization in small acts', in Andrew Hermann, ed., *Organizational Autoethnographies: Power and Identity in Our Working Lives* (New York, 2017), pp. 107–24.
21 Ibid., p. 112.
22 See, for example, Grace Wyler, 'The dark side of the Rainbow Gathering', *Vice*, 25 June 2014, https://www.vice.com/en_uk/article/gq8dy4/the-dark-side-of-the-rainbow-gathering.
23 The early history of the Kumbh Mela is explored in Kama Maclean's *Pilgrimage and Power: The Kumbh Mela in Allahabad, 1765–1954* (Oxford, 2008).
24 The research was published as Rahul

Mehrotra and Felipe Vera, eds., *Kumbh Mela: Mapping the Ephemeral Megacity* (Berlin, 2015). See also the project's website at http://kumbhmela2015mi.com.
25 Maclean, *Pilgrimage and Power*, pp. 27–33.
26 Mehrotra and Vera, *Kumbh Mela*, pp. 393–404; and Rahul Mehrotra, Feilpe Vera and José Mayorai, *Ephemeral Urbanism: Does Permanence Matter?* (Barcelona, 2017).
27 Julia Watson argues the case for low-tech solutions drawn from indigenous practices in *Lo-Tek: Design by Radical Indigensim* (London, 2019).
28 Nadine Anglin, *Slab City* (1997). See also the website https://slabcitystories.com for a more up-to-date account of the town's residents.
29 Charlie Hailey and Donovan White, *Slab City: Dispatches from the Last Free Place* (Cambridge, MA, 2018).
30 Philip Oltermann, 'The party city grows up: how Berlin's clubbers built their own urban village', *Guardian*, 30 April 2017, https://www.theguardian.com/cities/2017/apr/30/berlin-clubbers-urban-village-holzmarkt-party-city#img-1.
31 See https://www.huettenundpalaeste.de/work/holzmarkt-dorf/.

II. ESCAPE

1 Colin Ward and Dennis Hardy, *Arcadia for All: the Legacy of the Makeshift Landscape* (London, 1984).
2 Howard Marshall, 'The rake's progress', in Clough Williams-Ellis, ed., *Britain and the Beast* (London, 1937), p. 164.
3 See Lisa Goff, *Shantytown, USA: Forgotten Landscapes of the Working Poor* (Boston, 2016).
4 See Eve Blau, 'Learning To Live: 1919–1923', in *The Architecture of Red Vienna: 1919–1934* (Cambridge, MA, 1990).
5 Florian Urban, 'The hut on the garden plot: informal architecture in twentieth-century Berlin', *JSAH* 72: 2 (2013), pp. 221–49.
6 Charles Holland, 'Do It Ourself', conference paper presented at 'Government and housing in a time of crisis: policy, planning, design and delivery', AMPS, Architecture_MPS, Liverpool John Moores Uni, 8–9 Sept 2016.
7 Ward and Hardy, *Arcadia for All*, pp. 138–61.
8 For a comprehensive study of Nokken, see Tim Strange Jensen, Jun Philip Kamata and Line Thorup, 'Nokken – en klondike i systemet', 2010, Institut for Miljo, BA thesis.
9 Aliki Seferou, 'Nokken, Denmark's self-built wooden community,' *culture trip*, 8 March 2018, https://theculturetrip.com/europe/denmark/articles/nokken-denmarks-self-built-wooden-community/
10 April Anson, 'The world is my backyard: romanticization, Thoreauvian rhetoric, and constructive confrontation in the tiny house movement', in William G. Holt, ed., *From*

Sustainable to Resilient Cities: Global Concerns and Urban Efforts (Bingley, 2014), pp. 289–313.

11 See Carl Theodor Sørensen, 'Junk Playgrounds,' *Danish Outlook* 4:1 (1951), p. 314.

12 See John Bertelsen, 'Early experience from Emdrup', in Arvid Bengtsson, ed., *Adventure Playgrounds* (London, 1972), pp. 16–23.

13 Roy Kozlovsky, 'Adventure playgrounds and postwar reconstruction', in Marta Gutman and Ning de Conninck-Smith, eds, *Designing Modern Childhood: History, Space and the Material Culture of Children* (New Brunswick, NJ, 2008), pp. 171–90.

14 Colin Ward, 'Adventure playground: a parable of anarchy', *Anarchy* 7 (1961), pp. 193–201.

15 See Morgan Leichter-Saxby, *The New Adventure Playground Movement: How Communities Across the USA are Returning Risk and Freedom to Childhood* (London, 2015).

16 On post-1960s intentional communities in the USA, see Timothy Miller, *The 60s Communes: Hippies and Beyond* (Syracuse, NY, 1999); and Richard Fairfield, *Communes USA: A Personal Tour* (Baltimore, MD, 1972).

17 The most famous account of life in Drop City is resident Peter Douthit's book, written under the pseudonym Peter Rabbit, *Drop City* (New York, 1971).

18 See, respectively, Simon Sadler, 'Drop City revisited', *Journal of Architectural Education*, 59: 3 (2006), pp. 5–14; *Drop City* (Joan Grossman, 2012); and Mark Matthews, *Droppers: America's First Hippie Commune, Drop City* (Oklahoma City, 2010). Despite the title of T.C. Boyle's novel *Drop City* (London, 2004), it is in fact a caricature of another commune, Morning Star Ranch.

19 See Sadler, 'Drop City revisited', p. 12.

20 Steve Bauer, *Dome Cookbook* (Corrales, NM, 1968), p. 13.1.

21 See 'Drop City revisited', in Lloyd Khan and Bob Easton, *Shelter* (1973), p. 118; and William Yarnall, *Dome Builder's Handbook No. 2* (Philadelphia, 1978), p. 16.

22 See Cass Wester, "Steve Baer: the Plowboy interview," *Mother Earth News*, 22 (1973), http://www.motherearthnews.com/library/1973_July_August/The_Plowboy_Interview_Steve_Baer

23 See https://www.vanartgallery.bc.ca/the_exhibitions/exhibit_ken_lum.html for details of the exhibit.

24 See Alexander Vaseduvan, *The Autonomous City: A History of Urban Squatting* (London, 2017), pp. 184–202.

25 See Jean Walton, *Mudflat Dreaming: Waterfront Battles and the Squatters who Fought Them in 1970s Vancouver* (Vancouver, 2018).

26 See Rosemary Donegan, ed., 'Tom Burrows on squatting', *Borderlines* 1985, p. 10.

27 Yilin Wang, 'Finn Slough: an off-grid urban wilderness on the Fraser River', *theTyee.com*, 25 April 2015, available at https://thetyee.ca/Culture/2015/04/25/Finn-Slough-Off-Grid-Urban-Wilderness-Fraser-River/.

28 See Andrew Neef, 'ZAD battles thousands of police during attempted eviction of autonomous zone in France', *unicornriot*, 9 April 2018, https://unicornriot.ninja/2018/zad-battles-thousands-of-police-during-attempted-eviction-of-autonomous-zone-in-france/.

29 See Sonka Shuler, 'The Zone à Defendre of Notre-Dame-des-Landes in France: an ambivalent space for social critique', *Urbanities* 7: 1 (2017), p. 45.

30 See https://unicornriot.ninja/2017/greece-networks-resistance-part-1-zad-bure-hambach-forest/.

31 *Notre Dame des Luttes!* (Jean-Francois Castell, 2013), available at https://www.youtube.com/watch?time_continue=25&v=_Z0mfkeGp34. See also Oliver Ressler's more recent film *Everything's Coming Together While Everything's Falling Apart: The ZAD* (2017), available at https://vimeo.com/236277743.

32 The history of the ADM squat, and its eventual eviction, forms the subject of the independent documentary film *The (not yet) Lost Free-state* (2019), available at https://vimeo.com/showcase/5701040, 6 parts, created by local TV station AT5.

33 On the history of squatting in Amsterdam, see Nazima Kadir, *The Autonomous Life? Paradoxes of Hierarchy and Authority in the Squatters Movement in Amsterdam* (Manchester, 2016).

34 Former residents of ADM have set up a support and protest group 'WE are ADM' on Facebook, available at https://www.facebook.com/groups/WEareADM/.

35 *The (not yet) Lost Free-state* (AT5, 2019).

III. NECESSITY

1 The most important source on the *zone* is Jean-Louis Cohen and André Lortie's *Des Fortifs au Périf: Paris, Les Seuils de la Ville* (Paris, 1991). The most detailed in English is James Cannon, *The Paris Zone: A Cultural History, 1840–1944* (Farnham, 2015).

2 Atget's images of the *zone* were taken between 1910 and 1913 and published as part of two album projects of 60 photographs, each titled *Zoniers* and *Fortifications de Paris*.

3 On the Surrealists' response to the *zone*, see Ian Walker, *City Gorged with Dreams: Surrealism and Documentary Photography in Interwar Paris* (Manchester, 2002).

4 Cannon, *The Paris Zone*, p. 210.

5 See, for example, the 2019 documentary feature by Sputnik France, available at https://www.youtube.com/watch?v=LcdHkoGeOVs; and the 2018 news report 'Les oubliés du périphérique', available at https://www.youtube.com/watch?v=DIIYtyQW9cI.

6 Accounts of the Calais Jungle in both French and English are legion, but two excellent places to start are Michel Agier, et al.,

The Jungle: Calais's Camps and Migrants (Cambridge, 2019); and the edited collection *Voices from the 'Jungle': Stories from the Calais Refugee Camp* (London, 2017).

7 These drawings are reproduced in Agier, *The Jungle*, pp. 59, 63, 65, 67, 68.

8 See https://www.nbcnews.com/storyline/europes-border-crisis/banksy-dismaland-exhibition-houses-migrants-calais-jungle-n449856.

9 On the exhibit, see the architect's website at https://www.samjacob.com/portfolio/dar_abu_said/.

10 Quoted in Agier, *The Jungle*, p. 71.

11 See Anoma Pieris, *Architecture on the Borderline: Boundary Politics and Built Space* (Abingdon, 2019).

12 Chris Herring, 'Tent City, America', *Places*, December 2015, https://placesjournal.org/article/tent-city-america/?gclid=CjwKCAjwvOHzBRBoEiwA48i6Au1hgBzRJqN7rSRcipMvmjcPPYFcclK42Z-ActaRUI1ZP5S82FQfhxoC92sQAvD_BwE&cn-reloaded=1.

13 See Lisa Goff, *Shantytown, USA: Forgotten Landscapes of the Working Poor* (Cambridge, MA, 2016).

14 See https://dignityvillage.org for a history of the site. On the criminalization of the homeless in the US, see the National Law Center on Homelessness and Poverty's *No Safe Place: The Criminilization of Homeless and Poverty in US Cities* (Washington, DC, 2014).

15 See Susan Finley, 'The faces of dignity: rethinking the politics of homelessness and poverty in America', *International Journal of Qualitative Studies in Education*, 16:4 (2003), pp. 509–31.

16 Herring, 'Tent city, America'. See also www.tentcityurbanism.com.

17 The most well-known photographic account of the Walled City is Ian Lambot and Greg Girard's book *City of Darkness: Life in Kowloon Walled City* (Corby, 1993) which was republished in revised form in 2014. Documentaries include the German-language *Kowloon Walled City* released in 1988 and available at https://www.youtube.com/watch?v=S-rj8m7Ssow; and an Alan Whicker fronted BBC documentary aired in 1980, available at https://www.youtube.com/watch?v=JchVQMuxRVA.

18 On the history of Kowloon Walled City, see Elizabeth Sinn, 'Kowloon walled city: its origin and early history', *Journal of the Hong Kong Branch of the Royal Asiatic Society* 27 (1987), pp. 30–45; and Seth Harter, 'Hong Kong's dirty little secret: clearing the Walled City of Kowloon', *Journal of Urban History* 27: 1 (2000), pp. 92–112.

19 Many testimonies of residents are transcribed in Lambot and Girard, *City of Darkness*.

20 On the Kawasaki Warehouse, see Lambot and Girard, *City of Darkness*, pp. 215–16.

21 On afterimages of Kowloon Walled City, see

Alistair Fraser and Eva Cheuk-Yin Li, 'The second life of Kowloon Walled City: crime, media and cultural memory', *Crime Media Culture* 13: 2 (2017), pp. 217–34; and Lambot and Girard, *City of Darkness*, pp. 192–219.

22 See Martinh, 'In the shell of the old – Italy's social centres', *libcom* 11 March 2006, available at https://libcom.org/library/in-shell-old-italy-social-centres-wright; and Gabriella Kuruvilla, 'The biggest social centre in Europe', *abitare*, 31 July 2016, http://www.abitare.it/en/news-en/2016/07/31/the-biggest-social-centre-in-europe/.

23 Pierpaulo Mudu, 'Self-managed social centers and the right to urban space', in Isabella Clough-Marinaro and Bjørn Thomassen, eds. *Global Rome: Changing Faces of the Eternal City* (Bloomington, IA, 2014), pp. 246–64.

24 On the Autonomia movement, see Sylvère Lotringer and Christian Marazzi, eds., *Autonomia: Post-political Politics* (Los Angeles, 2007); and Steve Wright, *Storming Heaven: Class Composition and Struggle in Italian Autonomist Marxism* (London, 2002).

25 The book is available to download at https://www.forteprenestino.net/fortopia-il-libro/come-ottenerlo/ebook-fortopia.

26 See the website of Forte Prenestino at https://www.forteprenestino.net.

27 Sharon M., 'Occupied Rome. Where party revellers are world changers', romeing.it, 25 January 2014, https://www.romeing.it/occupied-rome-where-party-revellers-are-world-changers/.

28 Pierpaolo Mudu, 'Radical urban horticulture for food autonomy: beyond the community gardens experience', *Antipode* 50: 2 (2016), p. 567.

29 On the history of squatting in Barcelona, see Stephen Luis Vilaseca, *Barcelona Okupas: Squatter Power!* (Lanham, MD, 2013).

30 On the history of the Can Batlló and the background to the 2011 occupation, see David de la Peña, 'Beyond guerrilla urbanism: Can Batlló and the slowness of knowing, managing and making', *Urban Design International* 2019, pp. 1–11.

31 See the website of Can Batlló at https://www.canbatllo.org.

32 Peña, 'Beyond guerrilla urbanism'. As of March 2020, the extent of this municipal funding is in doubt as the city council had not yet allocated any of its budget to the continuation of the project.

33 G. Debelle et al., 'Squatting cycles in Barcelona: Identities, repression and the controversy of institutionalization', in Miguel A. Martínez López, ed., *The Urban Politics of Squatters' Movements* (New York, 2018), p. 68.

34 Ibid.

IV. PROTEST

1 See Charles Fager, *Uncertain Resurrection: The Poor People's Washington Campaign* (Grand Rapids, MN, 1969); and Gerald McKnight, *The Last Crusade: Martin Luther King, Jr., the FBI and the Poor People's Campaign* (New York, 1998).

2 See John Wiebenson, 'Planning and using Resurrection City', *Journal of the American Institute of Planners* 35: 6 (1969), pp. 405–11. Wiebenson was a member of Resurrection City's advisory committee on buildings and community.

3 Jill Freedman, *Old News: Resurrection City* (New York, 1970), pp. 71–2, 112.

4 See Robert T. Chase, 'Class Resurrection: the Poor People's Campaign of 1968 and Resurrection City', *Essays in History* 39 (1998), http://www.essaysinhistory.com/class-resurrection-the-poor-peoples-campaign-of-1968–and-resurrection-city/.

5 Freedman, *Old News*, pp. 1, 17–18.

6 Sources on the Greenham Common Women's Peace Camp are numerous, including many written by protestors themselves, such as Beth Junor's *Greenham Women's Peace Camp: A History of Non-Violent Resistance* (London, 1995), which brought together the personal diaries of several protestors. Other important accounts are Jill Liddington's *The Long Road to Greenham* (London, 1995); Sasha Roseneil's *Disarming Patriarchy: Feminism and Political Action at Greenham* (Milton Keynes, 1995); *Common Women, Uncommon Practices* (London, 2000); David Fairhall, *Common Ground: The Story of Greenham* (London, 2006). Amanda Richardson and Beeban Kidron's film *Carry Greenham Home* (1983) was probably the first first full-length documentary of a protest camp.

7 See Fairhall, *Common Ground*, pp. 44–47.

8 Sarah Hipperson, *Greenham, Non-violent Women v. The Crown Prerogative* (2005).

9 See Anna Feigenbaum, Fabian Frenzel and Patrick McCurdy, eds., *Protest Camps* (London, 2013), pp. 136–8.

10 The Newbury bypass protests were the largest of many anti-roads protests in the 1990s and were documented in Jamie Lowe's 2018 film *Tales of Resistance: The Battle of the Newbury Bypass.*

11 See George McKay, ed., *DiY Culture: Party & Protest in Nineties Britain* (London, 1998). See also the UK-produced pamphlet *Road Raging*, available at http://www.eco-action.org/rr/index.html.

12 Hank Chapot, 'Tree-sitting, since 1930', *Berkeley Daily Planet*, 26 June 2008, http://www.berkeleydailyplanet.com/issue/2008–06–26/article/30396?headline=Tree-Sitting-Since-1930.

13 See Merrick, *Battle for the Trees* (London, 1996) which documents the life of a protestor at the Newbury anti-roads camp.

14 Andy Griffiths and Terry Denton, *The 104–Storey Treehouse* (London, 2018). The first book in the series was published in 2011.

15 On the origins and development of Grow Heathrow, see Nicholas Ferguson, 'Dwelling as resistance', *Places*, September 2019, https://placesjournal.org/article/dwelling-as-resistance/?cn-reloaded=1.

16 Updates on the site can be found at https://www.facebook.com/transitionheathrow/.

17 For views inside the homes, see Jonathan Goldberg's photographs included in Alexandra Genova, 'Inside the off-the-grid ecovillage fighting London's airport expansion', *National Geographic,* 19 Sept 2018, https://www.nationalgeographic.com/culture/2018/09/heathrow-airport-protest-off-the-grid-community-england/.

18 Sources on the Arab Spring are numerous, but useful overviews are Paul Danahar, *The New Middle East: The World After the Arab Spring* (London, 2015); and Robert F. Worth, *A Rage for Order: The Middle East in Turmoil, from Tahrir Square to ISIS* (London, 2017).

19 Accounts of the events in Tahrir square include Ashraf Khalil's *Liberation Square: Inside the Egyptian Revolution and the Rebirth of a Nation* (London, 2014); and Steven A. Cook, *The Struggle for Egypt: From Nasser to Tahrir Square* (Oxford, 2012).

20 See Nabil Kamel, 'Tahrir Square: the production of insurgent space and eighteen days of utopia', *Progressive Planning* 191 (2012), pp. 36–40.

21 Ibid., pp. 38–39.

22 Rebecca Solnit, *A Paradise Built in Hell: The Extraordinary Communities that Arise in Disaster* (London, 2009).

23 For a map of the protest sites, see Simon Rogers, 'Occupy protests around the world: full list visualised', *Guardian*, 14 November 2011, https://www.theguardian.com/news/datablog/2011/oct/17/occupy-protests-world-list-map?newsfeed=true.

24 See Heather Gautney, 'Occupy x: repossession by occupation', *South Atlantic Quarterly* 111: 3 (2012), pp. 599–600.

25 Quoted in Feigenbaum, Frenzel and McCurdy, *Protest Camps*, p. 40.

26 First-hand accounts by participants at Zuccotti Park can be found in Lenny Flank's *Voices from the 99 Percent: an Oral History of the Occupy Wall Street Movement* (New York, 2011).

27 Stavros Stavrides, *Common Space: The City as Commons* (London, 2016), pp. 159–80.

28 On the privatization of public spaces in Hong Kong, see A. Cuthbert and K. McKinnell, 'Ambiguous space, ambiguous rights – corporate power and social control in Hong Kong', *Cities* 14: 5 (1997), pp. 295–311.

29 See Joyce Lau, 'Art spawned by Hong Kong protest: now to make it live on', *The New York Times*, 14 November 2014, https://www.nytimes.com/2014/11/15/world/asia/rescuing-protest-artwork-from-hong-kongs-streets.html. Although much of the artwork was destroyed by the authorities, the Umbrella Movement Art Preservation and the Umbrella Movement Visual Archive and Research Collective have worked together to preserve and document as much of it as they are able.

30 Daniel Matthews, 'Narrative, space and atmosphere: a nomospheric inquiry into Hong Kong's pro-democracy '"Umbrella Movement"', *Social & Legal Studies* 26: 1 (2017), pp. 25–46.

31 See https://rebellion.earth/the-truth/about-us/ for a summary of the movement's history and aims. XR have also published a best-selling 'guidebook' to civil disobedience *This is Not a Drill: An Extinction Rebellion Handbook* (London, 2019).

32 See Ben Smoke, 'Extinction Rebellion protestors who want to be arrested: be careful what you wish for', *Guardian*, 15 April 2019, https://www.theguardian.com/commentisfree/2019/apr/15/extinction-rebellion-protesters-arrested-stansted-15.

33 See Wretched of the Earth, 'An open letter to Extinction Rebellion', *red pepper*, 3 May 2019, available at https://www.redpepper.org.uk/an-open-letter-to-extinction-rebellion/; and Leah Cowan, 'Are Extinction Rebellion whitewashing climate justice?', *Gal-Dem*, 18 April 2019, http://gal-dem.com/extinction-rebellion-risk-tramplingclimate-justice-movement/. The XR book *This is Not a Drill*, published in June 2019, has explicitly addressed some of these criticisms.

V. ECOLOGY

1 The most thorough account of Street Farm is Stephen E. Hunt's *The Revolutionary Urbanism of Street Farm: Eco-Anarchism, Architecture and Alternative Technology in the 1970s* (Bristol, 2014). The Street Farmhouse was also built before the New Alchemy Institute (1971–91) built their first 'bioshelter', the Mini-Ark, in 1973.

2 *Street Farmer 1* was produced as a number of unbound pages in a cellophane bag and is only available in private collections. The full edition of *Street Farmer 2*, published in 1972, has been scanned and uploaded to Flickr by Stefan Szczelkun at https://www.flickr.com/photos/stefan-szczelkun/albums/7215762340436519.

3 Hunt, *The Revolutionary Urbanism of Street Farm*, p. 53.

4 See Lydia Kallipoliti, 'From shit to food: Graham Caine's eco-house in South London, 1972–1975', *Buildings & Landscapes* 19: 1 (2012), pp. 87–107.

5 'The house that grows', *Garden News*, 5 May 1972.

6 Caine's diagram was published in Stefan Szczelkun's *Survival Scrapbook, vol. 5: Energy* (Bristol, 1975).

7 Quoted in Kallipoliti, 'From shit to food', p. 104.

8 Quoted in *Clearings in the Concrete Jungle*. I'm grateful to Stephen E. Hunt for pointing this out to me.

9 See Timothy Miller, *The 60s Communes: Hippies and Beyond* (Syracuse, NY, 1999).

10 On the history and spiritual vision of the Lama Foundation, see https://www.lamafoundation.org/wp-content/uploads/2016–Lama-Alive.pdf.

11 On alternative communities and communes in New Mexico, see Carolyn C. Bennett's 'Alternative communities', available at http://online.nmartmuseum.org/assets/files/Maps/AlternativeCommunities.pdf.

12 On Baer's post-Drop City zomes, see Emily Silver, 'Manera Nueva, 1967–73', available at http://albuquerquemodernism.unm.edu/wp/manera-nueva-placitas/.

13 Almost impossible to source now in print, 11 pages of one edition of Baer's *Dome Cookbook* have been uploaded to https://november-books.blogspot.com/search?q=dome+cookbook.

14 See Simon Sadler, 'An architecture of the whole', *Journal of Architectural Education* (2008), pp. 108–29.

15 The new structures are documented in Oliver Croy and Oliver Elser's 2015 film *Counter Communities*, available at https://vimeo.com/127812338.

16 See https://www.earthshipglobal.com. In addition to running courses and acting as a consultant on many earthship projects around the world, Reynolds has also published widely with his own press in Taos, Solar Survival Architecture. See, for example, *Earthship: How to Build Your Own* (1990).

17 The Brighton earthship is the focus of Mischa Hewitt and Kevin Telfer's book *Earthships: Building a Zero Carbon Future for Homes* (Bracknell, 2007). A personal story of building an earthship is Alex Leeor's *Earthship Chronicles* (2019).

18 See, for example, Mischa Hewitt and Kevin Telfner, *Earthships in Europe* (Bracknell, 2012), p. 48.

19 Hewitt and Telfer, *Earthships* (2007), p. 78.

20 On the history and architecture of the Open City, see Rodrigo Perez de Arce, Fernando Perez Oyarzun, and Paul Rispa, *Valparaiso School: Open City Group* (Basel, 2003); and Ann M. Pendleton-Julian, *The Road that is not a Road and the Open City, Ritoque, Chile* (Cambridge, MA, 1996).

21 Over 200 individual projects for the Open City are listed in Rispa's *Valparaiso School*. Many are illustrated on the Open City's website at http://www.amereida.cl/Obras.

22 Charles Jencks and Nathan Silver, *Adhocism: the Case for Improvisation* (Cambridge, MA, 2013; original, 1972).

23 See the website of the community at http://landmatters.org.uk.

24 See Simon Farlie, *Low Impact Development: Planning and People in a Sustainable Countryside* (Oxford, 1996).

25 See the short film *Living in the Future: Part 11* (2007), available at http://livinginthefuture.org/episodes/11–land-matters.php.

26 See https://transitionnetwork.org/about-the-movement/what-is-transition/; and Rob Hopkins, *The Transition Handbook* (Totnes, 2008).

27 See http://lammas.org.uk/en/welcome-to-lammas/ for information on the community. Founding member Tao (Paul) Wimbush also recounts the history of Lammas in his book *Birth of an Ecovillage: Adventures in an Alternative World* (2012).

28 See Simon Dale's website 'Being Somewhere', http://www.simondale.net/index.htm.

29 A dozen or so sites in Wales, including Lammas, are documented in Mark Wighorn's MPhil thesis 'An investigation into the process of making do in ad hoc self-builds in rural Wales', Cardiff University, 2016. They include the largest, Tipi Valley, established in the 1970s and home to around 150 people, and the Brithdir Mawr eco-community close to Lammas, from which some of its members originated.

30 See Jana Wendler, 'Grassroots experimentation: alternative learning and innovation in the Prinzessinnengärten, Berlin' in James Evans, Andrew Karonen and Rob Raven, eds., *The Experimental City* (Abingdon, 2016), pp. 150–62.

31 On the building of The Arbour, see the short film at https://vimeo.com/234206237 and Clausen's blog post at https://prinzessinnengarten.net/home/blog/page/5/

32 See Marco Clausen, 'Urban agriculture between pioneer use and urban land grabbing: the case of Prinzessinnengarten, Berlin', *Cities and the Environment* 8: 2 (2015).

33 See Florian Urban, 'The hut on the garden plot: informal architecture in twentieth-century Berlin', *Journal of the Society of Architectural Historians* 72: 2 (2013), pp. 221–49.

34 On Teepee Land, see http://facesofberlin.org/in-a-teepee-on-the-spree/; on Kotti & Co., see https://kottiundco.net; on the YAAM, see https://www.yaam.de.

35 See https://www.casagrandelaboratory.com/portfolio/ruin-academy/.

36 Marco Casagrande, *Biourban Acupuncture: Treasure Hills of Taipei to Artena* (Rome, 2013), p. 11.

37 Ibid., p. 7.

38 See. See https://www.casagrandelaboratory.com/portfolio/ruin-academy/. In response to the first workshop, the Ruin Academy published two editions of its own magazine *The Anarchist Gardener*, issue 1 available at https://issuu.com/ruin-academy/docs/anarchist_gardener_issue_one.

VI. ART

1   Recounted in James Attlee, 'Towards Anarchitecture: Gordon Matta-Clark and Le Corbusier', *Tate Papers* 7 (2008), p. 16, https://www.tate.org.uk/research/publications/tate-papers/07/towards-anarchitecture-gordon-matta-clark-and-le-corbusier.

2   The many book-length sources on Matta-Clark's work include: Pamela M. Lee, *Object to be Destroyed: the Work of Gordon Matta-Clark* (Cambridge, MA, 2000); Corrine Diserens, ed., *Gordon Matta-Clark* (London, 2003); Stephen Walker, *Gordon Matta-Clark: Art, Architecture and the Attack on Modernism* (London, 2009); Mark Wigley, *Cutting Matta-Clark: The Anarchitecture Investigation* (Zürich, 2016); and Frances Richard, *Gordon Matta-Clark: Physical Poetics* (Los Angeles, 2019).

3   See Attlee, 'Towards anarchitecture'; and Wigley, *Cutting Matta-Clark*.

4   Quoted in Attlee, 'Towards Anarchitecture', p. 22.

5   See *Folke Köbberling and Martin Kaltwasser: City as a Resource* (Berlin, 2006); and *Hold it! The Art & Architecture of Public–Space–Bricolage–Resistance–Resources–Aesthetics of Folke Koebberling and Martin Kaltwasser* (Berlin, 2009). A full list of works by the duo can be found on their website at http://www.koebberlingkaltwasser.de/works.html.

6   On Istanbul's *gecekondu*, see Sebnem Eroglu, *Beyond the Resources of Poverty: Gecekondu Living in the Turkish Capital* (Abingdon, 2016).

7   Michael Braungart and William McDonough, *Cradle to Cradle: Remaking the Way we Make Things* (New York, 2002).

8   The most comprehensive account of the House of Mirrors is Gregg Blasdel, 'House of Mirrors: Clarence Schmidt', *Raw Vision* 56 (2004), pp. 24–31 ; see also http://spacesarchives.org/explore/collection/environment/journeys-end-house-of-mirrors-mark-11-silver-forest/ for additional sources on Schmidt, and also http://www.historicalsocietyofwoodstock.org/clarence-schmidt.

9   Roger Cardinal, 'The vulnerability of outsider architecture', *Southern Quarterly* 39: 1 (2000), pp. 169–87.

10 Ibid., p. 173. The most comprehensive global survey of outside architecture (termed 'art environments') to date is the SPACES website at http://spacesarchives.org.

11 Allan Kaprow, *Assemblage, Environments and Happenings* (New York, 1966), pp. 170–72.

12 Cardinal, 'The vulnerability of outsider architecture', p. 181.

13 See Robert Haney and David Ballantine, *Woodstock Handmade Houses* (New York, 1974). I am grateful to Gerry Straathof for bringing this book to my attention.

14 Boudicca Fox-Leonard, '"Some people get married, or a mortgage. I do this"': Meet the man pulling a raft from Liverpool to London', *Telegraph*, 1 May 2017, https://www.telegraph.co.uk/health-fitness/body/people-get-married-mortgage-do-meet-man-pulling-raft-liverpool/.

15 See Matt Fidler, 'Shed of the year 2018 shortlist – in pictures', *Guardian*, 15 August 2018, https://www.theguardian.com/uk-news/gallery/2018/aug/15/shed-of-the-year-2018–shortlist-in-pictures.

16 Spike Lee's documentary *When the Levee Broke: A Requiem in Four Acts* (2006) was an award-winning production aired on HBO in August 2006. The HBO series *Treme* (2010–13) focused on the lives of black residents in the Tremé district post-Katrina.

17 See the website of the Art House at https://1614esplanade.weebly.com.

18 Sarah Chase, 'NOLA Art house & insane treehouse listed for $475k', *Curbed New Orleans*, 27 Jan 2014, https://nola.curbed.com/2014/1/27/10150682/the-nola-art-house-its-insane-treehouse-just-listed-for-475k.

19 See Hazel Denart, 'Deconstructing disaster: economic and environmental impacts of deconstruction in post-Katrina New Orleans', *Resources, Conservation and Recycling* 54: 3 (2010), pp. 194–204.

20 Shannon Lee Dawdy, 'The taphonomy of disaster and (re)formation of New Orleans', *American Anthropologist* 108: 4 (2006), pp. 719–30.

21 On the decline of Detroit, see Thomas J. Sugrue, *The Origins of the Urban Crisis: Race and Inequality in Postwar Detroit* (New York, 1996).

22 A comprehensive account of recent arts projects in Detroit is Michael Arnaud, *Detroit: The Dream Is Now: The Design, Art, and Resurgence of an American City* (Detroit, 2017).

23 See the website of the project at https://www.heidelberg.org.

24 See M. H. Miller, 'Tyree Guyton turned a Detroit street into a museum. Why is he taking it down?', *New York Times*, 9 May 2019, https://www.nytimes.com/2019/05/09/magazine/tyree-guyton-art-detroit.html.

25 On Gates's gallery art, see *Theaster Gates: My Labor is my Protest* (London, 2013).

26 Gates's work is included in the broad survey of socially engaged art by Nato Thompson, *Living as Form: Socially Engaged Art from 1991–2011* (New York, 2012).

27 Kathleen Reinhardt, 'Theaster Gates's Dorchester Projects in Chicago', *Journal of Urban History* 41: 2 (2015), pp. 193–206.

28 See Hesse McGraw, 'Theaster Gates: radical reform with everyday tools', *Afterall* 30 (2012), p. 94. In 2009, Gates created an artwork in St Louis that was a direct response to the legacy of Matta-Clark.

29 Reinhardt, 'Theaster Gates', p. 202.

30 Marina Vishmidt, 'Mimesis of the hardened and alienated: social practice as business model', *E-flux* 43: 3 (2013), https://www.e-flux.com/journal/43/60197/mimesis-of-the-hardened-and-alienated-social-practice-as-business-model/.

VII. SPECULATION

1   The most significant books on New Babylon are Mark Wigley, *Constant's New Babylon: The Hyper-Architecture of Desire* (Rotterdam, 1998); Catherine de Zegher, ed., *The Activist Drawing: Retracing Situationist Architectures from Constant's New Babylon to Beyond* (Cambridge, MA, 2001); and Pascal Gielen, Laura Stamps, Willemjin Stokvis, Trudy van Der Horst, and Mark Wigley, *Constant: New Babylon: To Us, Liberty* (Berlin, 2016).

2   An introduction to the collection can be found at https://www.kunstmuseum.nl/en/collections/constant-new-babylon.

3   See, for example, Daniel Susskind, *A World Without Work: Technology, Automation and How we Should Respond* (London, 2020); and John Danaher, *Automation and Utopia: Human Flourishing in a World Without Work* (Cambridge, MA, 2019).

4   On the *Whole Earth Catalog*, see Andrew Kirk, *Counterculture Green: The Whole Earth Catalog and American Environmentalism* (Lawrence, KS, 2007).

5   Godfrey Boyle and Peter Harper, eds., *Radical Technology* (London, 1976).

6   Ibid., p. 166.

7   Simon Sadler, 'Design's ecological operating environments' in Kjetil Fallan, ed., *The Culture of Nature in the History of Design* (New York, 2019), pp. 19–30.

8   See Rick Watson, 'Living together 4: how to turn a row of terraced houses into a housing co-op', *noncorporate*, 1 August 2019, available at https://www.noncorporate.org/living-together-4-how-to-turn-a-row-of-terraced-houses-into-a-housing-co-op/; and 'Fireside Housing Co-op', https://www.diggersanddreamers.org.uk/communities/existing/fireside-housing-co-op.

9   William Gibson, *Virtual Light* (London, 1994), p. 58.

10 Ibid., p. 163.

11 See Amy Frearson, 'Megalomania by Jonathan Gales', *dezeen*, 7 March 2012. Available at https://www.dezeen.com/2012/03/07/megalomania-by-jonathan-gales/.

12 On architectural incompletion as ruins, see Paul Dobraszczyk, *The Dead City: Urban Ruins and the Spectacle of Decay* (London, 2017), pp. 189–213.

13 These earlier projects are illustrated in *Lebbeus Woods: Anarchitecture – Architecture is a Political Act* (London, 1992).

14 Lebbeus Woods, *Radical Reconstruction* (New York, 2004), p. 21.

15 Alexandra Overby and Brian L Jones, 'Virtual LEGOs: incorporating Minecraft into the art education curriculum', *Art Education* 68: 1 (2015), pp. 21–7.

16 See, for example, Kim O'Connell, 'Minecraft architecture: what architects can learn from a video game', *redshift* 2 Feb 2016, https://

www.autodesk.com/redshift/minecraft-architecture/.

17 See https://www.blockworks.uk.
18 See https://www.youtube.com/watch?v=pyNGDWnmXoU for the film.
19 Charles Leadbeater, *We-Think: Mass Innovation not Mass Production* (London, 2008).
20 Carlo Ratti et al, *Open-Source Architecture* (London, 2015).
21 Ibid., p. 30.
22 See https://en.wikipedia.org/wiki/Open-source_architecture as of 13 February 2020.
23 https://en.wikipedia.org/wiki/Open-source_architecture as of 13 February 2020.
24 See https://www.wikihouse.cc/Projects.
25 See https://www.urbanvillageproject.com.
26 See https://www.hassellstudio.com/project/xinqiao-open-source-city#0.
27 The full portfolio of the project can be viewed at https://issuu.com/akcm/docs/an_activist_artefact__a3_short_port.
28 See https://issuu.com/akcm/docs/dilemma_studio__2020.

VIII. PARTICIPATION

1 On de Carlo's work, see Benedict Zucchi, *Giancarlo de Carlo* (Oxford, 1992).
2 On the early work of Team X/Team 10, see Annie Pedret, *Team 10: An Archival History* (Abingdon, 2013).
3 Published as Giancarlo de Carlo, 'Il pubblico dell'architectura' ('Architecture's public'), *Parametro* 5 (1970). The lecture was also republished as the first chapter in Peter Blundell-Jones, Doina Petrescu and Jeremy Till, eds., *Architecture and Participation* (Abingdon, 2005), pp. 3–22.
4 de Carlo, 'Architecture's public'.
5 See Zucchi, *Giancarlo de Carlo*, pp. 106–14.
6 See Giancarlo de Carlo, *An Architecture of Participation* (Melbourne, 1972). On de Carlo's early plan for Urbino, see Giancarlo de Carlo, *Urbino: the History of a City and Plans for its Development* (Cambridge, MA, 1970; original, 1966); on the built projects, see Zucchi, *Giancarlo de Carlo*, pp. 42–103.
7 Zucchi, *Giancarlo de Carlo*, p. 125.
8 Lucien Kroll, *The Architecture of Complexity*. Trans. Peter Blundell Jones (Tiptree, 1986). See also Peter Blundell Jones, 'Sixty-eight and after', in Blundell Jones, Petrescu and Till, *Architecture and Participation*, pp. 134–36; and Lucien Kroll, 'Animal town planning and homeopathic architecture', pp. 183–86.
9 See John Habraken, *Supports: An Alternative to Mass Housing* (London, 1972; original, 1962).
10 Kroll, *The Architecture of Complexity*, pp. 48–9.
11 Ibid., p. 44.
12 See John McKean, *Learning from Segal: Walter Segal's Life, Work and Influence*. Trans. Olinde Riege (Basel, 1988).

13 Colin Ward, 'Walter Segal – community architect', available at http://www.segalselfbuild.co.uk/news/waltersegalbycol.html.
14 See Alice Grahame and Taran Wilkhu, *Walters Way & Segal Close* (Bristol, 2017).
15 See https://archtype.co.uk and http://jonbroome.co.uk.
16 See https://www.theruss.org/about/ for more details about the RUSS.
17 On the Bauhäusle, see Peter Blundell Jones, 'Student self-build in Stuttgart', *Architects Journal*, 27 July 1983, pp. 32–50; and Norbert Haustein and Thomas Pross, *Bauhäusle* (Basel, 1986).
18 See Peter Sulzer, 'Notes on participation', in *Architecture and Participation*, pp. 150–60.
19 See Alice Grahame, 'A playground for grown up kids': inside the student housing built by its residents', *Guardian*, 26 November 2018, https://www.theguardian.com/cities/2018/nov/26/a-playground-for-grown-up-kids-inside-the-student-housing-built-by-its-residents-bauhausle-stuttgart.
20 Colin Ward, *Talking Schools* (London, 1995), available at https://libcom.org/library/talking-schools-colin-ward.
21 Author's interview with student Clemens Mackensen in September 2019.
22 The festival brief, and calls for proposals, can be downloaded at http://raumlabor.net/wp-content/uploads/2019/02/afcul2019_crossroads.pdf.
23 See George Kafka, 'How a DIY Floating University in Berlin could be an unorthodox prototype for design education', *Metropolis*, 4 October 2018.
24 See http://raumlabor.net/floating-university-berlin-an-offshore-campus-for-cities-in-transformation/.
25 On the work of Assemble, see Angelika Fitz and Katharina Ritter, *Assemble: How we Build* (London, 2017) and their website https://assemblestudio.co.uk. On the Granby Four Streets project, see Assemble, *The Granby Four Streets* (Liverpool, 2013).
26 See Matthew Thompson, 'Between boundaries: from commoning and guerrilla gardening to community land trust development in Liverpool', *Antipode* 47: 4 (2015), pp. 1021–42.
27 See Lizzie Crook, 'Assemble transforms two derelict houses in Granby Winter Garden', *Dezeen*, 26 April 2019.
28 Frank Tonkiss, 'Austerity urbanism and the makeshift city', *City* 17: 3 (2013), pp. 312–24.
29 The work of aaa is documented on their website www.urbantactics.org.
30 See Doina Petrescu and Constantin Petcou, 'Tactics for a transgressive practice', *Architectural Design* 226 (2013), pp. 58–65.
31 For a comprehensive overview of the Agrocité and R-Urban's other projects, see Doina Petrescu and Atelier d'Architecture Autogérée, *R-Urban: A Participative Strategy of Urban*

Resilience (2015). Available at http://eprints.whiterose.ac.uk/98555/1/Rurban_Act_V2.pdf.
32 Author's interview with Nadia and Clarissa at Agrocité, Gennevilliers, 20 September 2019.
33 See http://www.naturerights.com/blog/?p=3062.
34 A full overview of their projects can be found at http://www.recetasurbanas.net/.
35 This project, documented at https://arquitecturascolectivas.net, currently includes practices in Spain, France, Italy, China, Mexico, Ecuador, Colombia, Brazil, Argentina and the USA.
36 See http://www.recetasurbanas.net/index1.php?idioma=ENG&REF=1&ID=0003 for the list of instructions. The practice's early projects are also illustrated in the exhibition catalogue *Urban Disobedience: The Work of Santiago Cirugeda* (New York, 2007).
37 The short film *Guerrilla Architect*, broadcast by Al Jazeera in 2014, provides an overview of these more recent projects. Available at https://www.aljazeera.com/programmes/rebelarchitecture/2014/06/spain-guerrilla-architect-20146299334895983.html.

STOP PRESS!

1 See https://www.dezeen.com/2021/06/26/antepavilion-police-raid-staff-arrested-london/.
2 https://www.theguardian.com/environment/2021/jun/26/12-arrested-raids-extinction-rebellion-london-protest.
3 https://www.dezeen.com/2020/09/16/extinction-rebellions-high-tech-stirling-prize/.

INDEX

This index is in alphabetical, word by word order. It does not include the Acknowledgements, Notes or Photographic Credits. Location reference is to page number. Illustrations are given in italics and follow the text page number, from which they are separated by a semi-colon.

ISBN 978-1-913645-17-5

British Library Catalogue in Publishing Data

A CIP record of this publication is available from the British Library

Produced by Paul Holberton Publishing
89 Borough High St, London SE1 1NL
PAULHOLBERTON.COM

Designed by Laura Parker
Printed by Gomer Press, Llandysul, Wales

Front cover: Perspective view of the connecting units of New Babylon, 1960
Back cover: Night-time view of the first Hausbau, 2004

PHOTOGRAPHIC CREDITS

The author and publishers wish to express their thanks to the below sources of illustrative material and/ or permission to reproduce it. Every effort has been made to contact copyright holders; should there be any we have been unable to reach or to whom inaccurate acknowledgements have been made, please contact the publishers, and full adjustments will be made to any subsequence printings.

All photographs ©Paul Dobraszczyk unless otherwise stated

p. 2 Non à l'aéroport Notre-Dame-des-Landes, Flickr CC; p. 7 Allan Henderson, Flickr CC; p. 10 Martin Kaltwasser and Folke Köbberling; p. 6 ©Antepavilion; p. 32 Dietmar Rabich, Flickr CC; p. 33 Thomas Ledl, Wikimedia CC; p. 34 Wikimedia CC; p. 35 Matthew T Rader, Wikimedia CC; p. 36 Kaspar Konrad, Wikimedia CC; p. 37 Ellie Pritts, Wikimedia CC; p. 38 Steve Jurvetson, Wikimedia CC; p. 39 Andrew Fresh, Wikimedia CC; pp. 40–41 Wikimedia CC; pp. 42-43, 45 Seba Della & Sole Bossio, Flickr CC; p. 44 Shak On, Flickr CC; p. 46 tuchodi, Wikimedia CC; p. 47 Rocor, Flickr CC; pp. 48–49 David Meyer, Flickr CC; p. 54 Tom Stohlman, Flickr CC; p. 57 Stefan Szczelkun, Flickr CC; pp. 64–65 ©Daily Mail/ Shutterstock; pp. 68–69, 71 ©Clark Richert; pp. 72–73 Jeff Hitchcock, Flickr CC; p. 75 ©Ken Lum; pp. 76, 77 Non à l'aéroport Notre-Dame-des-Landes, Flickr CC; p. 79 Dennis van Zuijlekom, Flickr CC; p. 80 Jchmrt, Wikimedia CC; p. 81 Robin Robokow, Flickr CC; p. 82 malachybrowne, Flickr CC; p. 84 Getty Museum, Wikimedia CC; p. 85 ©Geographicus Rare Antique Maps; pp. 87, 88 malachybrowne, Flickr CC; p. 89 Liam Stoopdice, Flickr CC; pp. 90–93 ©Todd Mecklem; p. 95 ©Adolfo Arranz; p. 96 ©Ian Lambot; p. 97 Ken Ohyama, Wikimedia CC; p. 99 GothEric, Flickr CC; pp. 101–03 ©Brian Rosa; p. 104 RachelH, Flickr CC; p. 105 zoetnet, Flickr CC; p. 107 ©David Solomons; p. 108 Dave Stevenson / Alamy Stock Photo; pp. 110–12 Collection of the Smithsonian National Museum of African American History and Culture ©Robert Houston; p. 113 Collection of the Smithsonian National Museum of African American History and Culture, Gift of Vincent DeForest; p. 114 The Photolibrary Wales / Alamy Stock Photo; p. 115 ©Janine Wiedel; p. 116 Janine Wiedel Photolibrary / Alamy Stock Photo; p. 118 ©Kate Evans; p. 119 Alan Feebery, Flickr CC; p. 120 Alan Feebery, Wikimedia CC; p. 124 Ithmus, Wikimedia CC; p. 125 Jonathan Rashad, Wikimedia CC; pp. 127–29 David Shankbone, Flickr CC; p. 130 Studio Incendo, Wikimedia CC; p. 131 Pasu Au Yeung, Wikimedia CC; p. 132 qbix08, Flickr CC; p. 136 AdDa Zei; p. 138 Stefan Szczelkun, Flickr CC; pp. 139, 140 ©Estate of Graham Caine; pp. 141–43 ©Jenny Pickerill; p. 145 Dameon Hudson, Flickr CC; pp. 146–47 Victorgrigas, Flickr CC; pp. 148–50 ©Archivo Histórico José Vial Armstrong; pp. 160–61 ©AdDa Zei; p. 162 ©Marco Casagrande; pp. 166–67 David Zwirner ©Estate of Gordon Matta-Clark; pp. 169–71 ©Martin Kaltwasser and Folke Köbberling; p. 173 ©David E. Johnson; p. 176, Infrogmation, Wikimedia CC; p. 177 lacraig819, Flickr CC; p. 178 Martin Gautron, Flickr CC; p. 179 Fen Labalme, Flickr CC; p. 180 David Yarnall, Wikimedia CC; pp. 182–83 Eric Allix Rogers, Flickr CC; p. 184 ©Anthony Ko; pp. 186–89 ©Collection of the Gemeentemuseum Den Haag; p. 193 ©San Francisco Museum of Modern Art; Hodgetts + Fung; photograph Don Ross; p. 194 Hodgett + Fung; pp. 196–97 ©Estate of Lebbeus Woods; p. 197 Het Nieuwe Instituut – Architecture Collection, Wikimedia CC; pp. 198–99 San Francisco Museum of Modern Art, Accessions Committee Fund purchase ©Estate of Lebbeus Woods. Photograph Katherine Du Tiel; p. 202 Andy Roberts, Flickr CC; pp. 205–07 ©Anthony Ko; p. 208 ©Santiago Cirugeda; p. 210–11 s.r.r., Flickr CC; pp. 213–14 ©Xavier de Jauréguiberry; p. 218 ©Architype; pp. 232–33 ©Santiago Cirugeda; pp. 234–35 ©Juan Gabriel Pelegrina; p. 236 ©Peter Brooks